FREEDOM AND RESPONSIBILITY IN REPRODUCTIVE CHOICE

What responsibilities, if any, do we have towards our genetic offspring, before or after birth and perhaps even before creation, merely by virtue of the genetic link? What claims, if any, arise from the mere genetic parental relation? Should society through its legal arrangements allow 'fatherless' or 'motherless' children to be born, as the current law on medically assisted reproduction involving gamete donation in some legal systems does? Does the possibility of establishing genetic parentage with practical certainty necessitate reform of current legal regimes of parenthood? And what limits, if any, should we set on parental procreative choices in the interests of future children, particularly with regard to genetic engineering and related techniques? These are the questions explored in this book by some of the foremost legal, biocthical and biomedical thinkers. Assembled with a view to assisting the reader to reflect critically on the ongoing social experiment which medically assisted reproduction is today, the essays in this collection highlight what are—and what else might in the nearby future become—possible reproductive options and respond to the difficulties we encounter in assessing these practices and possibilities from our traditional ethical vantage points.

Freedom and Responsibility in Reproductive Choice

Edited by

JR Spencer and Antje du Bois-Pedain

HART PUBLISHING
OXFORD AND PORTLAND, OREGON
2006

Published in North America (US and Canada) by
Hart Publishing
c/o International Specialized Book Services
920 NE 58th Avenue, Suite 300
Portland, OR 97213-3786
USA
Tel: +1 503 287 3093 or toll-free: (1) 800 944 6190
Fax: +1 503 280 8832
E-mail: orders@isbs.com
Web Site: www.isbs.com

Hart Publishing, Salter's Boatyard, Folly Bridge, Abingdon Rd, Oxford, OX1 4LB
Telephone: +44 (0)1865 245533 Fax: +44 (0) 1865 794882
email: mail@hartpub.co.uk
WEBSITE: http//:www.hartpub.co.uk

British Library Cataloguing in Publication Data
Data Available

ISBN-13: 978-1-84113-582-3 (paperback)
ISBN-10: 1-84113-582-8 (paperback)

Typeset by Compuscript Ltd, Shannon
Printed and bound in Great Britain by
TJ International Ltd, Padstow, Cornwall

PREFACE

Professor JR Spencer, QC

Law Faculty, University of Cambridge

This collection of essays grew out of a multi-disciplinary conference held in the Law Faculty in Cambridge on 2 and 3 July 2004. We wanted to explore some of the philosophical, sociological and legal questions raised by the medical possibilities of artificial procreation and the changing social setting in which both sexual and medically assisted reproduction take place.

These questions are profoundly important. Science when applied to procreation has the potential to radically affect the way we live our lives, and the way we think about our lives, and indeed about life itself.

Advances in medical and scientific knowledge have already led to changes in human procreation, child-bearing and child-rearing which have altered the face of society fundamentally—at any rate, in the western world. For thousands of years, sexual intercourse meant having children. For that practical reason, it was officially viewed as something that should take place only within marriage. For most of the population, family life would typically involve a child-birth every year, and in most years a child death too, until the mother's menopause—or commonly, her early death. The 18th and 19th centuries saw improvements in child-rearing, of which the result was that child-deaths became less frequent, though births for a time continued at their previous high rate. The consequence, of course, was a population explosion—notably in the United Kingdom and in Germany. (To add a personal note, at home I have a picture of my great-grandmother, taken around 1895, surrounded by her nine children; all of whom survived to adulthood, and five into old age, in which I remember them.)

The next stage in the story was the growth of contraception. Though known about in principle for centuries, its practice was, until comparatively recently, often regarded as immoral. In the later years of the 19th century it began to be tacitly accepted by the respectable. But long after it became widely tolerated it was disapproved of by influential and vocal people, not all of whom were Catholics. As late as 1934, the Anglican Bishop of London told a possibly astonished House of

Lords that 'when I hear of 400,000 [contraceptives] being manufactured every week, I would like to make a bonfire of them and dance round it.'[1] But today in Europe, and western society generally, it is almost universally accepted. This is true even among Catholics, most married Catholics practising it despite the continuing official disapproval of the Catholic Church.

In purely material terms, the main result of the general acceptance of contraception has been the return to a population that is stabilised in size—although now with a high standard of living. But contraception has brought other changes of a non-material sort that are perhaps even more significant.

Of these the most obvious is a dramatic alteration in the position of women. Until recently, a woman often had to choose between a career, and getting married. Far from being officially protected against discrimination, women in employment who got married were often formally required to resign. More fundamentally, the link between having children and having sex has, in one important sense, been severed. Sexual intercourse is no longer inseparably linked to having children. For those who are sexually active, sexual intercourse is something that is done primarily for pleasure, and not in order to have children—or even in the conscious awareness that the birth of a child might be the result. And this in turn has led to a revolution in public attitudes towards sexual morality. Sixty years ago, the view to which most respectable people publicly adhered was that sex outside the bounds of marriage was wrong, and when it happened—as of course it often did—those concerned, if they were detected, were said to be 'living in sin'. Today, I believe most people accept the idea that it is immoral to be unfaithful to your partner, if you have one; but few still accept the idea that it is immoral to have sexual relations with a person to whom you are not married.

Now reproductive medicine has the potential to produce social changes equally profound. If contraception means that having children is no longer the necessary consequence of having sexual intercourse, artificial procreation means that sexual intercourse is no longer the necessary precondition for having children. As Martin Johnson explains in his contribution to this book:

> Initially, this new scientific knowledge and understanding about human reproduction focused on controlling reproduction through more effective birth control (sex without babies or recreation without reproduction), but latterly reproduction without recreation (babies without sex) has also become an option. The type and number of babies, the time in parents' lives at which they are born and the range of parents responsible for producing them can be controlled. The genetic selection of early embryos *in vitro* is possible, and interventions by clinicians are the main cause of multiparity (multiple births). Medical assistance enables post-menopausal women to give birth, and gay

---

[1] Quoted by EJ Bristow, *Vice and Vigilance: Purity Movements in Britain Since 1700* (Dublin, Gill and Macmillan, 1977).

and lesbian couples, as well as women on their own, to become parents. Scientists now distinguish between four categories of parenthood (genetic, coital, uterine or gestational, and post-natal), each contributing to the establishment of an individual's identity and each susceptible to biomedical intervention. The discoveries of science have thus forced a major re-evaluation of social attitudes to reproduction, sexual expression, parenthood and the nature of families.[2]

All this brings an obvious need for philosophical reflection. It was with that in mind that the conference in July 2004 was held. And it was to stimulate this reflection further and more widely that this book of essays has been written.

As a member of the Cambridge Law Faculty, I feel a sense of collective pride that the conference took place in Cambridge and that this book is also in a sense a Cambridge project. Much of the basic science that made reproductive medicine possible took place in Cambridge. Two eminent Cambridge scientists working in this area whose names come instantly to mind are Professor Sir John Gurdon—and Martin Johnson, whose chapter has just been quoted. The legislative framework in which reproductive medicine in this country is practised is the Human Fertilisation and Embryology Act of 1990. This stemmed from the work of a Committee chaired by Baroness Mary Warnock—who, like Martin Johnson, has contributed a chapter to this book. The father of medical law in this country was another Cambridge scholar, Glanville Williams, for many years a professor in the Faculty of Law. In 1958 he critically examined the law on contraception, sterilisation and artificial insemination in the light of growing scientific knowledge and developments in philosophy in his pioneering book *The Sanctity of Life and the Criminal Law.*

But although I feel collective pride, I cannot claim much personal credit for either the conference or the book. The original idea for both came from my colleague Antje du Bois-Pedain, who worked on it with the help of another respected colleague who has contributed a chapter to this collection, Andrew Bainham. To draw an analogy with reproductive medicine, my role was, at the highest, to act as a facilitator, like the IVF consultant at the infertility clinic. It was my more expert colleagues who provided the gametes.

The main way in which I was able to facilitate this project was as a Manager of the Ver Heyden De Lancey Fund. Baron Cornelius Ver Heyden De Lancey (1889–1984) was a Dutchman, who lived and worked at various times in London, Rome and Jersey. He was astonishingly versatile. In the course of his very long life he was successively a dentist, a surgeon, a barrister, an expert on art history, a doctor, and finally once more a dentist. A wealthy man, in 1970 he founded the

---

[2] MH Johnson, 'Regulating the Science and Therapeutic Application of Human Embryo Research: Managing the Tension Between Biomedical Creativity and Public Concern' (in this collection; footnotes omitted).

De Lancey and De La Hanty Foundation, to stimulate studies in medicine and the law, and to promote links between these disciplines. The foundation endowed the Ver Heyden De Lancey Fund at Cambridge, which is used to promote lectures on medico-legal subjects, and to support the medical law collection in the Squire Law Library. This fund provided a grant to enable us to hold the conference. I hope the first Ver Heyden De Lancey Conference, and now this book, are fitting tributes to the memory of this learned, generous and public-spirited man.

CONTENTS

LIST OF CONTRIBUTORS

Andrew Bainham is a Reader in Family Law and Policy at the University of Cambridge and a Fellow of Christ's College, Cambridge. He is a founding member, and was the first chair, of the Cambridge Socio-Legal Group. His specialised interests are in family law and children's rights. He was Special Advisor to Baroness Nicholson of Winterbourne MEP in her capacity as Rapporteur for Romania in the European Parliament. In that role he was closely involved in the reform of Romania's child protection and adoption laws. He has published *Children: The Modern Law*, 3rd edn (Bristol, Jordans, 2005), and co-edited many publications by the Cambridge Socio-Legal Group, most recently *Children and Their Families: Contact, Rights and Welfare* (with Bridget Lindley, Martin Richards and Liz Trinder; Oxford, Hart Publishing, 2003); and *Sexuality Repositioned: Diversity and the Law* (with Belinda Brooks-Gordon, Loraine Gelsthorpe and Martin Johnson; Oxford, Hart Publishing, 2004). Most recently he has co-authored a report with Clem Henricson of the National Family and Parenting Institute, funded by the Joseph Rowntree Foundation, on the relationship between policies directed towards families and those directed specifically at children.

Thomas Baldwin is Professor of Philosophy at the University of York, a member of the Nuffield Council on Bioethics and of the Steering Committee of the UK Stem Cell Bank, and deputy chair of the Human Fertilisation and Embryology Authority. He is also editor of *Mind* and President Elect of the Aristotelian Society. His research interests are in 20th century philosophy, philosophy of language, philosophy of mind and bioethics. Recent publications include *Contemporary Philosophy. Philosophy in English since 1945* (Oxford, OUP, 2001); and *The Cambridge History of Philosophy: 1870–1945* (editor; Cambridge, CUP, 2004).

Lisa Bortolotti is Lecturer in Philosophy at the University of Birmingham. She was Research Associate and Honorary Lecturer in Bioethics at the Centre for Social Ethics and Policy at the University of Manchester, School of Law from August 2004 to September 2005. She studied Philosophy in Bologna (Italy), London and Oxford (UK) and holds a doctorate from the Australian National University in Canberra. Her research interests are in the philosophy of mind, philosophy of science, philosophy of psychology and applied ethics. She has written papers on rationality, theories of interpretation, delusions, animal cognition and the ethics of stem cell research and reproduction.

John Harris is Sir David Alliance Professor of Bioethics at the University of Manchester, School of Law, and joint editor-in-chief of the *Journal of Medical Ethics*. He was elected a Fellow of the United Kingdom Academy of Medical Sciences (FMedSci) in 2001 and has been a member of the United Kingdom Human Genetics Commission since its foundation in 1999. Recent books include: *Clones, Genes and Immortality* (Oxford, OUP, 1998); J Harris (ed), *Bioethics*, Oxford Readings in Philosophy Series (Oxford, OUP, 2001); JC Burley and J Harris (eds), *A Companion to Genethics: Philosophy and the Genetic Revolution*, Blackwell's Companions to Philosophy Series (Oxford, Basil Blackwell, 2002); and *On Cloning* (London, Routledge, 2004).

Martin H Johnson is Professor of Reproductive Sciences at the University of Cambridge (since 1992) and a Fellow of Christs's College, Cambridge (since 1969). He also is a founding member of the Cambridge Socio-Legal Group and is Distinguished Visiting Fellow at the Centre for Advanced Studies at La Trobe University, Melbourne, Australia, 2005–06. He was a Harkness Fellow (1971–73), Head of the Department of Anatomy in Cambridge (1995–99), Chairman of the British Society for Developmental Biology (1984–89), Hon. Secretary of the Professional Advisory Group for Infertility and Genetic Services (1989–94), member of the Human Fertilisation and Embryology Authority (1993–99) and Visiting Professor at the University of Sydney, Australia (1999–2004). He has published over 200 papers on the science, medicine, ethics and socio-legal impact of reproduction and early development, as well as papers on medical education. He is co-author, with Professor Barry Everitt, of *Essential Reproduction* (Blackwell Science, 6th edition forthcoming), and has co-edited *Sexuality Repositioned: Diversity and the Law* (with Andrew Bainham, Belinda Brooks-Gordon and Loraine Gelsthorpe; Oxford, Hart Publishing, 2004).

Judith Masson is Professor of Socio-legal Studies at the University of Bristol. Her main interests are family law and children's rights. She is co-author, with Stephen Cretney and Rebecca Bailey-Harris, of *Principles of Family Law*, 7th edn (London, Sweet and Maxwell, 2003); co-author (with Maureen Winn Oakley) of *Out of Hearing: Representing Children in Court* (Chichester, Wiley, 1999); and co-editor, with Christine Harrison and Annie Pavlovic, of *Lost and Found. Making and Remaking Working Partnerships With Parents of Children in the Care System* (Aldershot, Ashgate, 1999). She is an academic member of the Family Justice Council for England and Wales and an academic member of the Judicial Studies Board.

Martin Richards is Director of the Centre for Family Research and Professor of Family Research at the University of Cambridge. His research interests include marriage, divorce and family and, most recently, the psychosocial aspects of new genetic and reproductive technologies. His books include *Sexual Arrangements: Marriage and Affairs* (co-author Janet Reibstein; London, Heinemann, 1992); *The Troubled Helix: Social and Psychological Implications of the New Human Genetics* (co-editor Theresa Marteau; Cambridge, CUP, 1996); *What is a Parent? A Socio-Legal Analysis* (co-editors Andrew Bainham and Shelley Day Sclater; Oxford, Hart Publishing, 1999); *Body Lore and Laws* (co-editors Andrew Bainham and Shelley Day Sclater; Oxford, Hart Publishing, 2002); and *Children and Their Families: Contact, Rights and Welfare* (co-editors Andrew Bainham, Bridget Lindley and Liz Trinder; Oxford, Hart Publishing, 2003). He is a member of the Human Genetics Commission and the Ethics and Law Committee of the Human Fertilisation and Embryology Authority, and was a member of the Nuffield Council Working Party on genes and human behaviour.

Alison Shaw is a Senior Research Fellow at the University of Oxford in the Department of Public Health. She holds a doctorate in Social Anthropology and has specialist research interests in Britain's ethnic minorities, medical anthropology, kinship and social aspects of genetics. Her recent research has centred on kinship, marriage, health and genetic counselling issues among British Pakistanis. Her publications include *A Pakistani Community in Britain* (Oxford, Blackwell, 1988); *Kinship and Continuity: Pakistani Families in Britain* (London, Harwood Academic Publishers, 2000); and 'Interpreting Images: Diagnostic Skill in the Genetic Clinic' (2003) *Journal of the Royal Anthropological Institute*. From 2001 to 2005 she was engaged in research funded by the Wellcome Trust UK investigating the impact of genetic risk information on British Pakistani families referred for genetic counselling.

Sally Sheldon is a professor at the School of Law, Keele University. Her specialist interests are medical law and ethics, tort law, and legal regulation of gender and sexuality. She is an ESRC research fellow and a general editor of the journal Social & Legal Studies. Her publications include *Beyond Control: Medical Power and Abortion Law* (London, Pluto Press, 1997); *Feminist Perspectives on Health Care Law* (co-edited with Michael Thomson; London, Cavendish Publishing, 1998); and 'Fragmenting Fatherhood: The Regulation of Reproductive Technologies' (2005) *Modern Law Review*. With Richard Collier of Newcastle Law School she is currently writing a book on fatherhood.

Bonnie Steinbock is Professor of Philosophy at the University at Albany, New York State (SUNY). She is a fellow of the Hastings Center, and a member of the ethics committee of the American Society for Reproduction and Medicine. She has published widely on bioethical issues; her perhaps best-known book is *Life Before Birth: The Moral and Legal Status of Embryos and Fetuses* (Oxford, OUP, 1992; paperback 1996). She is the area editor in fertility and reproduction for the

3rd edition of the *Encyclopedia of Bioethics* (Basingstoke, Macmillan, 2003) and is currently editing the *Oxford Handbook of Bioethics*.

Mary Warnock For decades, Baroness Mary Warnock has held a prominent place as a philosopher, an educationalist and a figure in public life. She taught philosophy at Oxford and at Cambridge (where she was Mistress of Girton College from 1985 to 1991). She is an active member of the House of Lords, and has taken part in several governmental committees, notably the Committee of Inquiry into Human Fertilisation and Embryology (1984), which she chaired, and which prepared the ground for the legislation that currently regulates this area in the UK. Her passionate interest in this topic has remained with her: her recent writings include *Making Babies: Is There a Right to Have Children?* (Oxford, OUP, 2000).

INTRODUCTION

ANTJE DU BOIS-PEDAIN

What responsibilities, if any, do we have towards our genetic offspring, before or after birth and perhaps even before creation, merely by virtue of the genetic link? What claims, if any, arise from the mere genetic parental relation? Should society through its legal arrangements allow 'fatherless' or 'motherless' children to be born, as the current law on medically assisted reproduction involving gamete donation in some legal systems does? Does the possibility of establishing genetic parentage with practical certainty necessitate reform of current legal regimes of parenthood? And what limits, if any, should we set on parental procreative choices in the interests of future children, particularly with regard to genetic engineering and related techniques?

A pertinent feature of medically assisted reproduction is that it makes the 'when', 'where' and 'by whom' of reproduction more controllable. Increasingly, it also enables prospective parents to control what sort of children they will have: through genetic screening and embryo selection and through possible future techniques of genetic enhancement. It is thus becoming possible for parents to ensure that a child of theirs shares a trait they value about themselves (even if others or society in general may view that trait as a disability) or, conversely, that it does not share a trait which they deplore. Ultimately, we may even become technically able to create children who are largely genetic duplicates of ourselves.

Already, medically assisted reproduction is not only opted for by persons who find it difficult or impossible to beget or conceive a child without medical help, but seen and used by some as a valid, perhaps even superior, alternative to 'ordinary' sexual procreation[1]—particularly when there is a desire to make use of preimplantation genetic testing techniques. What does learning about the possibilities of genetic enhancement and trait selection and about certain genetic causes of disability mean for, and do to, those who find themselves confronted with this new scientific knowledge as they struggle to lead responsible lives, as prospective

---

[1] From a biological perspective, the term coital procreation might be more precise, since sexual procreation can not only, as in colloquial use, refer to procreation through sexual intercourse, but also more generally to procreation which involves the participation (and genetic endowment) of two sexually differentiated beings—a perspective from which any technique which creates embryos through the fertilisation of a human egg with human sperm is sexual as opposed to asexual procreation.

parents, biomedical doctors and scientists, or policy-makers? Can the concept of procreative autonomy help us to understand the moral setting in which reproductive choices are made? Or is the so-called right to procreative autonomy merely a reflection of our sexual freedoms and does it extend only as far as these freedoms go?

One reason why many people find the discussion of moral questions raised by the new scientific possibilities of procreation so utterly disconcerting relates to 'the overall structure of our moral and ethical experience'.[2] As the legal philosopher Ronald Dworkin explains:

> that structure depends, crucially, on a fundamental distinction between what we are responsible for doing or declining, individually or collectively, and what is given to us, as a background against which we act or decide, but which we are powerless to change. ... For everyone, the distinction, however they describe it, draws a line between who and what we are, for which either a divine will or no one but a blind process is responsible, and what we do with that inheritance, for which we are indeed, separately or together, responsible. That crucial boundary between chance and choice is the spine of our ethics and our morality, and any serious shift in that boundary is seriously dislocating.[3]

The essays in this book all can be read against that observation. But the dislocations they respond to are not merely those directly created by medical progress and the new kinds of choices which modern reproductive technologies bring in their wake. Considerable dislocation also results from the 'context' of medically assisted reproduction for those who opt for it: from the 'medicalisation' of procreation, the involvement of medical professionals in the 'making' of their child, and the end of intimacy for the procreative act. Provocatively, but not inaccurately, some biomedical scientists and doctors describe their involvement in the conception of 'test tube babies' as a kind of 'fatherhood'.[4] And even if the medical professionals involved still take a step backwards and view themselves merely as doctors discharging their duty to treat their patients, their presence and involvement profoundly affects the procreative experience which their patients have. No one has captured this better than Simone Bateman when she writes that:

> These techniques have [not only] created new options for persons who would otherwise not have had children, but they have also progressively altered the practices and relationships that condition and give meaning to reproduction in our society. This is primarily because reproductive technology is most often made available in a medical setting, where relationships are defined in therapeutic terms, where values give precedence to

---

[2] R Dworkin, *Sovereign Virtue. The Theory and Practice of Equality* (Cambridge, MA, Harvard University Press, 2000) 443.

[3] *Ibid*, 443–44.

[4] See MH Johnson, 'A Biomedical Perspective on Parenthood' in A Bainham, S Day Sclater and MPM Richards (eds), *What is a Parent? A Socio-Legal Analysis* (Oxford, Hart Publishing, 1999) 47.

the quality, security and efficiency of the technical act, and where physicians are held responsible for the appropriate management of procedures. Impregnation no longer has to do with the privacy of one's sex life, but with the accomplishment of a medical act.[5]

Moreover, background dislocations to our moral thinking of the kind Dworkin refers to also occur through broader social changes which affect the range of 'liveable lives' open to us. Our social practices, though always (in an abstract way) matters of choice, and hence subject to constant and ongoing moral scrutiny and reflection over centuries, are in another sense as much part of the backdrop for our moral decisions as scientific possibilities. Social mores, the accepted practices of society, have a profound and often determinative influence on what people view as choices they can make, as opposed to a destiny to endure and try to make the most of. They also colour the moral quality of making certain choices, such as to bring a 'fatherless' child into the world.[6] Human choices are always contingent upon a certain social setting, and any moral assessment must take account of this contingency. Different social practices and changing ways of life might allow and indeed compel us to re-conceptualise as a matter of choice behaviour which in earlier times could not have been seen as chosen in any meaningful way. To give but one example: in 17th century Britain, an unwed woman who found herself pregnant and without independent means had little if any prospect of getting the means by which to support her child through respectable gainful employment. She also had to contend with the fact that any child born out of wedlock would be discriminated against by society and be seriously disadvantaged throughout his life, a situation which she was powerless to change. The health risks which would have attached to any attempt to discontinue her pregnancy would also have affected the moral quality of any choice she might make. Her choice was located in the world in which she lived, with a profound impact on the morality of any resulting decision. In 21st century Britain, an unwed woman who finds herself pregnant and without independent means may well have a realistic option of finding gainful employment, or else may have access to state benefits or child support. She lives in a society where the marital status of any child born to her as such does not detrimentally affect this child's chances in life. She has, however, access to safe abortion. All these are colorants which affect the moral assessment of her choice.

There may be a further reason for the sense of moral panic with which we often react to the dislocating effects that new scientific possibilities have on our morality.

---

[5] S Bateman, 'When Reproductive Freedom Encounters Medical Responsibility: Changing Conceptions of Reproductive Choice' in E Vayena, P Rowe and D Griffin (eds), *Medical, Ethical and Social Aspects of Assisted Reproduction* (Geneva, World Health Organisation, 2001) 320.

[6] This is a point touched upon by John Harris and Lisa Bortolotti in their discussion of moral problems raised by the choice to have a child who will suffer from what is (in their terminology) a 'merely social disability' ('Disability, Enhancement and the Harm-Benefit Continuum'; in this collection).

In discussing these possibilities, we already find ourselves in a world different from the one we knew so far because we now live in a society where the chance/choice boundary has been irreversibly shifted, where something that was previously a matter of chance has become a matter of choice. But as we find ourselves called upon to re-think our moral obligations in the light of this change, we cannot escape the fact that the actual world which surrounds us is not yet shaped by multiple exercises of these new choices and their consequences. In our discussion of the moral obligations we face by virtue of the most recent shift in the chance/choice boundary we thus cannot rely, as background information, on our experience of 'the world we live in'. Instead, we struggle to imagine a social setting where the new kind of choice is really made by people on an everyday basis.

Again, an example might illustrate this point. In a world where sexual intercourse is inescapably linked to a risk of procreation this forms the backdrop against which sexual behaviour needs to be morally evaluated. It can be morally wrong to have sexual intercourse precisely because it would be inappropriate, and unfair to any resulting child, to run this procreative risk. In other words, the wrongness of running the procreative risk rebounds on the sexual act itself, making it wrong as well. Contrast this with a world where sexual intercourse need not be linked to procreative risk. Here too, of course, a sexual act could still be morally wrong because it would be inappropriate, and unfair to any resulting child, to run this procreative risk. But that—otherwise identical—sexual act would not be wrong if the procreative risk was eliminated from it (or reduced so much that it effectively counts as elimination). And living in this changed world where a sexual act may or may not carry a procreative risk has at least one further factual repercussion: our sexual partner might be mistaken about the fact that a particular sexual act is potentially also a procreative one, and this misapprehension we can either be aware of or not, and may even have had a hand in bringing about. That this profoundly changes the morality of sexual encounters should be obvious.[7]

The social and moral dislocations which follow upon the advent of safe and effective contraception may be largely behind us. The social and moral dislocations resultant from past, present and future advances in medically assisted reproduction are (notwithstanding the fact that already about 2% of babies born in

---

[7] It is interesting, and in a sense almost pitiful, to observe the initial reaction by many theologians and philosophers to this changed world in which procreative risk had become a matter of choice: to deny that they lived in a changed world. Many discussions in the 1970s stressed that no contraceptive method could be absolutely safe, thereby suggesting that there could be no morally significant difference between, on the one hand, a sexual act which carried the usual procreative risk associated with unprotected intercourse, and, on the other hand, a sexual act which carried, if any, only the infinitely much smaller procreative risk which attaches to protected intercourse. Other systems of morality—first and foremost, the teachings of the Catholic church—simply decreed that only unprotected sex was acceptable; shutting their eyes against the fact that the morality of unprotected sex can never be the same in a world where to have unprotected sex has become a matter of choice and not necessity (if one is to have any sex at all).

some European countries have been conceived with some form of medical assistance in their conception)[8] still largely ahead of us. They have begun to change the way we think about parenthood and procreative autonomy, and—together with other changes in our social landscape—they inspire legal and other regulatory changes. And increasingly they force us to reconsider the parameters of our debate; in particular whether—as Onora O'Neill suggests—'[r]eproductive choice is ... not best seen on the model of the exercise of a liberty right.'[9]

The essays in this book address these dislocations. Part I takes up O'Neill's challenge about the relationship between procreative autonomy and liberty rights. Chapter 1, by Mary Warnock, focuses on the limits of rights-based discourse about reproduction. She points to the fact that claiming a right is always a public act, and that it is always appropriate when someone claims a right to look out for the person or institution on which there is to rest a corresponding duty. She distinguishes between claiming something as a legal right and as a moral right, and discusses in the light of this distinction a recent court case where a woman who had begun fertility treatment with her then partner was forced to give up her not yet implanted embryos when her partner withdrew from the treatment.[10] She reads the judgment as saying that, in effect, even a moral right on the part of the claimant is difficult to uphold in this situation—procreation is too personal a matter not just for the claimant but also for her partner to tie her partner down to promises he made, unwisely but not callously, within an on-going relationship that has now ended.

She then addresses the difficulties, both factual and moral, which arise from the Human Fertilisation and Embryology Act's injunction to consider 'the welfare of any child who may be born' as a result of fertility treatment. On the factual side, there is the problem of: 'irremediable ignorance: We cannot know with any certainty how it will be for someone brought up as the child of two homosexuals, ... or two who are profoundly deaf.' And on the moral side, we have to ask ourselves: what standing, if any, should doctors, regulators, and society at large have to conclude that a person ought not to have the child they want?

This question has become particularly pertinent with regard to the possibilities of pre-implantation genetic testing and 'trait selection', and possible future techniques of genetic enhancement. While 'tissue typing' of embryos before implantation to ensure that the child who will be born will be able to act as a 'saviour sibling' for an existing child seems acceptable, can we say the same for genetic enhancements? If it were really possible for prospective parents to select a range of traits, physical attributes and characteristics which their future child might

---

[8] See MPM Richards, 'Genes, Genealogies and Paternity: Making Babies in the Twenty-first Century' (in this collection).

[9] *Autonomy and Trust in Bioethics* (Cambridge, CUP, 2002) 61.

[10] *Evans v Amicus Healthcare Ltd* [2003] EWHC Fam 2161; [2004] EWCA Civ 727; [2005] Fam 1.

have, would parents then have a right to make such choices? Warnock believes that they would not.

> It is not so much that the characteristics chosen might turn out after all not to be such a blessing to the child as the parents had supposed. It is rather that it would change the relation between the child and its parents in a potentially damaging way. ... [C]hildren are not like houses and horses, among the possessions of their parents. To insist that your child shall be born not with a unique and unpredictable mixture of genes passed on by both of its parents but with the characteristics you yourself would choose for it is to overlook this distinction.

Chapter 2, by Thomas Baldwin, addresses precisely this point: the morality of present and future efforts, through genetic selection and manipulation, to try and make 'better children'. For the purposes of his discussion, a child is 'better' than another if it is likely to lead a better life than a child who would otherwise have been born. This, in turn, is a function of how well equipped the child is for life: his health, range of talents, and so on. It is also, he acknowledges, very much a function of the environment in which the child grows up, and he is of the view that there can never be anything wrong with trying to make better children by supporting children and their families in their struggle for decent education, healthcare and housing. But the question he wants to concentrate on is whether prospective parents are morally entitled, or even morally obliged, to choose a child with the best genetic endowments it can have. Baldwin distinguishes between, on the one hand, strong procreative beneficence—the position that prospective parents are obliged to avail themselves of advances in medicine and technology to ensure that they are making the best child they can have—and, on the other hand, weak procreative beneficence—the view that it is always permissible to make children in ways which are likely to make their lives better than the lives of those children who would otherwise have been born. He thinks that strong procreative beneficence, as defended by Julian Savulescu, is unacceptable for the same reasons that make the similar 'obligatory' version of utilitarianism unsupportable: that we are not responsible for the state of the world, and that such a principle would be destructive of individual liberty. Objections to weak procreative beneficence, however, can only arise from deontological constraints—cases in which deontological principles are violated by liberal eugenic practices (a moral position which Baldwin defines as the combination of procreative autonomy and weak procreative beneficence). Ultimately, Baldwin does not think that there are any plausible cases of this sort: what comes closest to it is a hypothetical case in which parents 'select' the sexual preferences of their future child, since such a child may well have an 'alienating sense of another person intruding in her life' from knowing that her parents determined an aspect of her being which she cannot disavow: but if we were to conclude that such a feeling of alienation might result for certain (though not all) genetic enhancements, we can still understand this result as a new kind of harm which, being genuine harm, sets limits to the legitimate exercise of our personal freedom.

Chapter 3, by Lisa Bortolotti and John Harris, takes a different view of our moral obligations in respect of possible enhancements for our future child. They defend the claim that we owe our children more than just the avoidance of harm—part and parcel of which is to do what we can to avoid that they are born with a disability. They assume that there is: 'a continuum between harms and benefits. ... [T]he reasons we have to avoid harming others are continuous with the reasons we have for conferring benefits on others if we can', and argue that our moral obligation to do what is best for our children applies across a broad range of avoidable outcomes: from disabilities to mere disadvantages to characteristics the absence of which may not even be considered a disadvantage, so long as their presence (for instance, musicality or strong hair) is viewed as an asset for the individual concerned. This leads Bortolotti and Harris to face up to the question whether it is always wrong *not* to enhance: and they tentatively conclude that this would be so, provided the enhancement is safe and not too costly (in moral terms) for the prospective parent to provide.

Part II addresses the changing social conceptions and legal regulation of families and family-making. In chapter 4, Martin Richards provides an overview of the manifold ways in which 'making babies in the 21st century' is different from how it was like for previous generations, and the repercussions this has on our understandings of kinship and fatherhood in particular. He reviews the gradual rise in the frequency, and social acceptability, of the use of medical techniques to assist conception in humans—accompanied by a change in terminology from 'artificial insemination' to simply 'donor insemination' which is itself indicative of the changing social perception of these developments, of their normalisation. But while both patients receiving fertility treatment and the legislation which governs the use of (most) artificial reproductive technologies strive to assimilate families created through medically assisted reproduction into the model of the 'nuclear family', social changes within and outside that context continue to undermine and move beyond this ideal. The easy availability of paternity testing not only enables unmarried fathers to be tied, at least financially, to their genetic child: it also reveals many families with children conceived in the usual way to be 'as if' families, if with that term we refer to a family where the parents give their child the impression that they are its biological parents while at least one of them is not. And, increasingly, social understandings and the legal regimes of parenthood reflect the 'malleability' of families over time. At the same time, the realisation that biological and social fatherhood may easily diverge, and the 'cultural visibility' of DNA testing, has led both ordinary people and the courts to place more emphasis on the establishment of 'genealogical truth'. While it is doubtful that the 'new moral order of genetic parentage' that is being established will lead to 'a new moral order of paternity', social changes will continue to challenge, in both directions, the legal ascription of relevance to biological facts.

Chapter 5 takes us right into the reality of medically assisted reproduction, asking how prospective parents deal with genetic information they receive and to what extent this changes their traditional understandings of kinship. Alison Shaw's field work focuses on patients of Pakistani origin in British fertility clinics who receive genetic counselling about hereditary disorders. Many of these parents struggle to come to terms with the information they receive precisely because it is at odds with traditional understandings of 'blood relatedness' and heritage in their communities. Ideas about patrilineal inheritance often shape these patients' initial understandings of the inheritance of genetic illnesses, and clinicians may remain unaware that misunderstandings persist because patients are quick to pick up, and respond in terms of, the 'medical lingo'. Conversely, greater knowledge about 'biological facts', even when properly understood and 'digested' and even acted upon (for instance, by opting for pre-natal or pre-implantation genetic diagnosis or gamete donation) need not necessarily replace traditional understandings of kinship which are incompatible with it. To give but one example: the knowledge that each parent contributes an equal amount of 'genetic material' to a child does not displace the traditional view that the father contributes more; it may simply coexist with it. As Shaw concludes:

> the social ascription of relevance or irrelevance to a 'genetic link' cannot always be predicted in advance, and will depend, in part, on prior understandings of the connections between parents, children and siblings, and of what constitutes kinship, ethnicity and ancestry. This is so even in contexts in which concerns to establish parenthood or to establish the genetic basis of illness are routine.

Chapter 6, by Martin Johnson, looks at the potential of legal regulation to manage the 'tension between biomedical creativity and public concern' from the perspective of a biomedical scientist and doctor. He argues that biomedical scientists and doctors must understand that they 'are themselves part of a wider and diverse community and cannot arrogate to themselves exclusive powers of decisions over matters, the outcome of which affects others profoundly.' He sees the process which led to the adoption of the Human Fertilisation and Embryology Act 1990 as marked by a willingness by the biomedical community to engage in a wider ethical discussion, which resulted in an objective-driven regulatory regime reasonably open to biomedical innovation. He nevertheless highlights two problematic areas of this 'enlightened' regulatory framework: the time and nature of the evidence base in the light of which the Human Fertilisation and Embryology Authority approves new therapeutic research and new treatments, and the bureaucracy its procedures entail. For Johnson, however, these problems do not question the value for biomedical scientists and doctors of having external regulation:

rather, they point to a renewed need for the biomedical community to 'engage openly and constructively at all levels of society' in the debates about further legislative reform.

In chapter 7, Bonnie Steinbock raises the question to what extent the uses of medically assisted reproduction have already had an impact upon, and will continue to influence, changes in our legal recognition and definition of parenthood. She starts by reviewing the shift to intent-based conceptions of parenthood in the wake of procedures of medically assisted reproduction by taking the reader through a fascinating series of North American cases where courts had to decide between the competing claims of a range of 'new' types of 'candidate parents' for a child, be they gestational surrogates, gamete donors who, unusually, co-parent the resulting child, or commissioning couples with no genetic link to the child they set out to create. She compares the courts' approaches to these cases with that taken in cases of contested adoptions, questioning to what extent the 'best interests of the child' can and ought to serve as an appropriate and reliable guide for the determination of parental status, rights and duties.

This is also very much the question which drives the essays in Part III of this book on reproductive autonomy and parenthood. The first two chapters in this section are concerned with what Martin Richards, in his chapter, so poignantly refers to as this 'complex area of law, intended to sort out issues of parentage, parenthood and child support in the often confused social world of sex, love, relationships, parenting and kinship.'[11] In chapter 8, Judith Masson asks to what extent current English law gives, and as a matter of legal policy ought to give, legal recognition to the manifold ways of 'parenting by doing' and 'parenting by being'. She distinguishes between three interrelated concepts used to define the position of parents *vis-a-vis* their children in law: being a parent, having parental responsibility and having a right to family life with the child under Article 8 of the European Convention on Human Rights. With regard to each of these components of legal parenthood, she gives an overview of the current legal regimes which govern their ascription to progenitors and others involved in the upbringing of a child, and in this context questions the coherence of the regimes of legal fatherhood for children conceived with donated gametes. She takes the view that '[t]he desire to maintain the special status of marriage, and to impose a father in every possible arrangement has produced an incoherent system for establishing parenthood, and one which leaves unprotected a large minority of children whose parents cohabit rather than marry'. The law is clearly in need of further reform.

Chapter 9, by Andrew Bainham, focuses on the rights and obligations associated with the birth of a child. Bainham is concerned that a number of rights which

---

[11] 'Genes, Genealogies and Paternity: Making Babies in the Twenty-first Century' (in this collection).

the child is supposed to enjoy from birth, such as that to knowledge of its parents and to an ongoing relationship with them, depend for their realisation on effective birth registration and are easily undercut by adults who, in pursuit of an agenda of their own, keep the child in the dark about its origins and, in particular, the identity of its biological father. He questions the ease with which commentators and courts assume that a 'right to knowledge' of one's genetic parents, if one accepts that such a right exists, can be respected by giving children access to certain identifying information when they reach age 18. Surely, at that point, the chance for an ongoing relationship with a birth parent previously unknown to the child may be largely lost. What is more, knowledge attained only at this age may prove unsettling rather than supportive for the child. In essence, Bainham rejects the position that children can ever benefit from growing up in an 'as if' family in the sense in which this term is used by Richards: a family where at least one non-biological parent is presented as a biological parent to the child. He thinks that the law should further openness, not secrecy, in this respect, and that one of the ways of achieving this is by ceasing to confuse social and legal parentage:

> The purpose of legal parentage is to recognise the fundamental kinship connection between the child and the parent and the child and that parent's wider family. The effect of making social parents legal parents is ... to create a legal fiction by hiding the fact that the child's genetic parents are not the social parents.[12]

And, one may add, it is perhaps part of the procreative responsibility of mothers to reveal the identity of the genetic father to their child.

In chapter 10, Sally Sheldon focuses on a different aspect of reproductive responsibility: that of men as 'reproductive bodies'. She suggests that there may be a shifting understanding of how a man's biological contribution to the resulting child may affect the health and welfare of that child, which leads us, on the one hand, to see men increasingly as bearers of reproductive responsibilities, while, on the other hand, we also increasingly understand their bodies and psyches as both vulnerable and continuingly involved in reproduction. Sheldon acknowledges that 'biological asymmetry does exist and, moreover, it provides a clear basis for suggesting that men's and women's responsibilities in the context of reproductive decision-making must therefore also be asymmetrical.' But, in her view, 'biological asymmetry itself cannot adequately explain the differences in how we think about men's and women's reproductive responsibilities: gender is an important prism through which these are read.' She argues that 'a number of dominant and highly gendered assumptions have had a clear impact on the way in which we think about such responsibilities'. But she also suggests that men, like women, increasingly 'find themselves called upon to make "responsible" reproductive choices, not

---

[12] Original footnote omitted.

just in avoiding unwanted pregnancy, but also in taking appropriate measures to safeguard their own reproductive health and to avoid conception of a child likely to suffer from illness or disability.' Sheldon believes that the changing understandings of male and female reproductive responsibilities which she outlines are paralleled by the rethinking of men's and women's responsibilities with regard to parenting. Her essay is a forceful reminder that the changes to social expectations and legal regimes of fatherhood are an ongoing process which may eventually lead to greater fairness and gender equality in matters of reproduction.

The essays in this collection were assembled with a view to assisting the reader in reflecting critically on the ongoing social experiment which medically assisted reproduction is today. Read together, they do not only highlight what are—and what else might in the nearby future become—possible reproductive options; they also bring out the difficulties we encounter in assessing these practices and possibilities from our traditional ethical vantage points. The perhaps most important message of these essays is that in expanding human choices, medically assisted reproduction also brings with it new responsibilities. We should, in my view, value it for both these reasons: shifts in the chance/choice boundary which increase human choices are welcome changes, even if human beings need time to think through these new possibilities and to learn to use them responsibly.

TABLE OF CASES

TABLE OF LEGISLATION

TABLE OF INTERNATIONAL
INSTRUMENTS AND CONVENTIONS

Part I

The Rights and Wrongs of Reproduction

1

The Limits of Rights-based Discourse

MARY WARNOCK

I hope you will forgive me if I start with some absolutely general and blindingly obvious remarks about rights and the discourse of rights. First, put negatively, if someone's right has been violated, he has suffered an injustice. So, since justice and injustice are essentially social or public concepts, to claim a right is a public, or at least potentially public, act. If I knew that I was the last person left alive on earth there would be no point in my claiming a right. Suppose that I said to myself before swimming out to sea and drowning: 'I have a right to die as I choose'. This would be a last rhetorical flourish. It would have no real meaning. For if someone has a right, then someone else has a duty to ensure that he has what he claims, or, more modestly, that he is not actively prevented from having it.[1]

Putting the discourse of rights thus in the public domain, we can at once distinguish between claiming a right to something and expressing a strong desire for it. The latter is a private matter of wishes, aspirations and longings, arguably even needs. If I long for something that I have not got and which it is in your power to give me, how we judge your refusal to do so will depend on the circumstances. If you are to be blamed for not letting me have it, this will be a moral condemnation. You may be thought mean, hard-hearted, insensitive, lacking in loving-kindness—all moral attributes. You will not be condemned as unjust. You have no strict duty to concede to my wishes.

Everything that I said so far about rights and duties seems to suggest a positivistic, indeed Benthamite view of rights, that unless you can cite the law that confers the right and imposes the duty, such a right cannot exist even if you think it ought to. The discourse of rights outside the framework of laws that confer

---

[1] You sometimes hear it said that rights imply duties, and this is true in precisely the sense I have proposed. However there are those who seem to believe that if I have a right it is I who must also have a duty. This is false. It is someone else who has a duty not to put obstacles in the way of my doing what I claim it is my right to do. Thus, if a keen rambler I claim the right to roam, although it is reasonable and morally proper to assert that I also have a duty not to leave gates open or vandalise your property, this duty is not entailed by my possession of the right. It is you, the property owner, who has the duty.

them is 'nonsense on stilts'.[2] And I have to confess that even after all the arguments I have had over the Human Rights Act 1998 now firmly on the statute book, I still have strong positivistic leanings. For I still believe that wherever there is a right, it is always proper to ask by whom or what it was conferred, and on whom the correlative duty falls, even if the answer is only that it is derived from a general moral consensus. We all know, more or less, what is meant by saying of a particular regime that it has a bad human rights record. We know that people living under this regime are deprived of things that are generally agreed to be necessary to their well-being; they may live in appalling poverty, be forbidden to own property, have no access to fair trial or healthcare, and so on. Such deprivations are morally abhorrent and no human beings should have to suffer them; and those who inflict them on others have a moral obligation to change their ways. The language of rights has become extremely familiar to us in such contexts, because it is easy to point to the general, shared, moral principles according to which we can agree that no one ought to be treated as these people are treated. But I believe we need to be very careful, in using such language, not surreptitiously to borrow the certainty that belongs to the discourse of rights in its legal context where the existence of a right entails that it is someone's legal obligation to see that it is not infringed. However, I also recognise that with the passing of the Human Rights Act a new era began; and however fogeyish or Benthamite I might like to be, I have to acknowledge that claims that something is a human right, that is a right that belongs to everyone who is human, regardless of the legal system under which they live, are made and upheld or rejected, even if, in the last analysis, it has to be in the courts of law that disputed cases must be decided. Does this mean that courts are inevitably turning more frequently into courts of morals? Lord Bingham, in a lecture delivered at Ditchley Park in 2003, suggested that this is indeed one of the ways in which a judge's task has changed in the last few years.[3] There is no approved list of human rights, and not much in the way of precedent (or not yet). Decisions must be made as a matter of judgment: and it is difficult not to suppose that such judgments, as often as not, are moral judgments, to the making of which a judge has to bring an understanding of what is an accepted moral principle. And of course any such judgment may be disputed.

In any case, it is against this general background that I want to consider the question of rights in connection with reproduction. The Universal Declaration of Human Rights,[4] drawn up in 1948 in the aftermath of the Second World War, and

---

[2] This expression comes from Jeremy Bentham's critical analysis of the French Declaration of the Rights of Man and Citizen in a work usually known as *Anarchical Fallacies*. Bentham's claim is that language which looks as if it is describing what rights there actually are is in fact suggesting what rights there ought to be (see R Harrison, Entry on 'Bentham' in T Honderich (ed), *The Oxford Companion to Philosophy* (Oxford, OUP, 1995) available online at http://www.benthamlinks.com/oxford.htm).

[3] The text of Lord Bingham's lecture is published in 68 *Journal of the Ditchley Foundation*, and can be found online, at http://www.ditchley.co.uk/news/newsletter_summer03.htm.

[4] Adopted and proclaimed by General Assembly Resolution 217 A (III) of 10 December 1948.

one of the first outcomes of the newly established United Nations Organisation, set out the freedoms to which every human being was entitled. Backed up by the World Health Organisation, it was agreed that one such freedom was that of establishing a family.[5] Though the Declaration was not, strictly speaking, a source of international law within the meaning of Article 38 paragraph 1*lit*(a) of the Statute of the International Court of Justice in The Hague, the rights it formulates, at least in their core, can today be taken to reflect customary international law,[6] and supposed infringements by any member of the United Nations which has also accepted the jurisdiction of the International Court of Justice over such matters could be brought before the International Court at The Hague.[7] Thus any country that tried to prevent a particular group of people from having children, by enforced sterilisation of, say, the mentally disabled could be held to be in breach of international human rights law.

Compulsory sterilisation of individuals is of course a highly controversial issue, giving rise to questions about the definition of competence, which fall to be settled in the context of particular circumstances and particular patterns of behaviour in the individuals concerned. The taken-for-granted right to autonomy in matters of procreation has to be weighed against the social consequences and the possible harm to the unborn child of leaving a woman to have children irresponsibly, or a man to inseminate women criminally. However, it is extremely unlikely that there will ever be an attempt to have recourse to programmes of wholesale sterilisation of those deemed mentally or racially unfit to have children, such as were instituted in the USA at the beginning of the 20th century,[8] and were even advocated by such jurists as Oliver Wendell Holmes as late as the 1930s.[9] The history of the

---

[5] Universal Declaration of Human Rights, Art 16 para 1. The same right was later enshrined in an international treaty, the International Covenant on Civil and Political Rights (adopted and opened for signature, ratification and accession by General Assembly Resolution 2200 A (XXI) of 16 December 1966 and entered into force on 23 March 1976), Art 23 para 2. Many of the States Parties to this Convention have submitted themselves to the jurisdiction of the Human Rights Committee, which adjudicates complaints by individuals against States Parties, under the Optional Protocol to the International Covenant on Civil and Political Rights, which was adopted, and later entered into force, on the same date as the Covenant.

[6] See RKM Smith, *Textbook on International Human Rights*, 2nd edn (Oxford, OUP, 2005) 39.

[7] The judicial enforcement of human rights at the international level continues to be difficult. The situation of individuals affected by human rights violations is much improved under some regional conventions for the protection of human rights, like the European Convention on the Protection of Human Rights and Fundamental Freedoms and the American Convention of Human Rights. See RKM Smith, *ibid* 92 ff, and more generally A Cassese, *International Law* (Oxford, OUP, 2000) 349 ff.

[8] See D Micklos and E Carlson, 'Engineering American Society: The Lesson of Eugenics' (2000) 1 *Nature Reviews Genetics* 153–58.

[9] In upholding the right of the State of Virginia to sterilise the mentally disabled compulsorily, Holmes's judgment read 'It is better for all the world, if instead of waiting for their imbecility, society can prevent those who are manifestly unfit from continuing their kind. Three generations of imbeciles are enough.' *Buck v Bell* 274 US 207 (1927). See further PA Lombardo, 'Taking Eugenics Seriously: Three Generations of ??? Are Enough' (2003) 30 *Florida State University L Rev* 191–203.

20th century in Europe, and the dramatic growth in our insistence (sometimes reluctant) on the equal worth of all human beings has made it virtually certain that eugenics on this sort of scale will not recur. I shall return to the concept of eugenics later.

To return to rights, people are prone to deploy the language of rights most vociferously when they have not got that to which they claim they are entitled; thus the question of an individual's right to choose to have a child is perhaps most frequently heard in the context of infertility treatment. In my book *Making Babies. Is There a Right to Have Children?*[10] I tried to draw a distinction between claiming a right to assistance in conceiving a child and claiming a right to receive this assistance free of charge, under the National Health Service. In fact *in vitro* fertilisation and donor insemination are theoretically available under the National Health Service, up to the limit of three attempts,[11] though it may be that clinics or hospitals that provide it are pretty widely geographically scattered and differ from one another in their success rates. But the situation is little different from that of dental treatment these days. Theoretically residents in this country are entitled to free dental treatment; but few are legally entitled to or qualified for a totally free service, and this has been true now for many years; moreover now few even if they are qualified can get access to a dentist practising under the National Health Service. We have therefore to be content not with a right to free treatment, but with a right to treatment, even if we have to pay for it. Our right is not to be refused treatment if we come with the money in our hand (as we might claim a right to be served in a pub as long as we can pay for our drink). We have long given up claiming a right to free spectacles or free prescriptions. So, though people doubtless do not welcome being told that they cannot have fertility treatment unless they pay for it, they are perhaps little inclined to argue that to cause them to pay is to infringe a right.

Indeed, we in the UK are gradually beginning to realise that the state has a limited duty to provide free treatment to us for all our ills. In 1995 there was a case in which the Cambridgeshire Health Authority refused a third course of chemotherapy and a second bone marrow transplant for a child (known as child B) whose previous treatments for leukaemia had been unsuccessful.[12] This was taken up by the tabloid press as a scandal. It was held that the Health Authority

---

[10] (Oxford, OUP, 2002).

[11] See National Institute for Clinical Excellence (NICE) guidelines *Fertility: assessment and treatment for people with fertility problems* (February 2004), available at http://www.nice.org.uk/page.aspx?o=104435, and further information provided by the British Fertility Society at http://www.fertility.org.uk/public/factsheets/keyfacts.html.

[12] The decision was judicially reviewed, the Court of Appeal eventually ruling that the Health Authority's decision was reasonable and properly made (*R v Cambridge Health Authority, ex parte B* [1995] 1 WLR 898).

was denying to the child what they described as 'the most fundamental right of all, the right to life'; and this, they alleged, was on 'purely financial grounds'. Some would-be benefactor came forward with money to pay for child B to have the treatment privately; and the child lived a few more months and then died. But the confusion about rights, to what precisely we are entitled, should, if possible, be clarified. In what contexts, and with a view to what outcomes, does it make sense for a terminally ill person to claim 'the right to life'? It seems to me that there cannot be a right to something that it is impossible we should have. A right secures a freedom which no one must prevent my enjoying: but there may be other factors besides some dereliction of duty that prevent my enjoying that freedom. As a rambler, my right to roam over the rocky and uneven terrain of your grouse moor is at best a hypothetical right if I have my legs amputated or become confined to a wheel-chair. In the case of child B, it was exceedingly improbable that she would long survive a third course of chemotherapy; which would in any case cause her great suffering; and she had already suffered almost unbearably. The treatment was judged to be futile by the Health Authority. They were not refusing to pay for a life-saving intervention. Had child B been a competent adult she would have had the right, as we all have, to refuse further treatment which she judged unlikely to succeed.

I mention this case only to illustrate a common muddle in the claim to rights in matters of health treatment, including the provision of assisted conception. Sometimes people may be claiming a right to reproductive autonomy; sometimes they may be claiming a right to free medical assistance; sometimes they may be claiming a right to have a baby which with the best medical help in the world they still cannot have.[13] But there are some signs that our claims to rights in respect of medical treatment are undergoing a change. It may be that the case of child B would not cause such outrage if it arose today (though the Daily Mail would still love it). We may gradually be beginning to realise that rights to treatment are limited, certainly by what money is available, but also by what counts or does not count as acceptable risk or probability of success.

However, even if in some respects people may be more hesitant than once they were to claim their supposed rights (or at any rate more realistic), there are still many situations in which the question of rights does arise. I want to look at some

---

[13] Rights to particular state-funded services are sometimes claimed as instantiations, or concretisations, of a broader human right. In the jurisprudence of the European Court of Human Rights, such rights are then conceptualised as reflecting the positive obligation of Member States to 'ensure' the enjoyment of the human rights enshrined in the Convention. It may, however, be better to understand such rights to services as new and separate rights which are generated by the broadly formulated human right in question, when it is read in conjunction with the inherently dynamic obligation on the part of the state to 'ensure' that human rights can be enjoyed by the people within their jurisdiction, rather than as an aspect, or part, of the human right itself.

of them now, in order to try to assess the usefulness, even intelligibility of the discourse of rights in their connection. I will start with the case of Ms Evans.[14] This
case began in 2003. Ms Evans and her partner had intended to use embryos
brought into existence by *in vitro* fertilisation and stored in a hospital to start a
family when they were ready. However, at this hospital, Ms Evans had been diagnosed as suffering from early-stage ovarian cancer. She was told that she could
become pregnant, using the frozen embryos in about a year or so, but that she
would first need surgery that would involve oophorectomy, and that therefore
using the embryos would be her last chance to have a baby. By the time that the
right moment in the cycle to use the embryos had come round she had separated
from her partner; but she wanted to start a pregnancy anyway. Now the law is
absolutely clear on this point. In order to use frozen embryos to start a pregnancy, the hospital or clinic where they are stored has to obtain written consent from
both partners. The man and the woman are treated by the law as having equal
rights of decision. Ms Evans's partner, however, now refused his permission. Ms
Evans brought a case against the hospital and based her case largely on the admitted fact that her ex-partner had promised her, in front of witnesses, that she could
use the embryos at any time that she was ready, and that he would never stand in
her way. These facts were not disputed. However, in his evidence the man claimed
that he had uttered the words only to comfort Ms Evans when she was distressed
by her diagnosis, and that since then circumstances had radically changed. He had
left Ms Evans for someone else with whom he was starting a family, and so his
promise was no longer binding. It had been uttered in an emotional moment in
the doctor's office, and had certainly never been repeated in writing. Ms Evans had
committed to writing an undertaking that if she had the baby he should have no
responsibility for it, financial or otherwise: but such an undertaking is not recognised in law and had to be overlooked as irrelevant. The judge in the case, Mr
Justice Wall, in finding against her said that in this sort of case what was needed
in law was certainty, and it was certain that without the consent of both parties in
writing, Ms Evans had no legal right to use the embryos in order to become pregnant, nor, more accurately, to attempt to become pregnant. The hospital on the
contrary had the right to dispose of the embryos, either for use in research or for
immediate destruction. If the requirement of written consent could be waived in
some cases the hospital, whose statutory duty it was to release the embryos to the
couple only with their written consent, might find itself involved in litigation, followed perhaps by withdrawal of their licensed status for failure to comply with the

---

[14] For the decision of the High Court discussed in the text, see *Evans v Amicus Healthcare Ltd* [2003]
EWHC Fam 2161. The Court of Appeal has meanwhile confirmed Wall J's ruling: *Evans v Amicus
Healthcare Ltd* [2004] EWCA Civ 727; [2005] Fam 1. The case is discussed by S Sheldon, '*Evans v
Amicus Healthcare; Hadley v Midland Fertility Services*—Revealing Cracks in the "Twin Pillars"?' (2004)
16 *Child and Family Law Quarterly* 437–52.

law. As to the promise, Mr Justice Wall agreed that it had been made only as a means of reassurance to Ms Evans at a particularly fraught time, and could not be held to override the law. That her partner may have been morally wrong to make such a promise to Ms Evans simply as vacuous words of comfort was held to be neither here nor there. Ms Evans, however, took the case to appeal. In the Court of Appeal Lord Justice Thorpe and his colleagues turned down the appeal, upholding Mr Justice Wall's judgment. The destruction of the embryos is to be stayed for four weeks, giving Ms Evans time to decide whether or not to carry her case to the House of Lords. But at present it looks as though Ms Evans will lose her appeal, and with it her last chance to have a child genetically related to herself.

I have spelled out the details of this case because there could hardly be a clearer instance of the difference between a legal right and what Ms Evans doubtless thought of as a moral right, indeed a human right, not to be prevented from becoming pregnant. Interestingly, in his very long judgment, Mr Justice Wall had gone into the question of the promise in detail, and considered by way of analogy some cases of promissory estoppel, where a verbal undertaking had been deemed so strong as to compel the overriding of the normal course of law. The cases he considered were all of them concerned with the disposal of property where, let us say, a nephew had given up his employment to manage his aunt's estate and to look after her and her affairs, and she had repeatedly told him that the estate would be his when she died, and that all the work he was putting in would in the end be to his own benefit. When the aunt died and her will was read it turned out that she had left all of her estate to the local cats' home. In such a case the will might be overturned (estoppel on grounds of promise) because the injustice caused by honouring its terms would be 'unconscionable'. In correspondence with Mr Justice Wall, who had sent me a copy of his judgment in full, I asked him the precise meaning of the word 'unconscionable' (a word that I have now adopted as part of my moral vocabulary) and he replied that he did not really know, but that he accepted my suggested definition that it meant 'what would be generally agreed to be morally outrageous'. If this is a correct definition, it shows that there are cases, though that of Ms Evans was not among them, when the rights conferred by law are overridden on moral grounds. Moreover, in the matter of the disappointed nephew Mr Justice Wall said that the *injustice* would have been unconscionable. The word 'injustice' implies that, if the will had been upheld, he would have been deprived of something not merely that he badly wanted, even needed, but something to which he was in some manner entitled. The estoppel was not grounded on pity or compassion, but on something at least akin to a human or moral right. By the use of this analogy, which turned out to be non-analogous, Mr Justice Wall was saying, in effect, that though Ms Evans might be thought, on grounds of compassion, to deserve to have her baby, she not only had no legal right (which was beyond dispute) but no moral right either.

I want now to return to the matter of eugenics and to raise two different questions about rights in this connection. The first is the question whether or not the medical profession is entitled to refuse requests for assisted conception to people or classes of people on grounds other than clinical grounds or grounds of scarcity of money or resources. Have they the right, in other words, to say of a particular applicant, or a category of applicants that they are not fit to be parents, and are not therefore entitled to help? As I have said already, I think it most unlikely in the present climate of opinion that any doctor or clinic could pursue a policy of refusing infertility treatment to members of specific racial or religious groups, however undesirable they privately believe it is to increase the numbers of these groups. This would be illegal under anti-discrimination laws, and they would undoubtedly lose their license to practice if such a policy were discovered. But what about a refusal to treat an infertile couple who were convicted child-abusers? What about providing assisted conception to couples who were not infertile, but were homosexual? Do these individuals, or categories of people possess a right to treatment? After all, what distinguishes assistance to conceive from other forms of medical treatment is that if it is successful, there is not just the patient or patients to consider but the child who will be born. Whenever the question of fitness for parenthood is raised, it is the good of the child that must be taken into account and indeed which by law is to be paramount.[15]

The difficulty, however, of applying such a test is that of irremediable ignorance. We cannot know with any certainty how it will be for someone brought up as the child of two homosexuals, any more than we can know what the outcome will be for a child brought up as the child of two blind people, or two who are profoundly deaf. The case of the child-abusers may seem clear-cut but what about applicants for assisted conception who have less obviously relevant criminal records? What about those who want a child together, have failed to conceive and are manifestly on the very border of mental competence to take decisions? Are we here embarked on a slippery slope? I believe that hospitals and clinics are probably unwilling to turn down applicants for assistance on the basis of personal, one-off moral judgments. There is a case here, I think, for hospital ethics committees, often bodies of dubious utility, to draw up guide-lines (but not rigid criteria) to inform individual decisions; but above all, it seems to me morally right that applicants for assisted conception should be told honestly what are the reasons for their application's being turned down if it is (and not have them disguised as a matter of 'clinical judgment'), and that they should be given a list of hospitals where their

---

[15] See s 13(5) Human Fertilisation and Embryology Act 1990: 'A woman shall not be provided with treatment services unless account has been taken of the welfare of any child who may be born as a result of the treatment (including the need of that child for a father), and of any other child who may be affected by the birth.'

application might be assessed differently. Apart from this I think that current laws against sexual, racial or religious discrimination should be enough to protect applicants from any infringements of their legal rights to fair treatment, in whatever contexts these infringements occur.

I come finally to what will be an increasingly contentious question about parental rights. Should parents be allowed to exercise choice not only over whether to have or not to have children, and when to have them, but over what sort of children they will have? We all of us have a right to choose what sort of property we acquire. Even if sometimes we have to make compromises, and make do with a house, say, or a horse, which falls short of our ideal, but is the best available, and seems good enough, in the end the decision is ours. We cannot yet do quite the same with the children to whom we give birth. But, we are told, we are moving in that direction. The concept of the 'designer baby', deliberately engineered to possess the characteristics we would wish for in our children has become a Shibboleth, a criterion to distinguish the virtuous from the vicious in autonomy over conception, and genetic choice. There is, as usual, a high degree of media rhetoric surrounding the possibility of such choices. The Times leading headline on 26 June 2004 read 'Gene tests to start era of Baby-to-Order'. In fact this story referred to two applications for licenses to carry out preimplantation genetic diagnosis for two particular genes, BRCA1 and BRCA2, which give rise to inherited early-onset breast cancer. Preimplantation genetic diagnosis (PGD) is already widely used, followed by IVF, especially to select female embryos from among those fertilised in the laboratory in the case of families at high risk of having babies with Duchenne's muscular dystrophy or haemophilia, both conditions affecting only males. There is nothing new in the concept, only in the discovery of the particular gene that can now be identified in the eight–cell embryo. It seems to me beyond doubt that once the new diagnostic techniques are available then those families that are at risk have a right to seek the diagnosis, if they are prepared to accept the inherent intrusiveness and relatively low success rate of IVF treatment. They have to weigh these immediate disadvantages against the manifest long term advantages (for the child as well as for themselves) of not having a child who will in all probability die painfully and young. This seems to me no more than the right we all have, if we can afford to exercise it, to seek up-to-date medical treatment. The arguments of those who say that thereby some rejected embryos are denied the right to life are not to be taken seriously. In the first place thousands of embryos fail to implant in the uterus in the natural course of events, and thus have no chance of life, let alone a right to it. Secondly, most people now accept that IVF is a morally acceptable method of assisted conception, and that more embryos than are actually inserted into the uterus are routinely produced by IVF, and are destined for destruction, either after being used for research or immediately. Again, there is nothing new, and if further tests are devised for other late-onset diseases such as Alzheimer's or Parkinson's, then so much the better for the humane practice of medicine.

But, as the same Times leader points out, there are those who argue that such advances 'make it harder to resist efforts to use PGD to screen for socially desirable traits such as good looks or intelligence'. And here we have the real horror of designer babies, the possibility of choosing our babies as we choose our houses or our horses—turning our children, as we are often told, into mere commodities. Well, first it must be said that such possibilities of choice are very far from being realised at present. No one has any idea what genes or combinations of genes express themselves in high intelligence or beauty. And this is not just a matter of current ignorance which can predictably be overcome by further research. It is more deeply rooted than that. Although we may be fairly sure what factors contribute to a profound lack of intelligence, or some kinds of physical deformity, intelligence and physical beauty are unpredictable, and in the known combination of genes 'for', as they say, intelligence, still what might be expressed by these genes might turn out to produce less than we hoped. Numberless factors of nurture as well as nature go into the making of what we regard as an intelligent person. And, again, it is well-known that some people with impeccably regular features are less beautiful than those who are idiosyncratically and unexpectedly attractive by reason of their psychological as much as their physiological inheritance. So I do not myself see that the progress in eliminating rogue genes that cause or contribute to certain undoubtedly disastrous diseases is necessarily a step in the direction of the kind of enhancement that those who talk of designer babies so much dread.

Before considering that issue further, I should briefly refer to a kind of case which falls between selection of embryos in order to avoid giving birth to a sick baby and selection of embryos to enhance their prospects in life, and that is the case of selecting an embryo by PGD whose bone marrow would be compatible with that of a sibling in need of a bone marrow transplant to save his life. One such case arose a few years ago in the UK, and permission for the procedure was refused by the Human Fertilisation and Embryology Authority (HFEA) on the grounds that it would amount to the creation of a baby not for its own sake but simply as a means to be used for the sake of another child, and that no one had a right to request something that was so morally objectionable and so harmful to the new child.[16] Others argued against it on the grounds that it was yet one more

---

[16] The case concerned the child Charlie Whitaker. The HFEA based its decision on the fact that Charlie suffered from a non-hereditary disease (Diamond Blakfan anaemia), and hence there was no need to screen the embryo 'in its own best interest' in order to make sure that it was free from the disease. The HFEA has since changed its policy on the issue. See further S Sheldon and S Wilkinson, 'Hashmi and Whitaker: An Unjustifiable and Misguided Distinction?' (2004) *Medical L Rev* 137–63 and the discussion of the HFEA's policy considerations by M Johnson, 'Regulating the Science and Therapeutic Application of Human Embryo Research: Managing the Tension Between Biomedical Creativity and Public Concern' (in this collection).

step in the direction of the designer baby. I think that both objections are profoundly mistaken, but especially that of the HFEA. There is nothing, as Aristotle knew, to prevent something's being valued both for the sake of something else and for its own sake (health was the example he took). I think that this baby would have been equally valued for himself and for what he could do for his sibling, and if the transplant after all failed, he would not be rejected but loved all the more for his very existence. Children who have been born sometimes donate organs for a sibling; they are admired for their heroism and loved the more even if the attempt fails. I cannot see that to select an embryo that might turn out to perform this function is any less acceptable.

But this is by the way. To return to the fantasy of designer babies, let us try to imagine that there will come a time when people can select the characteristics that they want for their child: they can choose whether he is to be amiable or irascible, ambitious or a contented sluggard, a classical violinist or a jazz saxophonist or tone-deaf. Let us try to imagine at least that they can select a proneness to such characteristics, which may emerge if the environment is right (and this is a big qualification). The theoretical question is: would parents then have a right to make such choices? I do not believe that they would. It is at this point I think that the argument that turns on the good of the unborn child comes into force. No one could claim a moral or human right (and it could not conceivably become a legal right) to do something that would be manifestly contrary to the interests of the child who would be born. It is not so much that the characteristics chosen might turn out after all not to be such a blessing to the child as the parents had supposed. It is rather that it would change the relation between the child and its parents in a potentially damaging way (of course this is a theoretical response to the question, no empirical evidence being available).[17] The basis of my conviction on this point is, however, the non-theoretical fact that children are not like houses and horses, among the possessions of their parents. To insist that your child shall be born not with a unique and unpredictable mixture of genes passed on by both of its parents but with the characteristics you yourself would choose for it is to overlook this distinction. And, as the expression 'designer babies' suggests, the parents' motivation for having such a child becomes suspect. It must surely be so that they can take pride in the achievements or the beauty of their child, glory reflected on themselves, rather than so that they bring up a new human being, with perhaps unexpected and often less than ideal characteristics of his own, with an identity separate from that of his parents. And then there is the further point, that if, as would be highly likely, the genes in their new admixture did not express themselves as it had been hoped, the disappointment and disapproval of the parents in

---

[17] See further T Baldwin, 'Choosing Who: What is Wrong With Making Better Children?' (in this collection).

their refusnik child, who declined to play the violin or whatever he was supposed to do would be terrible in its effects on the child. Here again one has to observe the crucial distinction between things that one wants, perhaps passionately, even unreasonably (such as success for one's children) and things to which one is entitled under the law, or, by extension, under the natural or moral principle that confers human rights. And, as I have argued, this very extension carries the danger that it may entice us into blurring that distinction.

2

Choosing Who: What is Wrong with Making Better Children?

THOMAS BALDWIN*

A. Making Better Children

Sometimes people talk about the possibility of making a 'perfect' child. Taken literally this is misconceived: we can speak of a perfect circle but not of a perfect child, since the diverse strands of human life cannot be captured by a single formula which would enable us to specify what it would be for a child to be perfect. It is an *a priori* truth and not just an empirical one that no one is perfect. So it is preferable to talk of one child being 'better' than another, in the sense that one child is likely to have a better life than another, as in Julian Savulescu's principle of procreative beneficence: '[C]ouples (or single reproducers) should select the child, of the possible children they could have, who is expected to have the best life, or at least as good a life as the others, based on the relevant available information.'[1]

But even this type of judgment is one concerning which we should be cautious: in many cases the question, 'has X had a better life than Y?', when asked of two people who have had reasonably decent but very different lives, is surely not a question to press. Nonetheless we can be confident in some cases that there are ways of making life better, of improving life for people. We are rightly suspicious of the ability of politicians to deliver such improvements but at least the claim that some improvements are possible makes sense. So a sensible reformulation of the original question would be this:

What is wrong with making children in such a way that they are likely to have better lives than would otherwise have been the case?

---

* This is a revised version of a paper given at the Cambridge conference. I am much indebted to Matthew Kramer for his helpful comments on the original paper.
[1] J Savulescu, 'Procreative Beneficence' (2001) 15 *Bioethics* 415.

—except that we need to allow for the fact that some of our interventions would create children different from those who would otherwise have been born. There is no neat idiom to add this disjunct to the question unequivocally, but I shall take it that the following idiom does so:

What is wrong with making children in such a way that they are likely to have better lives than the lives of those children who would otherwise have been born?

(*ie* the phrase 'those children who etc' is to be understood to apply both where an intervention leads to the birth of different children and where it does not).

B. Procreative Beneficence

This question suggests that in some circumstances it might be wrong to act in this way; and the denial of this suggestion is the assertion that under no circumstances is this wrong, *ie*:

It is always permissible to make children in ways which are likely to make their lives better than the lives of those children who would otherwise have been born.

Savulescu's principle of procreative beneficence embodies a stronger claim, to the effect that such interventions are not only permissible, but 'morally required' *ie* obligatory;[2] so his principle can be formulated as follows:

It is obligatory to make children in ways which are likely to make their lives better than the lives of those children who would otherwise have been born.

To label this distinction, I shall call Savulescu's principle 'strong procreative benef- icence', and the permissive principle that procreative beneficence is never wrong 'weak procreative beneficence'.

These two principles can be compared with those which express the generalised beneficence of ideal utilitarianism. The strong principle is:

It is obligatory to do whatever one can to make the world better than it would other- wise have been. (So one does wrong if one does anything else).

---

[2] *Ibid.*

The weak principle is:

It is always permissible to do whatever makes the world better than it would otherwise have been. (So one does no wrong if one does that; but it is not obligatory to act in that way).

Now let us think briefly about standard objections to utilitarianism. The standard objections to the strong principle are that we are not responsible for the state of the world and that any such responsibility would be destructive of individual liberty since the strong principle eliminates the possibility of actions which are permitted but not obligatory. Plainly, these objections do not apply to the weak principle; in this case the standard objection is that there are situations in which it would be wrong to perform some action despite the fact that by doing the action one would bring it about that the world is better overall than it would otherwise have been. This objection is usually filled out by more or less imaginary cases such as the following: suppose one were to find oneself in a situation in which one is invited by a powerful evil gangster to perform an action which violates a strict moral prohibition such as that on killing the innocent while the gangster makes it clear that he will attach even worse outcomes to one's refusal to violate the prohibition than flow from the act by itself.[3] Critics of the weak principle hold that one should not allow oneself to be coerced in such cases; thus they hold that there are cases in which an act would not be permissible because it violates a 'deontological constraint', such as not killing the innocent, despite the fact that its potential consequences are maximally beneficial overall.

These familiar points provide a way of approaching the dialectic that applies in the restricted sphere of procreative beneficence. Consider first the strong principle; indeed consider not just Savulescu's principle, which applies only to potential parents, but a super-strong principle which applies to everyone:

It is obligatory for everyone to do what they can to ensure that children who are born are those who are expected to have the best life.

It seems clear that this is too strong. We do not have that responsibility to children in general, and it would be very destructive, not only of our own liberty, but also of the rights of potential parents, if we did have this responsibility. So the objections to strong utilitarianism apply across here, although, as I shall argue below, there is a weaker obligation on us to have a concern for the welfare of children in general.

---

[3] See B Williams 'A Critique of Utilitarianism' in J Smart and B Williams (eds), *Utilitarianism: For and Against* (Cambridge, CUP, 1973) esp at 98–99.

What, now, about Savulescu's strong principle, which applies to potential parents? Here again (as Savulescu acknowledges[4]) there is an issue about liberty: take a case where there is an intervention which would enable parents to have a 'better' child than would otherwise be the case. Is this intervention obligatory? If it is, it potentially conflicts with the parents' procreative autonomy, which permits them to act as they choose as long as their choice does not harm anyone. The conflict is clear where there is a potential enhancement in the offing whose absence would not harm a child by damaging its fundamental interests. For such an enhancement would be obligatory under the strong principle, whereas it would be a legitimate exercise of parental autonomy not to provide it. To think about the issue here let us imagine that there is a genetic way of making a child a bit more musical. Strong procreative beneficence implies that, other things being equal, this enhancement is obligatory. But does one harm a child by not equipping it with this enhancement? Well, do parents harm a child by not providing it with music lessons? Surely not, even though it is generally beneficial for children to have music lessons. Thus while parents who fail to provide their child with the imagined enhancement to its musical abilities violate the strong principle of procreative beneficence, their conduct is an exercise of their procreative autonomy; and in a case of this kind, as with the provision of music lessons, the balance of reasons surely favours autonomy over obligatory procreative beneficence.

A different type of case is that in which one is not aiming at an enhancement, but rather at avoiding something awful, such as the birth of a child with Tay-Sachs disease.[5] Is it morally required, where both parents know that they are carriers, to take steps to ensure that they do not create a child with this terrible disease? Or does their procreative autonomy make it permissible for them to take the one in four risk of creating such a child? In a case of this kind an important consideration is that the usual ways for a couple to ensure that they avoid having a child with Tay-Sachs is to employ either pre-implantation genetic diagnosis (PGD) or pre-natal diagnosis (PND). PGD requires the creation of embryos *in vitro* and is likely to lead to the disposal of unwanted embryos; PND is likely to lead to a termination of pregnancy where Tay-Sachs is diagnosed. Thus both techniques involve a step that many people regard as morally unacceptable; and one does not have to agree with those who think that abortion or the disposal of embryos is

---

[4] Savulescu, 'Procreative Beneficence', above n 1, 418.

[5] Tay-Sachs disease is a fatal inherited disease of the central nervous system. Babies with Tay-Sachs lack an enzyme necessary for breaking down certain fatty substances in brain and nerve cells. These substances build up and gradually destroy brain and nerve cells, until the entire nervous system breaks down. Symptoms appear at 4 to 6 months of age when an apparently healthy baby gradually stops smiling, crawling or turning over, and eventually becomes blind, paralysed and unaware of its surroundings. Death occurs by age five.

wrong to hold that it cannot be morally obligatory, as the strong principle implies, for potential parents to have to take such a step where they would never willingly consent to it. So here too, even though it is obviously highly desirable that the chances of the birth of a child with Tay-Sachs be minimised, the moral basis of procreative autonomy provides a good reason for rejecting the demands of strong procreative beneficence.

But what about weak procreative beneficence, the principle that doing what one can to bring it about that one has better children is always permissible? This thesis is less demanding than the strong one, and for that reason more readily compatible with procreative autonomy. 'Liberal eugenics' can be thought of as the conjunction of these two principles. The comparison with weak generalised utilitarianism then suggests that the objection to this position should come from deontological constraints—cases in which there are deontological principles which are violated by liberal eugenic practices. Are there plausible cases of this kind?

C. Improving the Environment

Before discussing this, however, I want to go back to a point left over from the previous discussion of 'super-strong' procreative beneficence, the thesis that there is a general obligation on us to support the birth of better children, children whose chance of a good life is better than it would otherwise have been. This thesis is, I think, important when one considers one general type of intervention that helps to support the birth of better children: environmental interventions. I mention this here because bioethical discussions of this issue are typically conducted in the context of a tacit genetic exceptionalism whereby all the attention is focused on genetic interventions and none on environmental ones. But the truth is that although more or less hypothetical genetic interventions raise more 'sexy' issues, potential environmental interventions are from a practical perspective overwhelmingly more important. In the real world, as opposed to the science fiction of bioethical discussions about human genetics, there is no genetic determinism and single-gene disorders or characteristics are very unusual; the more we learn about human genetics, the more it appears that the connections between genes and health or welfare are mediated by environmental conditions and involve multi-factorial genetic interactions. So the chances of significant genetic interventions, either by PGD and embryo selection or gene therapy, are limited. By contrast we know from the work of David Barker that the relationship between maternal health, especially nutrition, during pregnancy and the subsequent health of a child born after that pregnancy is very intimate; the notorious famine of the Dutch winter of 1944–45 was disastrous for the welfare of the children whose mothers were affected by it.[6] It is also known that children who miss out during early infancy on early windows for the development of movement, language, and play have much poorer life chances thereafter. Almost anyone who becomes familiar with this work, I think, acknowledges a 'negative' version of my 'super strong' principle of procreative beneficence, that there is a general obligation to take steps to ensure that these evils are minimised. We do need a state which is prepared to put serious resources into parenting so as to protect the interests of unborn children and early infants. This would not be literally a 'nanny state', a state which takes over direct responsibility for parenting; for family life is in general much better for children than no family at all. What is required instead is provision to prepare young adults for parenting and to help them look after their children through the crucial early years. The delicate issue here is one of intervention into the 'private' sphere of family life: the need is to find ways of supporting families without undermining their dignity.

Thus from a practical perspective the most important exercise of procreative beneficence lies in this area of 'environmental' interventions. Some genetic disorders are of course awful, but far more common than genetic disorders is the social misfortune a child endures by being conceived and then brought up by a couple who are financially poor, with poor education and poor health. There's surely nothing wrong about making life better for those children.

D. Liberal Eugenics

I return now to liberal eugenics, the combination of procreative autonomy and weak procreative beneficence. The initial issue here is whether the practice of liberal eugenics, thus understood, is liable to violate any deontological constraints. To think about this I return to the use of PGD to avoid the birth of a child with Tay-Sachs. It will be obvious from the previous discussion where the question of a potential deontological constraint arises: PGD involves the creation *in vitro* of several human embryos some of which, almost certainly, will not be used—either because they have the 'bad' gene, or because they are of poor quality, or simply because they are surplus to requirements. So: if all human embryos ought to be implanted, because they are all equally human beings whose lives are not to be terminated merely by a human decision to dispose of them, then PGD is inherently wrong. The argument here is similar to the argument against weak utilitarianism: where that argument relies on the claim that people have a fundamental right to

---

[6] See D Barker, *The Best Start in Life* (London, Century, 2003); and ACJ Ravelli *et al*, 'Glucose tolerance in adults after prenatal exposure in the Dutch famine' (1998) 351 *Lancet* 173–77.

life which makes it wrong to kill the innocent, this argument relies on the thesis that all human embryos have a similar right to life which makes it wrong to dispose of unwanted ones. The difference between the arguments, however, is that this latter thesis is highly contentious and since it raises a range of difficult points which it would not be sensible to discuss here, the question at issue here can only be answered in a conditional format: if the human embryo is a human being with a fundamental right to life, then genetic techniques such as PGD are wrong, even if they are ways of making better children. But if the antecedent of this conditional is false then this argument falls, and with it, I think, the strongest case for supposing that liberal eugenic practice violates a deontological constraint. It should also be noted that the fact that PGD is in this way conditionally questionable does not imply that any genetic intervention with the same result raises a similar moral issue. A hypothetical technique of gene replacement for Tay-Sachs can be envisaged which could be applied to a single embryo *in vitro*, thereby eliminating the creation of any unused embryos. So even if PGD is wrong, with another technique it need not be wrong to make children who are better in the same respect.

Liberal eugenics does not just face a challenge on the grounds that it violates the right to life of human embryos. For even when that point is set aside, there are other important issues that need to be faced. Consider a genetic disability such as Down's syndrome: the liberal eugenicist will say that couples at risk of this should be permitted to use genetic interventions to ensure that they avoid having a child with this disability. Some disability groups object to this, however, on 'expressivist' grounds—to the effect that this kind of intervention expresses and thereby encourages prejudice against people with this disability. This argument is basically consequentialist: it asserts that there is a causal link between genetic interventions to prevent the birth of children with the disability and popular prejudice against such people. As such, the argument is open to the objection that popular prejudices against people with Down's syndrome long predate interventions such as PGD and PND, and that there are other, and better, ways of combating such prejudices. Furthermore, once one appreciates the very substantial commitment to long-term care typically required of parents of children with Down's syndrome, the liberal case appears very strong. Not permitting parents to avoid the birth of a child whose care will require this long-term demanding commitment from them when they find themselves, even after counselling, unwilling to make such a commitment is a tremendous imposition on them; it is also a poor policy for ensuring the welfare of the child.

Further issues arise from the application of a liberal eugenic policy to achondroplasia.[7] This disorder is the result of a genetic mutation and because the gene

---

[7] Achondroplasia is the most common form of short-limb dwarfism, an incurable developmental disorder in which bone tissue does not develop properly in the long bones of the arms and legs. Affected individuals reach a maximum height of 120 cm. The torso develops normally, but the head may be larger than normal with a prominent forehead and flat nose.

involved is autosomal dominant, where just one parent has this mutation, there is a 50% chance that any child s/he has will inherit it; if both parents have it, there is again a 50% chance that their child will be similarly affected, but only a 25% chance that their child will be altogether unaffected, since there is also a 25% chance that their child will inherit the mutation from both parents, with fatal results for the infant. Because of this last possibility, where both parents are achondroplasic the situation is similar to that which applies in the case of Tay-Sachs discussed above: setting aside the deontological concerns arising from the destruction of embryos and fetuses, the use of PGD or PND to avert the birth of a fatally damaged child is morally acceptable. What is more difficult to assess, however, is the situation where just one parent is achondroplasic; is it acceptable for the parents to use PGD or PND to avoid having a child who is similarly achondroplasic? Or is such a practice an unacceptable form of discrimination?

An initial question here is whether such a practice would be a form of procreative beneficence at all, a way of having children likely to have a better life. I said right at the start that judgments of the form 'A has a better life than B' are ones concerning which we should be cautious, and this is an area where this warning certainly applies. For there is no question but that many achondroplasics lead fulfilling lives which, so far from being obstructed by their condition, are unimaginable without it. On the other hand, achondroplasia is a disorder affecting more than size which makes life more difficult in many respects, and if one imagines a world from which it is absent altogether one would surely not regard its subsequent evolution as a way in which human life has become better. One way to think further about the matter is to suppose there to be a reliable technique of gene therapy which enabled achondroplasia to be treated; would such an intervention, whether pre-natal or post-natal, be beneficial? One can certainly imagine someone whose achondroplasia had not been treated in this way feeling resentful later of those responsible for neglecting their situation; equally one can imagine others in the same situation who might feel that their life would not have been improved by an intervention which would have removed an aspect of their life that has become central to much of what they value. By removing a physical impediment to many familiar possibilities, treatment would bring with it many opportunities that are not available to achondroplasics (and not just because of obstacles that could also be removed by social action); but, equally, it would close off the possibility for a life whose distinctive perspective brings its own opportunities. On balance (and this is a tentative judgment), I take the view that because the result of the imagined treatment would be to significantly increase opportunities of many kinds available to a child (artistic, athletic and vocational, for example), it would in principle be beneficial for the child. If this is right, it follows that the use of PGD or PND to avoid having a child who is achondroplasic would be a case of procreative beneficence and, *prima facie*, a legitimate application of a liberal eugenic policy.

Again it may be objected on expressivist grounds that permitting couples to avoid having an achondroplasic child is likely to encourage prejudiced attitudes and discrimination against achondroplasics, and thus that the practice would give rise to significant indirect harm. But there is a powerful reply to this: couples who have a genetic reason for fearing that a child they will have will be achondroplasic will themselves include a potential parent with achondroplasia. So, if they wish to avoid having a child with this condition, it is not likely to be because they are themselves prejudiced against such people; the expressivist case against permitting liberal eugenic practice is in this case undermined by the fact that among its supposed victims are precisely those who might seek to undertake the eugenic practice in the first place. And if one thinks of such a family who have already had one child with achondroplasia, and who wish to ensure that their second child will not be similarly affected, it is very hard not to accept that they should be allowed to take this action. There is, however, a further consideration to be introduced here. Most cases of achondroplasia are not in fact inherited: about 80% of cases arise from an unpredicted spontaneous mutation. At present where couples are not themselves achondroplasic there is no programme of genetic screening to enable them to avoid having an achondroplasic child with this unpredicted mutation; but one can envisage the possibility of a pre-natal test for achondroplasia being included in a batch of tests for more or less serious rare disorders that is offered to pregnant women generally. In this situation, the couple involved themselves would not include someone who is achondroplasic, so the previous argument against the expressivist thesis that the availability of such a test would reinforce prejudice no longer applies. But if the previous argument has been accepted, and it is accepted that it is morally permissible for a couple where one partner is achondroplasic to use PND, it is hard to see how it can be fair to prevent other unaffected couples using PND in the same way. So, on balance, even in this hypothetical new situation, liberal eugenic practice seems acceptable.

But there is a further question here: if it is acceptable for a couple to choose to use PGD or PND to *avoid* having an achondroplasic child, is it also acceptable for them to use to PGD to *ensure* that they have an achondroplasic child? This would be, *prima facie*, an exercise of procreative autonomy by the parents, but not a case of procreative beneficence, given the tentative conclusion of the previous discussion. But the weak principle of procreative beneficence affirms only that beneficence is sufficient for permissibility, not that it is also necessary. So, on the face of it, the proposed intervention would be a legitimate application of liberal eugenic principles. The only way to query this is to appeal to the familiar constraint on the exercise of autonomy, namely that it should not lead to harm to others and then to argue that choosing to have an achondroplasic child is a way of harming the child. But the positive selection of an affected embryo for implantation is obviously not a way of harming that embryo, nor, on the face of it, the child thereby born; and although the disposal of any unaffected embryos is, arguably, a way of harming them, this point is just a reiteration of the general issue of whether PGD is ever morally permissible. Given the tentative conclusion of the previous discussion one can argue that because the proposed intervention will lead to the birth of a child whose opportunities will be more restricted than those of an unaffected child, it is an intervention whose result is the birth of a child who is likely to have a less good life than the lives of those children who would otherwise have been born. But to make it a requirement that this result be avoided, *ie* that one is not permitted to make children in ways which are likely to make their lives worse than the lives of those who would otherwise have been born, is to go beyond the familiar restrictions on autonomy. As indicated above, one way to impose this requirement would be take procreative beneficence to be necessary as well as sufficient for permissibility; but this takes one straight back to Savulescu's strong principle of procreative beneficence. And that principle is too strong. So a better suggestion is that there be a requirement of 'procreative non-maleficence', that one is not permitted to make children in ways which are likely to make their lives worse than the lives of those who would otherwise have been born; normal methods of conception satisfy this requirement even though they may in many cases fail to satisfy Savulescu's strong principle.

One key question concerning liberal eugenics, therefore, is whether this extra requirement of non-maleficence is appropriate, or whether it represents an unwarranted intrusion into the private life of a couple. In thinking about this, it is worth remarking that the 'no harm to others' element of legitimate autonomy does already rule out hypothetical perverse interventions intended to bring about the birth of a very seriously handicapped child. For where a child's life is not worth living at all, it was harmed by being created in the first place. But these cases are extreme and hypothetical; the difficult cases involve the creation of a child whose life is certainly worth living but where there is an element of procreative maleficence. In any case of this kind which is seriously imaginable, the issue of procreative maleficence will itself be disputed, for the couple in question (such as an achondroplasic couple seeking to have a similar child) must be assumed to hold sincerely that the proposed intervention is actually one which is likely to advance the welfare of the child thus born. If that assumption is not satisfied, then deliberate maleficence is involved, and since this is a type of harm it is ruled out by the 'no harm to others' aspect of legitimate procreative autonomy. The difficult issue arises where maleficence is not deliberate, since the implementation of any prohibition on procreative interventions such as PGD in this situation will involve overriding the judgment of a couple about the likely welfare of their own future child, and although parents are not authoritative in this regard there must be a strong presumption that their judgment should be respected.

We are here in very tricky territory. My present judgment is that the presumption in favour of respecting the wishes of the parents should be overridden only when they fail to make a strong case for the claim that their proposed intervention will bring significant benefits to a child thus created which would not be otherwise available and where fulfilling their wishes is likely to lead to the birth of a child whose life is in fact likely to be much worse than the life of a child who could otherwise have been born. Possible cases then need to be worked through in detail, but my inclination would be to permit achondroplasic couples to select an achondroplasic child (though only after extensive counselling), but not to permit a deaf couple to select a deaf child. If this is right, then liberal eugenics does need an extra, though significantly qualified, requirement of non-maleficence.

E. Positive Enhancements

So far I have discussed a liberal eugenic policy in relation to more or less serious genetic disorders. But consider now the case of sexuality. Despite Hamer's work there is at present no genetic test for homosexuality;[8] nonetheless it is conceivable that a combination of alleles giving rise to a significant predisposition to homosexuality might be discovered, thereby making possible a genetic test for it. If there were one, would we want potential parents to be able to use PGD to decrease the chance of having a child who develops into a homosexual adult? As ever, there is a large element of make-believe about the very idea of such a test, since there is every reason to think that environmental conditions play a large part in the development of sexuality; but the question is nonetheless worth discussing. There is, I think, a strong intuition that such a practice would be wrong, and thus that if liberal eugenics were to imply that this practice is permissible, that fact would count against liberal eugenics. But does it imply this? The primary way for the liberal eugenicist to argue that such an intervention is not permissible is by showing that it would lead to harm. Yet there is no obvious direct harm here. At present one might use the expressivist argument to make the case that such a practice would give rise to indirect harms. We can imagine, however, that the world in which there is a genetic test of this kind is also a world in which there is no significant public prejudice against homosexuality (even though the prospective parents in this case can be assumed to have such a prejudice). In such a world, then, the expressivist argument would have no purchase—and yet it would still seem to me wrong for parents to select the sexuality of their children. Furthermore, in such a world there would be no reason to regard the intervention as maleficent, since there would be no reason to think that sexuality makes a significant difference to

---

[8] See D Hamer and P Copeland, *Living with Our Genes* (New York, Doubleday, 1998) but then also G Rice *et al*, 'Male Homosexuality: Absence of a Linkage to Microsatellite Markers at Xq28' (1999) 5451 *Science* 665–67.

the quality of life. So the further requirement of non-maleficence is also satisfied. Hence if such an intervention is indeed wrong, further considerations are required to show why this is so. Before considering these, however, I want to discuss briefly the related issue of positive interventions that are genuinely beneficent, *ie* positive genetic enhancements.

In thinking about such interventions it is best, I think, not to think in terms of superlatives, interventions which bring very high IQ etc. For are we confident that people with such characteristics have better lives than ordinary folk? No doubt they have different lives, but are they clearly better? Probably better in some ways and not in others—*eg*, in terms of successful achievement vs. friendship; yet who is to rank these against each other? That kind of doubt does not apply if we think of more modest enhancements, of the kind we might wish for ourselves. I wish that I was able to play music in time and to sing in tune. I have no doubt that my life would have been better with modest enhancements of this kind. So, assuming the science fiction that relevant genetic interventions are available and do not bring with them a substantial risk of other harms, the issue is whether there is anything wrong with a liberal eugenicist practice which permits such enhancements.

One anxiety here is egalitarian: would the introduction of such practices create a division of society between the 'gene-rich' and the 'gene-poor' which, given assortative mating, tended to replicate itself over generations and to lead to a 'genism' comparable to racism in which the gene-poor were predestined to a poor condition of life?[9] One response to this anxiety is just to observe that this result is very unlikely since the connections between genes and significant abilities are much too indeterminate, complicated, and environment-dependent to be stratified merely by the availability of modest genetic enhancements. But a more important point is that the social implications of a liberal eugenic practice depend on the way in which the background socio-political system is assumed to be structured. If genetic enhancements were made available at a low cost and information about them was effectively distributed, the feared inegalitarian outcome would be largely avoided. Thus the problem here, such as there is, is contingent on the ways in which a society deals with other inequalities, in particular those that arise from inequalities of wealth, as inequalities in education and opportunity usually do. If a society already has good ways of dealing with those inequalities, then adding in the availability of genetic enhancements of the kind envisaged here is not going to make a major difference. Whereas if a society does not have satisfactory ways of dealing with existing inequalities, then permitting genetic enhancements will perhaps make things worse. But that is primarily an objection to a socio-political system that is already basically unfair and not to liberal eugenics.

---

[9] L Silver, *Remaking Eden* (London, Weidenfeld, 1998).

A different anxiety arises from Joel Feinberg's important work on the need to preserve an 'open future' for children.[10] His starting point is that parents and others have a duty to protect a child's 'rights-in-trust', *ie* those rights which the child will only be able to exercise fully when the child becomes an adult. The rights on which Feinberg then concentrates are the right to self-determination and the right to opportunities for self-fulfilment, which, following Aristotle, he takes to be the ultimate human good. Since the exercise of these rights presupposes that the child's life-choices and character are not irrevocably fixed before she becomes an adult, Feinberg argues that it is essential that those with responsibility for the child's rights-in-trust should ensure that when she becomes an adult she is still in a position to explore a broad range of possibilities for herself—*ie* that her future remains 'open'. The implication of this thesis which Feinberg then explores concerns parental obstacles to education. He argues that because education is an essential prerequisite for a child's development into a young adult with an open future who can exercise the rights to self-determination and to opportunities for self-fulfilment, parents violate their duty to their children if they prevent them from completing their education.

So far the argument does not address the issue of genetic interventions, and Feinberg himself did not seek to make any connections here. Since some genetic enhancements can be thought of as similar in their aims to education, it would seem at first that Feinberg's argument should favour a liberal eugenic policy of making them readily available. But it might also be argued that, on the contrary, because some genetic interventions fix aspects of a child's character they pose a threat to the child's later capacity for self-determination.[11] This argument is capable of a very broad range of application, but if one concentrates just on modest genetic enhancements of the kind envisaged above, it does not seem persuasive. For where an enhancement just provides one with a basis for developing the ability to play music in time and to sing in tune, no particular future is determined. Someone who has developed their genetically enhanced musical predispositions can put the resulting musical abilities to any use they like, or they can just leave them to wither through disuse. What one might fear here is that parents who have paid for a child to have such an enhancement might as a result be over-inclined to direct the child towards musical lessons and other activities. There is a familiar stereotype of musical parents who seek to impose themselves on their children; and one can imagine such practices being exacerbated by the availability of interventions which provide genetic enhancement of musical predispositions. But, as things are, beyond a certain stage children with musical 'gifts' (as we say) have to be left to take control of this aspect of their lives themselves if they are to develop

---

[10] J Feinberg, *Freedom and Fulfillment* (Princeton, Princeton University Press, 1992) ch 3.
[11] This suggestion is proposed by Dena Davis in *Genetic Dilemmas* (London, Routledge, 2001) 64ff.

their abilities; and as long as the child has a liberal education in which a variety of possibilities for self-fulfilment are provided, its musical abilities will not close off any of these possibilities. So as long as the main message of Feinberg's insistence on the importance of providing an open future for children has been secured through political insistence on making a liberal education available to all children, modest genetic enhancements pose no significant threat to a child's welfare.

F. Enhancement as Alienation

But what about the hypothetical genetic test for a predisposition to homosexuality envisaged earlier? In this case the threat to a child's open future seems at first more significant, for the intervention is not intended to enhance a worthwhile ability, but to decrease the chance of an unwanted outcome. It is an attempt by potential parents to determine the sexuality of their child, and thus, on the face of it, a challenge to the child's capacity for self-determination. Yet when conceived in this way, the issue is not entirely straightforward: for sexuality is not a matter of choice for most people. It is more a matter of self-discovery than self-determination. So a liberal eugenic policy that permitted parents to select the sexuality of a child is not exactly a case of parental determination imposing itself on the child's potential for self-determination in this respect; instead it is a matter of parental intervention replacing the genetic lottery in the determination of a child's future sexuality. And if there is something wrong here, it is not well diagnosed as a threat to the child's open future.

I think therefore that we do better here to turn away from Feinberg and to consider instead the criticisms of liberal eugenics that have been advanced by Jürgen Habermas.[12] Discussing the kind of case envisaged here, Habermas argues as follows:

> Insofar as the genetically altered person feels that the scope for a possible use of her ethical freedom has been intentionally changed by a prenatal design, she may suffer from the consciousness of sharing the authorship of her own life and her own destiny with someone else. This sort of *alienating* dilution or fracturing of one's own identity is a sign that an important boundary has become permeable—the deontological shell which assures the inviolability of the person, the uniqueness of the individual, and the irreplaceability of one's own subjectivity.[13]

Habermas' claim is therefore that genetic interventions are liable to induce a profound sense of alienation from oneself. I doubt whether this claim can be

---

[12] J Habermas, *The Future of Human Nature* (London, Polity, 2003).
[13] *Ibid*, 82.

substantiated in the case of most of the types of interventions discussed in this chapter, such as those undertaken to enable a couple to avoid having a child with a serious inherited disorder. For all that the young adult whose conception has involved PGD will think when she learns about the manner of her conception is just that she was selected as free from a serious inherited disorder which might well have affected a child conceived normally in her place; and that thought should not lead to a loss of 'ethical freedom' or to 'a consciousness of sharing the authorship of her own life', a claim which needs to be understood anyway in a way which accommodates our inescapable dependence upon our parents. But the situation is different in the case of interventions intended to avoid having a homosexual child. Plainly, our sexuality shapes at the most profound level the kind of person we are. At present, by and large, we just accept ourselves as we find ourselves: we are not 'authors' of our own sexuality—we just find ourselves with one predominant orientation or the other (or, sometimes, both equally). But now suppose one were to discover that one's sexuality was not the result of the genetic lottery; instead, we are to imagine, one discovers that this outcome was the result of a deliberate intervention by one's parents, either through genetic manipulation or embryo selection (I will discuss later whether it makes a difference which alternative is employed). Then, I think, Habermas' charge of alienation does have application: for one of the most profound aspects of our character turns out to have been imposed upon us in a way that we cannot disavow. It is not like, say, being made to play the violin before one could express a choice about the matter: for one can just put that behind oneself later. In the case of one's sexuality, the normal situation is one in which one becomes 'author' of oneself by accepting, and then building onto, an orientation that is initially just given; in the genetically manipulated case, the same process of acceptance and self-consciousness is radically disrupted by finding that this aspect of oneself has been deliberately inserted or selected by someone else.

It seems to me that Habermas does here point to a genuine form of alienation, in which one finds that one's own character is in a profound respect someone else's handiwork. This situation is quite different from that which arises from education, at least where this is conceived as a relationship in which a child's character is taken as a starting point and the process is intended to enable a child to fulfil its own potential. Instead the genetic determination of sexuality resembles an extreme form of indoctrination, in which a 'teacher' manages to insert into the pupil's psyche some dogma or prejudice that lives on as an alien presence which cannot be rejected even when it has been discovered for what it is. The remaining question, therefore, is quite how far this criticism goes. As I have indicated, I do not see how it applies to negative interventions which remove dispositions to serious disorders; what, however, about the modest enhancements which would have enabled me to be better at music, etc? Habermas, I think, would criticise these on the grounds that they are an external intervention intended to alter the child's abilities rather than to develop abilities which were already there, though it is not clear that the facts will support a substantial distinction here. So he would say that the young adult might come to feel that her own 'authorship' of her life has been damaged. Yet, as I indicated earlier, as long as the young adult's capacity for self-determination is not compromised by the modest enhancements one might envisage, coming to appreciate that they were selected for, or inserted into one, by one's parents should not induce the alienation of which Habermas writes. They provide new opportunities for self-fulfilment without imposing a destiny.

What I take from Habermas, therefore, is just the existential thesis (in both senses of 'existential') that there are some types of potential genetic intervention, such as that to determine sexuality, which threaten a new form of alienation. Hence it looks as though there is here a different kind of deontological constraint on procreative beneficence or liberal eugenics, that expressed, in Habermas' language, as respect for 'the deontological shell which assures the inviolability of the person, the uniqueness of the individual, and the irreplaceability of one's own subjectivity'. But in truth that is the wrong way to think about the matter. For if Habermas is right, these are interventions which are not beneficent at all, or even merely neutral, but positively maleficent or harmful. In which case they do not show the need for a further deontological constraint on weak procreative beneficence, for they are not beneficial; and they do not threaten liberal eugenics, for procreative autonomy is of course constrained anyway by the 'no harm to others' condition, and these interventions are, it is argued, harmful. So, despite what he says, Habermas' argument does not threaten liberal eugenics; it just shows that there are other forms of harm than those normally taken into account.

Finally, I need to address the question as to whether the distinction between direct gene alteration and embryo selection makes a difference to Habermas' argument. The reason for thinking that it does make a difference is that where embryo selection alone is involved the young adult cannot complain that her parents made her the way she is in some respect (*eg* in respect of her sexuality). She cannot justify the thought, 'if my parents had not intervened I might have been different in that respect'; for in all worlds in which she exists, she has that character. Instead, however, she can justifiably think 'if I had been different in this respect I would not have existed at all', and she knows that the truth of this counterfactual is dependent upon her parents' deliberate choice. Hence the alienating sense of another person intruding in her life returns. For in learning of the manner of her conception the young adult learns that her own being, with this aspect of her character, is not the result of the genetic lottery, but of her parents' decision to have a child with that character. She comes to learn that this aspect of her character is the result of her parents' decision to have a child of that kind. If the aspect is as profound as one's sexuality, this thought is surely alienating.

3

Disability, Enhancement and the Harm–Benefit Continuum*

LISA BORTOLOTTI AND JOHN HARRIS

Suppose that you are soon to be a parent and you learn that there are some simple measures that you can take to make sure that your child will be healthy. In particular, suppose that by following the doctor's advice, you can prevent your child from having a disability, you can make your child immune from a number of dangerous diseases and you can even enhance its future intelligence. All that is required for this to happen is that you (or your partner) comply with lifestyle and dietary requirements. Do you and your partner have any moral reasons (or moral obligations) to follow the doctor's advice? Would it make a difference if, instead of following some simple dietary requirements, you consented to genetic engineering to make sure that your child was free from disabilities, healthy and with above-average intelligence? In this paper we develop a framework for dealing with these questions and we suggest some directions the answers might take.

First, we shall contrast our own 'harmed condition' account of disability[1] with the social conception of disability put forward by Reindal[2] and Koch[3] by revisiting the distinction between conditions which are 'socially disabling' and conditions which are disabling irrespective of any particular social environment. In our framework, it makes sense to claim that certain conditions of the person can be

---

* The authors acknowledge the stimulus and support of the 'European project on delimiting the research concept and research activities (EURECA)' sponsored by the European Commission, DG-Research as part of the Science and Society research programme–6th Framework in the preparation of this paper.

[1] J Harris, *Wonderwoman and Superman: Ethics and Human Biotechnology* (Oxford, OUP, 1992) 84–97 and J Harris, 'Is Gene Therapy a Form of Eugenics?' (1993) 7 *Bioethics* 178, 180.

[2] SM Reindal, 'Disability, Gene Therapy and Eugenics—A Challenge to John Harris' (2000) 26 *Journal of Medical Ethics* 89–94.

[3] T Koch, 'Disability and Difference: Balancing Social and Physical Constructions' (2001) 27 *Journal of Medical Ethics* 370–76.

regarded as disabling given the physical or social environment in which the person is embedded when they are harmful conditions that a rational person would have a preference not to be in. Our account is preferable to the social conception of disability, because it can explain how certain conditions of the person remain disabling even after issues of discrimination are addressed and society is free from prejudice which harms the subjects. Moreover, the 'harmed condition' account of disability does not rely on the problematic assumption that disability is a deviation from normal species functioning or from species typical functioning.

From the perspective of a 'harmed condition' account of disability, we shall then proceed to explore the relation between disability and enhancement, given our commitment to the harm–benefit continuum. The harm–benefit continuum is the idea that: '[T]he reasons we have not to harm others or creating others who will be unnecessarily harmed are continuous with the reasons we have for conferring benefits on others if we can.'[4]

It would appear that, if we have moral reasons to prevent people from being in disabling conditions, we might also have moral reasons to improve their conditions, whether they are disabling or not. Further questions are whether these moral reasons are (in at least some cases) moral obligations and whether it is wrong not to enhance individuals whom we could thus benefit. We shall assess some common objections to enhancement and conclude that there are at least three possible ways of conceiving the 'morality of enhancement' that are compatible with our account of disability.

A. Against Social Conceptions of Disability

John Harris has suggested that conditions are disabling if they are physical or mental conditions that constitute a harm to the individual which a rational person would wish to be without.[5] According to this account, disabling conditions are not necessarily harmful relative to normal species functioning or species typical functioning. In what sense, then, are conditions such as deafness and Down's syndrome disabling? What all disabling conditions have in common is that, to some extent, they cause harm to the people who are in them (by exposing them to risks, impairing them in what they do, limiting their opportunities or preventing them from having experiences that are worthwhile). On this view, disabling conditions constitute a disadvantage with respect to relevant alternatives, not

---

[4] J Harris, 'One Principle and Three Fallacies of Disability Studies' (2001) 27 *Journal of Medical Ethics* 383, 386.

[5] J Harris, *Wonderwoman and Superman: Ethics and Human Biotechnology* (Oxford, OUP, 1992) 84–97 and J Harris, 'Is Gene Therapy a Form of Eugenics?' (1993) 7 *Bioethics* 178, 180.

necessarily with respect to the conditions of the typical human. The reason why the notion of 'normal species functioning' is unhelpful in defining disabilities is that it would make disability too narrow. Changing environmental factors, or new discoveries about the onset of serious diseases, for instance, might make it the case that typical conditions of our species become disabling.

Consider the case of white-skinned people in an environment where the ozone layer is seriously depleted. They would probably be much more vulnerable to skin-cancer than brown- or black-skinned people and this would constitute a disadvantage. Being white-skinned is no more or less 'normal' than being black-skinned relative to our species functioning. Indeed, if we had evidence that women live longer because they are less vulnerable to heart disease than men,[6] we might consider being a man rather than a woman a disabling condition!

What reasons are there to adopt this conception of disability? First, it is sufficiently broad to cover all the harmful conditions that we might intuitively regard as disabling, whether the harm be primarily caused by medical conditions of the person, genetic or environmental factors or social context. It has clear advantages compared to a *merely* social conception of disability, as it is not committed to the rather implausible claim that all disabling features of the condition would disappear if society were inclusive and free from discrimination or prejudice. The definition of disability formulated by the Union of the Physically Impaired Against Segregation is an example of how disabilities can be conceived of as effects of social organisation:

> Disability: disadvantage or restriction of activity caused by a contemporary social organization which takes no or little account of people who have physical impairment and thus excludes them from the mainstream of social activities.[7]

Whereas it is certainly true that certain attitudes in society towards people who are perceived as different cannot but make things worse for disabled people, in many cases, perhaps most cases, their harmful condition—for instance, deafness or Down's syndrome—would persist once society had been reformed.

The only case in which a disabling condition would cease to be harmful if society were reformed is the case of a disability entirely caused by the adverse social context. For instance, history teaches us that being born female in 19th century Europe would have been a disabling condition when compared to being born male. Exceptions apart, women were prevented from exercising any form of autonomous decision-making, often did not have the opportunity to have a

---

[6] *The Guardian*, 11 January 2005, reports that: 'A group of scientists may finally have solved the mystery of why wives outlive their husbands after discovering that women's hearts age better than men's.'

[7] Reported by M Oliver, 'Defining Impairment and Disability: Issues at Stake' in C Barnes and G Mercer (eds), *Exploring the Divide: Illness and Disability* (Leeds, The Disability Press, 1996) 29–54.

proper education and so on. Similarly, being born today in a developing country rather than in a developed country is, for most, a disabling condition. These harmful conditions would cease to be regarded as disabling if we could operate on the social, political and economic context. The 'harmed condition' conception of disability can recognise that disabling conditions might have a variety of causes without being committed to the view that by operating appropriately on social factors all disabilities would disappear.

B. Moral Reasons against Creating Individuals with Disabling Conditions

What are the consequences of this account of disability for the morality of reproductive choices? According to the definition of disability that we have defended in this chapter, a condition is disabling if it constitutes a harm to the individual which a rational person would wish to be without. Moreover, we argued that disabling conditions constitute a disadvantage with respect to relevant alternatives. Given this account, it is easy to see how we have moral reasons to prevent or eradicate disabling conditions, as part of our commitment to the basic moral principle of avoiding unnecessary harm. This means that, when we have the choice, we should bring into existence people without (known) disabling conditions rather than people with such conditions.

But this of course says nothing about whether these moral reasons give rise to a moral obligation or about the way in which we should carry out such a moral obligation. There are many different ways in which creating a person with a disability can be avoided, including postponement of conception, behaviour modification, gene therapy, selection between pre-implantation embryos and abortion.[8] One might recognise the moral obligation to prevent or eradicate disabilities and still object on moral or other grounds to the methods by which the obligation can be carried out. Moreover, the strength of the obligation might vary relative to the context of the disabling condition, and to the degree of harm that the disabling condition is likely to cause to future persons.

1. Serious Disability

In the case of a person with a very serious disability, there would be moral reasons not to bring her into existence. Imagine a child diagnosed in early pregnancy with

---

[8] For a more comprehensive list and discussion, see J Harris, 'Should We Attempt to Eradicate Disability?' (1995) 4 *Public Understanding of Science* 233–42.

holoprosencephaly,[9] a structural brain disorder in which the two halves of the brain have failed to separate. In the full blown condition which we are imagining here to be present, there is severe brain damage and a high risk of intractable seizures. The condition is incompatible with long term survival. In such a case the child would have a hopeless prognosis and a brief life distressing for the child and the family with no hope of palliation, prevention or cure. Here there are surely strong moral reasons not to bring such a child into existence.

2. Slight Disability

In the case of a person with a very minor disability, which is not thought of as a truly disabling condition, there might none the less be moral reasons to eradicate the disability by selecting between pre-implantation embryos for example but perhaps not by abortion.

Suppose that a woman has six pre-implantation embryos *in vitro* awaiting implantation. Pre-implantation genetic diagnosis (PGD) has revealed that three have asthma and three seem healthy. Which should she implant?[10] Does she have any moral reasons to avoid implanting those who will develop asthma? Notice two features of this case. The woman is under no moral, nor any legal obligation to implant *any* of the embryos. The decision to implant some or none is entirely within her unfettered discretion. She doesn't have to offer legal, moral or any other justifications to anyone if she decides to implant none of the embryos. Can she say, 'It is a matter of moral indifference whether or not my resulting child has asthma and therefore I have no reason to select the healthier embryos'?

This seems implausible. True, her choice is relatively free. None of the embryos has a right or an entitlement to be chosen rather than the others, since none is a person, none has begun the sort of biographical life that would give it interests, none has become a moral agent or a legal person.[11] Nevertheless, she has a reason to do what she can to ensure that the individual she chooses is as good an individual as she can make it. She has a reason therefore to choose the embryo that is not already harmed in any particular way, however slightly, and that will have the best possible chance of a long and healthy life and the best possible chance of contributing positively to the world it will inhabit. If on the other hand she chooses to implant an individual destined to suffer an illness, however mild, she will have created that illness and any harm that it will do.

---

[9] We are indebted to our colleague Dian Donnai for information about this condition. Further facts may be found at: http://www.ninds.nih.gov/disorders/holoprosencephaly/holoprosencephaly.htm.

[10] This example is borrowed from J Harris, 'Reproductive Liberty, Disease and Disability' (2004) *Reproductive Medicine Online*.

[11] See the judgment of the Grand Chamber of the European Court of Human Rights in *Vo v France*, Appl no 53924/00, ECHR 2004, judgment of 8 July 2004.

Notice that this woman has the same reason to select against an embryo with asthma as her sister who is told that if she conceives immediately she will have a child with asthma but that if she postpones pregnancy and takes a course of treatment she will have a healthy child.[12] The sister and her partner in this case have a reason to maximise the opportunities and minimise the disadvantages of any child they will have and therefore to modify their behaviour so as to try and conceive the healthiest embryo possible. But if they only learn in the course of an already established pregnancy that the child the woman is carrying will develop asthma, the parents might consider that avoidance of asthma does not justify an abortion, since the problem is relatively slight and life with asthma is well worth living.

3. Merely Social Disability

Social factors can be disabling but this does not imply that the person making reproductive choices has an obligation, or even a reason, to prefer creating an individual without socially disabling conditions such as those determined by gender or skin colour. In these circumstances the choice that needs to be made, *ie* whether to attempt to change society or to avoid creating individuals with features that will be socially disabling in the expected social or political context, is not value-free or politically neutral. The strategy of choice for minimising expected disability may be difficult to arrive at for individuals. Reforming society of course is never an easy option or a fast process, and there are known cases of mothers who chose to, say, have white-skinned children to prevent them from being harmed by prejudice and discrimination.

Notice that these considerations make social factors significantly different from environmental factors. Recall the example of white-skinned people in an environment where the ozone layer is so depleted that their chances to get skin cancer are significantly increased when compared to darker-skinned people. In that case, it seems that we would be happy to acknowledge the need to 'adapt' to the changed environmental conditions to have a better and longer life. However, in the case of (merely) socially disabling conditions it is not at all obvious that we have the same need to adapt to the current organisation of our social environment and there is no morally neutral way to deal with the problem so as to minimise or eliminate

---

[12] This situation is often discussed with a view to the so-called 'non-identity problem', which trades on the possible moral significance of the fact that any child with asthma which the sister conceives now would not have existed at all if the sister had waited and only had a child later. Some would argue that this prevents us from viewing the child with asthma as having been harmed by its mother's choice not to wait, and perhaps also from viewing her choice as morally wrong. For an exposition and discussion of the 'non-identity problem', see D Parfit, *Reasons and Persons* (Oxford, Clarendon Press, 1984) part 4 especially 358ff, and specifically in the context of disability J Harris, *Wonderwoman and Superman: Ethics and Human Biotechnology* (Oxford, OUP, 1992) ch 3.

the disadvantage of the individuals who are likely to be harmed by prejudice or discrimination. Many, including the present authors, might feel a moral obligation to affirm the entitlement to equal concern and respect of society and their fellow citizens both for themselves and for their children; but the rationality as well as the morality of this can have limits. Many European Jews, for example, made a conscious decision not to reproduce during the Nazi period because they knew that whether or not their children chose to identify themselves as Jews, the mere fact of 'having Jewish parents' was enough to render their children liable to terrible cruelty and premature death.

Another consideration in making these decisions is whether the factors that render a certain condition disabling can be altered. In the case of social organisation, alteration is always possible, though perhaps not realistic in a short span of time. In the scenario with the seriously depleted ozone layer the assumption is that we cannot do anything about the environmental change. But we can imagine scenarios in which the environmental factors in relation to which a condition becomes disabling can be altered and therefore the same choice that we have in the case of merely socially disabling conditions can present itself.

C. Disability and Enhancement

Suppose we accept that there are moral reasons to prevent or eradicate disability when possible. Does this commit us to recognising that we also have moral reasons to enhance? This question arises with particular force for those who believe that there is a continuum between harms and benefits. On this view the reasons we have to avoid harming others are continuous with the reasons we have for conferring benefits on others if we can. All actions are re-describable as omissions and vice versa. The decision to save a life is the decision not to allow someone to die. The decision to kill is a decision not to refrain from killing. This is not just a semantic quibble but is rooted in both theory of action and theory of responsibility. Where we can protect people from harms, to elect not to do so is to become responsible for the harms we might have prevented. Suppose a child can be protected from risk of polio in an environment where polio is rife. The enhancement (a polio vaccination) is available free of charge but the parents refuse. The child contracts polio. The chain of causation as well as the chain of moral responsibility is as clear as it could be.[13]

If we accept the view that there is a harm–benefit continuum, and we have a moral reason to avoid causing unnecessary harm to others, we also have a moral

---

[13] See J Harris, *Violence and Responsibility* (Kegan Paul London, Routledge, 1980) and J Feinberg, *Harm to Others* (Oxford, OUP, 1984) ch 3.

reason to confer benefits on others, and this moral reason can become a positive obligation where the costs to ourselves are reasonable given the level of benefit. This is supported by the intuitive analogy between disability and enhancement. If disabling conditions constitute a *disadvantage* with respect to some relevant alternatives, enhanced conditions constitute an *advantage*. For instance, enhancing strategies such as taking a 'longevity pill' are likely to confer a benefit on those who appreciate life and want to live as long as possible. When we save a life, by whatever means, we simply postpone death. Life-saving is just death postponement. This is a truth from which it follows that life-extending therapies are, and must always be, life-saving therapies and must share whatever priority life saving has in our morality and in our social values. So long as the life is of acceptable quality (acceptable to the person whose life it is) we have a powerful, many would claim an overriding, moral imperative to save life, because to fail to do so when we can would make us responsible for the resulting death.[14]

Moreover, one can easily imagine scenarios in which not enhancing a person's condition amounts to creating a disability. In an environment in which most people have had their long-term memory enhanced by 20%, people whose memory has not been enhanced are at a disadvantage in some contexts. Or, if a safe and effective vaccine against HIV/AIDS were to be developed, those not protected would be at a severe disadvantage.

It is true that there are situations where it is more difficult to re-describe the choice to provide a person with an enhancement as a choice to prevent or avoid risk of harm. If there existed a free-of-charge vitamin supplement which a pregnant woman could take to prevent future ageing-related hair loss of the male child she is carrying, and if she nevertheless chose not to take it, she does perhaps cause, and become responsible for that person's hair loss in late adulthood. But some would still baulk at describing ageing-related hair loss as a *harm* or a debilitating disadvantage, even if we imagine a society where hardly anyone still loses their hair at an advanced age.

We nevertheless believe that our argument concerning the harm–benefit continuum also applies to these situations. First, it is clear that a reason such as 'wanting the best life possible for one's child' applies equally to the avoidance of harm, to enhancements that prevent risks of harms and to 'pure' enhancements, which are merely likely to make the life of the child happier or better in some small but significant way. Secondly, in any consideration of 'harms'—even if one rejects, as we do, a purely circumstantial or 'social' conception of harm and disability in which harms are simply 'conditions considered disadvantageous by society'—the difference between a harm and a mere neutral condition is often one of degree only. The line between harms and non-harms fluctuates and is malleable over

---

[14] See J Harris, *Violence and Responsibility* (London, Routledge and Kegan Paul, 1980).

time. We therefore think that any differentiation between, on the one hand, harm-preventing enhancements, and on the other hand, further enhancements, is unwarranted and that the harm–benefit continuum applies to any change that can be brought about in a person that a rational person would consider a change for the better.

D. Who is Afraid of Enhancement?

In the bioethical literature, the press, and even in recent cinematography, enhancements are viewed with great suspicion.[15] In this section we are going to briefly review some of the most common arguments that are often employed to show that enhancing is unethical. By 'enhancement' we refer to any procedure aimed at conferring benefits on people by improving their conditions, from immunisation against serious diseases to increases in intelligence or memory. We shall come back to the distinction between different types of enhancement in the next section. Here it will suffice to note that many of the following considerations have been relied on to argue against the prevention of disabling conditions.

1. Safety

This family of arguments includes two main empirical worries. First, there are concerns about the safety of the procedures involved. Secondly, there are worries about the limited amount of knowledge even experts have about the consequences of, say, genetic engineering in certain domains. Although there might be very good reasons to decide against enhancement out of concern about safety, this is not an argument that could ever by itself show that enhancing is unethical. Should the science improve and with it the safety of the procedures, there would be no objection left to proceeding with enhancement.

Notice that in some cases you can have a sophisticated 'safety' objection to enhancement. Norman Daniels gives an interesting example.[16] Suppose that we learn that an enhancement of short-term memory would benefit many of our cognitive processes and that we have the opportunity to enhance short-term memory by operating on embryos. This is how Daniels argues that we should not do it:

---

[15] Let us offer just one example. In the movie 'Gattaca' (1997), a world where most people are genetically enhanced is presented as cold and soulless and those who are not enhanced are discriminated against by being prevented from playing certain valued roles in society.

[16] N Daniels, 'Can Anyone Really be Talking About Ethically Modifying Human Nature?' in J Savulescu and N Bostrom (eds), *The Enhancement of Human Beings* (Oxford, OUP, in press).

What else might we have to know to proceed ethically with the modification? We would have to know a lot more. We would have to know that the increased short-term memory involved here actually plays a role in enhancing the more complex cognitive task rather than, in the case of this pattern, interfering with it. Perhaps it creates too much noise that interferes with the complex task, or does so in some range of environments not tracked in the original finding of the association. ... Without some clear sense of these complex issues, we could not have any confidence that improving the component capability has the intended or desired effect on the more complex one. And all of this information goes well beyond the standard worry that the intervention itself carries with it risks that non-interference lacks.[17]

Daniels' concern is that enhancements might not really improve the quality of life.

Here the objection is context-specific. Daniels does not just reiterate the idea that there are always risks involved in changing something that is working well enough. He is saying that, given the nature of genetic modifications and the complex way in which we would need to assess their consequences, the fact that the capacity or trait to be enhanced is a necessary condition for better performance does not mean that by enhancing it we would produce an overall better offspring. Although his concerns are definitely to be taken into account, we do not believe that they justify the extremely conservative conclusion that enhancement should never be tried out. And this leads us to a brief examination of the precautionary principle.

2. The Precautionary Principle

There is widespread acceptance of the (nonetheless incoherent) precautionary principle.[18] The idea is the *status quo* has done well for us and is likely to continue to do well for us. Therefore in the absence of reliable data, any proposed changes are to be considered of uncertain consequence and presumed disastrous or, more weakly, dangers that are to be considered more probable and of greater magnitude than the expected benefits. The precautionary principle therefore applies and requires that we leave things well alone. A number of questionable assumptions are involved here. If enhancements might alter the course of evolution, or even effect permanent change, then one assumption that the precautionary principle requires is that our present point in evolution is unambiguously good and not susceptible of improvement. Secondly, it is assumed that the course of evolution, if left alone, will continue to improve things for humankind or at

---

[17] *Ibid.*

[18] In this section we draw on J Harris and S Holm, 'Extended lifespan and the paradox of precaution' (2002) 27 *The Journal of Medicine and Philosophy* 355–69 in which the incoherence of the principle is detailed.

least not make them worse. The incompatibility of these two assumptions is obvious. The *status quo* is a result of evolutionary change. Unless we can compare the future progress of evolution uncontaminated by manipulation of the human genome with its progress influenced by any proposed genetic manipulations we cannot know which would be best and hence where precaution lies.[19] Put more prosaically, it is unclear why a precautionary approach should apply only to proposed changes rather than to the *status quo*.[20] In the absence of reliable predictive knowledge as to how dangerous leaving things alone may prove we have no rational basis for a precautionary approach which prioritises the *status quo*. This point re-enforces our earlier remarks about the continuum between removal of disadvantage and implementation of advantage.

3. Priority of the Natural

There is a strong and tenacious view that the natural is good and the unnatural bad, that we should, in short, give priority to the natural over the artificial. This seems untenable, as the following extract from a recent paper by Julian Savulescu and John Harris shows:[21]

> Witness the obsession with natural foods over genetically modified and other artificial, Frankenstein foods. The belief that the natural should have priority over the artificial, though common, is mistaken. A child born by assisted reproduction is of the same kind with the same moral status as a child born by natural reproduction. In so far as naturally occurring foods are safer or healthier, there is a reason to prefer them. But in many cases, artificial preparations are healthier and safer. Indeed, they are preferred. The drug digoxin is used for heart conditions. It is always given in a highly purified pharmaceutical form as digoxin even though it occurs naturally as digitalis in the foxglove plant. Natural reproduction may be more fun than artificial reproduction. That is a reason to prefer it. Natural processes may be less costly or do less damage to the environment. These are reasons to prefer them. But there is no reason to prefer a natural process *per se* to an artificial process. Human beings are, after all, a part of the natural world. The mere fact that something is natural is not a reason to prefer it.
>
> The natural *per se* is morally neutral. Sometimes natural events are good, like a brilliant sunset or an abundant harvest. But often the natural does great harm—disease, pestilence,

---

[19] While some maintain that human evolution of the Darwinian sort is at an end because most humans now survive long enough to reproduce, this view overlooks the role of parasites in evolution. It also of course ignores our deliberate interventions in the evolutionary process.

[20] See FM Cornford, *Microcosmographica Academica* (London, Bowes and Bowes, 1908) ch 7: 'Every public action which is not customary, either is wrong, or, if it is right, is a dangerous precedent. It follows that nothing should ever be done for the first time.'

[21] J Savulescu and J Harris, 'The Creation Lottery: Final Lessons from Natural Reproduction: Why Those Who Accept Natural Reproduction Should Accept Cloning and Other Frankenstein Reproductive Technologies' (2004) 13 *Cambridge Quarterly of Healthcare Ethics* 90–96.

floods, hurricanes, fire, landslides and the like can cause massive loss of human life. One might characterize the practice of medicine as the comprehensive attempt to frustrate the course of nature, because people naturally fall ill, are invaded by natural organisms like viruses and bacteria, and naturally die at a young age, often as babies. If we always prioritized the natural we would have to abjure the practice of medicine and the discoveries of medical science including vaccines and antibiotics.

Our current fascination and worship of the natural should be tempered. We should remember how Thomas Hobbes so famously described life in a state of nature, '... and which is worst of all, continual fear, and danger of violent death; and the life of man, solitary, poor, nasty, brutish and short.'[22]

4. Self-evolution and the Post-human Future

There are two objections that are often run together. One is the 'playing God' objection, the idea that by enhancing in certain ways we are guilty of hubris. Humans are not supposed to create better humans, because that would be arrogance on their part. They should just accept what God or Nature has given them without attempting to better it. This is not a very interesting objection and has been discussed at length, so we propose to move on to the second point. What are the consequences of playing God? By intervening on the genes, we might change human nature and self-evolve. What is wrong about that?

One idea is that the human species as it is should be preserved. This stems from the belief that there is something intrinsically good about being human. As it happens, we also think that there is something very valuable about *human* persons, but we believe that what is really valuable in them is the capacity of persons to be aware of themselves, make decisions for themselves in a rational and autonomous way and have complex feelings and emotions. The fact that all the persons we know are human is just an accident. If we did find those characteristics of persons in non-humans, we would (or should) still appreciate them and cherish them. Our value and moral status does not depend on the species we belong to, but on the fact that we are persons and, as such, have interests of a certain kind.

Some worry that, say, genetic prejudice might ensue and *human* rights might be denied to those who are no longer human as a consequence of genetic modification or self-evolution.[23] But being human is neither necessary nor sufficient for having rights, as Juengst himself notices. Dead humans have no rights, whereas arguably intelligent animals do. If we recognise that what justifies granting rights

---

[22] T Hobbes, M Oakeshot (ed), *Leviathan* (Oxford, Blackwell, 1960) 82, cited in Harris and Savulescu *ibid*.
[23] E Juengst, '"Alter-ing" Human Nature? Misplaced Essentialism in Science Policy' in J Savulescu and N Bostrom (eds), *The Enhancement of Human Beings* (Oxford, OUP, in press).

to individuals is not the species they belong to but the interests they might have, then the question of whether to grant rights to post-humans is easily solved. The 'human' in the phrase 'human rights' is just supposed to highlight that differences of race, gender and wealth are not relevant to the question whether someone should be granted those rights. If we take seriously the concern that some philosophers have for another kind of prejudice or discrimination, speciecism, then the 'human' has to go and 'human rights' will just be the 'rights of persons'.

These objections, like the arguments in the next sub-section, refer to the political and social consequences of widespread enhancements and can be partially if not completely addressed if we operate in a framework in which we recognise the validity of the principle of genetic equity.[24] This principle is simply an elaboration of principles of equality that have become well recognised and articulated in recent years. Such a principle highlights the requirement that each of us be treated as an equal, shown the same concern, respect and protection as is accorded to any other person.[25]

As John Harris and John Sulston have recently argued:[26]

> All democratic societies must treat their citizens as equals, according to each the same concern, respect and protection as is accorded to any, both in the protection of their laws and customs but also in the allocation of public resources or indeed in the ways in which private resources are deployed to secure public goods. For example, if a private commercial organization, say a pharmaceutical company, develops a vital treatment or vaccine it is the obligation of societies to ensure that access to this drug or treatment is available in a way that does not unfairly discriminate against some sections of society, for example is not available only to those of a particular race or religion or to members of the governing party. The scope of this principle might of course be contested, for example as to whether or not it covers discrimination on the basis of ability to pay, or the degree of benefit to be derived from the treatment.[27]

Both in view of the above arguments but also because we believe equal respect for all persons is an integral and ineradicable part of democratic theory and

---

[24] See J Harris and J Sulston, 'Genetic Equity' (2004) 5 *Nature Reviews Genetics* 796–800; and C Farrell, 'The Genetic Difference Principle' (2004) 4 *American Journal of Bioethics* 21–28.

[25] See S Giordano, 'Do Elderly People Have Human Rights? Respect for Equality and the Treatment of the Older Person. Declarations of Human Rights and Age-Based Rationing' (2005) 14 *Cambridge Quarterly of Health Care Ethics* 83–93; J Harris, 'Does Justice Require that we be Ageist?' (1994) 8 *Bioethics* 74–84; J Harris, 'Could We Hold People Responsible for their Own Adverse Health?' (1996) 1 *Journal of Contemporary Health Law and Policy* 100–6; J Harris, 'What is the Good of Health Care?' (1996) 10 *Bioethics* 269–92; and generally R Dworkin, *Taking Rights Seriously* (London, Duckworth, 1977). For early philosophical discussion of the principle of equality, see Plato, AD Lindsay (tr), *The Republic* (Dent, Everyman, 1993) Book V, 451–57 [Stephanus]; JJ Rousseau, *Du Contract social, ou Principes du droit politique* (Amsterdam, Chez Rey MM, 1972); JS Mill, Mary Warnock (ed), *Utilitarianism* (London, Collins Fontana, 1960).

[26] J Harris and J Sulston, 'Genetic Equity' (2004) 5 *Nature Reviews Genetics* 796–800.

[27] Original footnote omitted.

hence an essential feature of all liberal democracies, we believe that a principle of genetic equity should be explicitly added to our understanding of the requirements of both equity more generally and of the requirements of democratic polity. Societies have a fundamental obligation to ensure the protection of the life, liberty and health of each citizen impartially, and to provide access to beneficial health care, and to the fruits of research, on the basis of individual need so that each has an equal chance of flourishing to the extent that their individual genome and personal health status permits. This equal chance of flourishing should be protected by the state, regardless of such arbitrary features as race, gender, genome, degree of disability, wealth and power, religious belief, skin colour etc.

Genes (or genetic constitution) are clearly some of the most important examples of those personal characteristics which most clearly make a difference to both how people are able to function and often also as to how they are perceived, but they are also features that as yet have not been adequately incorporated into our understanding of the requirements of both equity and democracy.

Harris and Sulston therefore propose a 'principle of genetic equity', which they formulate as follows:

> Humans are born equal; they are entitled to freedom from discrimination and equality of opportunity to flourish; genetic information may not be used to limit that equality.

> It follows that neither genetic constitution nor genetic information should be the basis of discrimination or stigmatization of an individual, family or group. No one's genes, or genetic information about them, can or should derogate from their equal standing and dignity in the human community and their equal entitlement to the concern, respect and protection of others or of society.[28]

5. Unfair Advantage and Diminished Agency

It is a common thought that some enhancing strategies such as genetic engineering are going to be very expensive and only the better-off in society will be able to afford them. As a consequence, the current divisions in society will become even less bridgeable. Notice that this is not an ethical objection to enhancing as such, but a concern about the distribution of resources. Actually, the worry about the ways in which enhancements will be distributed implies that enhancements are perceived as a good thing.

Some believe that the practice of enhancing and genetically engineering capacities will lead to a revision of our conception of agency.[29] Agents typically enjoy a certain

---

[28] *Ibid*, 798.

[29] M Sandel, 'What's Wrong with Enhancement' (2002), Council of Bioethics, available online at http://www.bioethics.gov.background.sandelpaper.html.

amount of freedom of action and are subject to judgments of praise for their achievements and of blame for their failures. But if the physical or intellectual achievement of the agent is only marginally due to effort and discipline and main-ly produced by, say, a powerful drug, the achievement might no longer be a good reason to admire the agent. The argument is supposed to show that a pervasive use of enhancement might lead to a diminished sense of agency and responsibility.

To assess the force of this argument one needs to be able to account for what the consequences of the practice of enhancement would really be for our concep-tion of agency. Partly, this is an empirical question. We know what our current psychological reactions to illicit drug-taking by athletes are; we feel it is cheating. But the scenario in which everybody is given an opportunity to enhance their con-dition is significantly different and so our reactions might reflect that. It is not at all obvious that we would lose the sense of ownership of our own actions if the capacities that made it possible for us to achieve something desirable with our actions had been enhanced. One possible consequence of pervasive enhancement could be a 'raising the bar' effect that would subtract little from the merits of the personal achievements of the individual.

That said, it seems as if the diminished agency objection is on to something. Suppose you are a runner and want to increase your speed by 20%. Also suppose that there are two methods by which you can achieve this target. You can take a pill that has an immediate enhancing effect on your speed or you can train for two months, three hours a day. (Notice that these are both *enhancing* strategies.) Now, you might have a morally relevant reason to prefer the hard way to the easy way. You might value self-discipline and think that you will grow as a person if you achieve this target by making a conscious effort to perfect your body during the next two months. You might believe that the sense of satisfaction you would get at the end of the training for having achieved the target is worth the time and the effort that are required. But all these valuable considerations do not amount to judging that it would be unethical for you to choose the easy option.

E. Types of Enhancement

It is not easy to provide a clear classification of types of enhancements. There are different ways in which the enhancement can be achieved and different aims that the enhancing strategies can have.

1. Methods

One thought is that natural enhancing strategies are better than non-natural or artificial ones. But, first, the dichotomy between natural and artificial is not very clear. Second, there don't seem to be any good arguments for the view that the natural has moral value.

Recall the example of the runner who wants to increase her speed by 20% and has a choice: she can either train for two months, three hours a day, or take an enhancing pill. What is the most natural of these two strategies? 'Natural' can refer to (1) the endowments we are born with and we have not acquired, (2) the features we regard as normal as opposed to those which result from illness, (3) the features which have remained the same as opposed to those that we have altered and (4) something that belongs to the world of nature and has not been processed or manufactured.

One strategy does not strike us as obviously more natural than the other. It is true that regular training might not involve any of the artificial processing that might go into preparing the pill, but we do not seem to ethically object to this kind of artificial processing when we take medicines or eat food that we haven't grown ourselves. Of course we might have preferences for avoiding excessive processing and opt for so-called 'natural' remedies or home-grown food when possible, but these preferences do not necessarily track moral reasons. We do no think that it is morally wrong to buy vegetables from a supermarket. And neither strategy is natural from the other points of view. Both strategies are aimed at the alteration of a feature (running speed) which is not innate but acquired. And running three hours a day is not something people normally do.

2. Aims

There can be enhancing strategies whose main aim is disease prevention and increasing life expectancy and enhancing strategies that are aimed at improving cognitive abilities or physical appearance. While many feel an intuitive difference between these different goals for enhancement it is difficult to draw a clear line between them from an ethical perspective. Other things being equal, if it is not wrong to wish for something, it is not wrong, if we have the technology, to play fairy Godmother to ourselves and grant our wishes. So if it is not wrong to wish that our child were healthier, more intelligent or more beautiful it is difficult to see how it might become wrong to grant our own wish if we could, or of course for our fairy Godmother to grant it on our behalf.

The difference of course between the various aims or goals of enhancement might rather lie in the risks that it would be worth running or justifiable to run in pursuit of them. While for example considerable risks might be justifiable in order to cure a terrible disease or protect ourselves from almost certain death in a pandemic, it would be difficult to justify exposing our children to risks simply to change the colour of their eyes or make them better tennis players.

F. Is it *Always* Wrong not to Enhance?

In the previous two sections, we have considered some standard objections to enhancements and challenged the view that, from a moral point of view, there is a sharp distinction between those enhancing strategies that have as their main objective a healthier and longer life and those enhancing strategies that are aimed at improving the cognitive capacities of a person.

Here we face the question whether we have a moral obligation to eradicate disabilities and to enhance capacities where we safely can in human reproduction. Given our discussion so far, there are at least three positions that could be defended given the conception of disabling and enhanced conditions that we have presented, although not all of them seem compatible with the harm–benefit continuum and the thesis that we are responsible for both what we do and what we omit to do.

1. The Clear Moral Duty to Confer Benefits Option

On this view, no matter how slight the disability or insignificant the enhancement, parents have powerful reasons, which are always *moral* reasons, to minimise harm for, or confer benefits to, the person they are bringing into existence (subject of course to a safe method of achieving this and to the unambiguously beneficial nature of the proposed outcomes). We can note that at the moment selecting between pre-implantation embryos in the context of medically assisted reproduction is reasonably safe. Dietary manipulation (folic acid for example) and avoiding smoking or alcohol are also safe. Genetic manipulation is as yet untried and unsafe although that may change in time. These moral reasons stem from the basic principles of beneficence and non-maleficence.

2. The Threshold Option

On this view, parents have powerful moral reasons to prevent a disabling condition or enhance only when by not doing so they cause considerable harm to their children. This is a threshold option. In the context of reproductive choices, the parents' actions cease to be morally neutral and become subject to moral approval or condemnation when their actions have significant effects on the person they are bringing into existence in terms of harmed conditions that can be prevented or other conditions that can be enhanced. If the disadvantage caused by not preventing a disabling condition or not enhancing another condition is below a certain threshold, then there are no moral reasons to act. However, if the disadvantage is significant, then there are.

3. The Sliding Scale Option

On this view, all actions are subject to moral scrutiny, not only those which have significant effects in terms of benefits and harms for future people. The idea is that parents always have powerful moral reasons to enhance and prevent disability, but there is an important difference between the clear-moral-duty option and the sliding scale. In the former, to confer benefits or to prevent harm is right and to withhold benefits or cause harm is wrong, no matter how slight the disability or valuable the enhancement. Here, whether the reason to act is a moral reason and the degree of moral appraisal or condemnation for our actions co-vary with the degree of benefit conferred or harm prevented. Therefore, the reasons to prevent the disabling conditions caused by holoprosencephaly have a much greater moral impact than the reasons to enhance intelligence by say 15%. We are not talking here about the degree of strength of the motivating reasons, which can of course vary equally in the three options described, but about their being *moral* reasons in the first place.

Which of these positions is preferable? An advantage of the clear-moral-duty option is that it is a coherent and simple option that seems to be compatible with our conception of disability as a harmed condition and with the harm–benefit continuum. The problem with this option is that from a moral point of view some distinctions that many find intuitively strong (distinctions between preventing serious disability and enhancement for the purpose of minor benefits) are not transparent. Not to prevent disability where possible is clearly wrong, but so is withholding an enhancement, and both are moral issues. Of course where there are risks to the preventive or enhancing strategy, then the smaller the benefit the less it will rightly seem to be worth running risks. But apart from safety concerns, can the distinction between the two cases, which is intuitively recognised by many, be rationally justified, given our commitment to the harm–benefit continuum? We think that the distinction between preventing serious harm and preventing minor harm matters, but we believe that it is sufficient to mark such a distinction by considering the relative weight of the moral reasons we have. The moral reasons to prevent serious harm will be always stronger, all things being equal, than the reasons to confer minor benefits, although both sets of reasons will be morally relevant.

There are two serious problems with the threshold position. One is epistemological. It is never easy to measure how harmful or beneficial a condition is, as it cannot always be done out of context or inter-subjectively. This kind of calculation becomes even harder when applied to future people, whose interests and inclinations we ignore. The loss of a finger might be more significant for someone who may develop the ambition to become a great pianist than for someone who will have no interest in playing musical instruments, although it is disabling for both. The other problem is whether this option is really compatible with the harm–benefit continuum. If we recognise that a condition is harmful for someone, it would seem to follow that there are moral reasons to prevent that condition independently of the extent to which it is harmful. Can actions aimed at preventing harm ever be morally neutral?

The sliding scale option shares some of the epistemological problems that affect the threshold option but is overall more compatible with the harm–benefit continuum. What seems unattractive about this option is the conclusion that some reasons to act can be only *partially* moral reasons. Although it is perfectly reasonable to claim that we might have a variety of reasons to act in a certain way, it is more puzzling to believe that each of our reasons to act is only partially a moral reason.

G. Conclusion

In this chapter we defend the view that there are moral reasons to prevent disabling conditions and to adopt enhancing strategies in reproduction, on the basis of our conviction that there is a clear moral duty to confer benefits and avoid harms. This duty is of course moderated by the usual risk/benefit calculation that we all have to make about every decision we face.

First, we have defended a 'harmed condition' account of disability. Although there is always a social element to the disabling conditions people suffer from, some conditions seem to remain disabling even when the social context changes for the better. Since disabilities are harmed conditions, the moral reasons we have to prevent harm are also reasons to avoid creating disabling conditions.

Our commitment to the harm–benefit continuum also suggests that we have moral reasons to confer benefits on our children when this can safely be done. This brings us to the debate on enhancements. We have assessed some of the common arguments against enhancements and found that either they were unjustified or that they did not offer any *moral* reason to reject enhancements.

Finally, we have reviewed three possible approaches to the morality of enhancements and suggested that the most coherent option is to maintain that there are always moral reasons to enhance, although of course the strength of those moral reasons depends on the extent to which the condition to be enhanced would be an advantage to the future person.

Part II

Social Conceptions and Legal Regulation of Families and Family-making

4

Genes, Genealogies and Paternity: Making Babies in the Twenty-first Century

MARTIN RICHARDS*

The microscope has made visible aspects of the process of reproduction that were previously hidden. We have become familiar with images of egg meeting sperm; conception, the fertilised egg dividing and differentiating as embryo grows into fetus. The fetus, too, has become visible in the ultrasound scans which mark the progress and surveillance of pregnancy. Biologists have taught us that genes preside over these processes of development and that the equal contributions of the two parents combine in unique and unpredictable mixtures to produce our children. Biologists have also provided new techniques to assist our reproduction when our own efforts fail. There are other new DNA techniques which can reveal whose sperm met whose egg. The internet has many sites which offer to provide the genetic 'truth' of parentage at ever cheaper prices. Companies offer 'peace of mind' to those who have concerns about parentage and 'lie busters' to those who might otherwise be taken for a ride by women's 'paternity fraud'. For those too impatient to wait for a birth, the truth tellers have now added prenatal paternity testing to their dropdown menus.

Are these new biological techniques changing our ideas of parenthood and kinship? Kinship is, of course, not a matter of biology but rather of our culture,

* I would like to thank Katherine Vine and Laura Riley for their assistance with some of the research related to this chapter, and Tabitha Freeman and Helena Willén for their helpful comments on an earlier draft. Jill Brown and Sally Roberts provided excellent technical assistance, while Hazel Dickens, Alice Gerrard, JD Crowe, the Cox Family, Roy Acuff, Bill Monroe and the Flatlanders provided support and stimulation while I was writing. The author's research on everyday understandings of inheritance has been supported by a grant from the Wellcome Trust.

actions and social understanding. We acquire kin through marriage and cohabitation as well as reproduction and adoption. It is social understanding rather than biological facts of reproduction that govern kinship. Assisted reproductive technologies (ARTs), it has been said, create babies and not parents. Parentage rests with the legislation governing practice in the fertility clinics. But, of course, the spheres of biology and kinship are not independent, as our kinship system assigns parenthood and parentage to children, and it is that interrelation which is the focus of this chapter. My concern will be with paternity and not maternity. Historically, while conception was always hidden and the actions that may lead to it are generally private, pregnancy and birth are socially acknowledged and visible.[1] This is reflected in English law where maternity is signalled by the act of birth while paternity is generally a matter of social status and relationship. Even in the world of assisted fertilisation, where a woman may bear a child at the behest of a couple who provide their own eggs and sperm, she is the legal mother and legal procedures have to be carried out to reassign the parentage to the commissioning couple when the baby is handed over.[2] In contrast, while men have a duty to support (almost) any child conceived with their sperm, they are only able to achieve parentage through marriage, a joint birth registration or a court order.[3] However, things are rather different in a Human Fertilisation and Embryology Authority (HFEA) licensed fertility clinic. There a sperm donor has no social connection[4] with any child that may be conceived with his sperm, while other men may gain legal parentage simply as partners or companions of women who 'receive treatment' (*ie* are inseminated).[5] When a woman receives treatment on her own, clinics may be able to perform a quiet miracle of virgin birth and a legally fatherless child is created. All of this now occurs in a context of readily available DNA testing which can provide a more or less certain evidence-trail linking a man to a

---

[1] There are exceptions. In France, at least since the French Revolution, women have had the right to give birth secretly and anonymously; see N Lefaucheur, 'The "Tradition" of Anonymous Birth: The Lines of Argument' (2004) 18 *International Journal of Law, Policy and Family* 319–42. More recently, there have been attempts to introduce anonymous birth in other European countries; see B Willenbacher, 'Legal Transfer of French Traditions? German and Austrian Initiatives to Introduce Anonymous Birth' (2004) 18 *International Journal of Law, Policy and Family* 343–54.

[2] Human Fertilisation and Embryology Act 1990, s 27(1); R Lee and D Morgan, *Human Fertilisation and Embryology: Regulating the Reproductive Revolution* (London, Blackstone, 2001). In other jurisdictions, intent-based parenthood of the non-genetic and non-gestational 'commissioning mother' may instead be decisive; see B Steinbock, 'Defining Parenthood' (in this collection).

[3] A Bainham, *Children: The Modern Law*, 3rd edn (Bristol, Jordan, 2005).

[4] Matters are somewhat different for donations carried out after 1 April 2005 when donor anonymity ceased, as discussed further below.

[5] The Human Fertilisation and Embryology Act (HFE Act) 1990 was novel in its introduction of unmarried fatherhood for men who had neither a biological link to a child nor a formal relationship with the mother. However, this does create complications, when, for example, a relationship ends before a treatment programme is complete. For discussion, see J Masson, 'Parenting by Being; Parenting by Doing—In Search of Principles for Founding Families' (in this collection).

child conceived with his own sperm. And this trail has been firmly enshrined in legislation in the Child Support Act 1991 which, in effect, uses shared DNA sequences to determine a man's obligation to pay child support—though in law (if not always in the minds of some of the men involved) there is no connection between this obligation to support and fatherhood. And we should emphasise that liability to pay child support is not the same as parentage.

In this chapter I shall approach the issue of the relationship between genetic links and fatherhood by considering the history and development of artificial insemination by donor and then move on to discuss wider issues concerning fatherhood and parentage and DNA paternity testing.

A. From Artificial Insemination to Donor Insemination

Artificial insemination probably has had a very long but a little known history. In the modern era we know that various experiments with domestic animals were carried out in the late 18th century. In Britain the first recorded human case is attributed to John Hunter in 1790.[6] These early recorded cases involved insemination using the sperm of husbands who were unable to achieve intercourse. The first recorded case of 'heterologous insemination', *ie* insemination with donor sperm, comes a century later. Bartholomew records a survey of the world medical literature in 1928 reporting 185 cases of which 65 successfully produced pregnancies.[7] However, in a general climate of disapproval, such figures for artificial insemination (AI) are likely to be a very considerable underestimate. It would seem that both in Britain and elsewhere there were doctors who offered donor insemination to infertile couples but neither they, nor the couples they sought to help, would wish these activities to become public.

Matters became a little more open in the eugenic era. Some eugenicists promoted what they called 'eutelegenesis'[8] or 'germinal choice'.[9] By the 1930s, there were a number of birth control clinics as well as individual practitioners who also offered assistance to infertile couples and this might include AI. For eugenicists, indications for artificial insemination by donor (AID) would include risks of

---

[6] GW Bartholomew, 'The Development and Use of Artificial Insemination' (1958) 49 *Eugenics Review* 187–95.

[7] *Ibid.*

[8] H Brewer, 'Eutelegenesis' (1935) 27 *Eugenics Review* 121–26. Stedman's Medical Dictionary explains the term as 'artificial insemination by semen from a donor selected because of certain desirable characteristics for the development of superior offspring' (http://medical-dictionary.thefreedictionary.com/eutelegenesis).

[9] HJ Muller, *Out of the Night. A Biologists's View of the Future* (New York, NY, Garland, 1936). Muller received the Nobel Prize in Physiology/Medicine in 1946. He supported the idea of voluntary 'germinal choice', *ie* the choice of gametes from which to produce offspring.

hereditary 'taint' in the husband's family as well as infertility. However, such evidence as we have suggests that most cases were of infertile couples. Of course, artificial insemination does not require the involvement of medical practitioners and, particularly by the 1930s when AI had become common practice in agriculture, it seems likely that the idea and practice were more widespread. And, of course, in addition to home AI, there are also more traditional means for women with infertile partners to achieve pregnancy.

Marie Stopes founded her birth control clinic under the banner of the Society for Constructive Birth Control and Racial Progress in 1921. In addition to the clinic, she wrote letters to numerous people who enquired about their sexual and reproductive problems. She was not a great fan of the medical profession and she would suggest to those who had infertility problems that they should avoid 'expensive doctors' and go for 'DIY' (do-it-yourself) AID. Her letters contained detailed instructions. Husbands were advised to elicit the help of their best friend or a relative who would act as a donor. The donor should go to a room near the wife's bedroom. The husband might take the semen in a glass to the wife who could inseminate herself with a wedge of cotton wool. After this she was advised to lie on her front with her arms under her chin and hips held high for at least half an hour to achieve the maximum chance of conception. Marie Stopes claimed her DIY method was more likely to achieve conception than going to a doctor for advice.

By 1948 the practice of AID had become sufficiently well known and for some sufficiently a matter of concern for the Archbishop of Canterbury to set up a commission to examine the issues. This concluded that the practice should be criminalised on the grounds that it was adulterous, involved masturbation[10] and created an illegitimate child.[11] Indeed, until the Family Law Reform Act 1987, women who conceived through donor insemination were treated in law as if they had had intercourse with a third party. Typically, the whole matter would be shrouded in secrecy. The donor's name was usually not recorded. The birth would be registered in the husband's name and children generally would not be told of their origins. In 1960 the Feversham Committee, set up by the government, decided that, though artificial insemination by a husband (AIH) might be acceptable, artificial insemination by donor (AID) was not.[12] But attitudes were changing with a growing medical recognition of problems of infertility. In 1968, the then Minister of Health decided that both AIH and AID should be available on the NHS in appropriate cases. However, it was not until the coming of the Human Fertilisation and Embryology Act 1990 that the practice was established on a

---

[10] Though a suggestion was made that this difficulty could be avoided by collecting sperm from the donor's wife's vagina.
[11] E Haimes, 'Issues of Gender in Gamete Donation' (1993) 36 *Social Science and Medicine* 85–93.
[12] *Report of the Departmental Committee on Human Artificial Insemination* (1960 Cmnd 1105).

medically regulated basis. At this time, as had been the case for birth control, the word 'artificial' was dropped and the practice became known as donor insemination (DI). But we may note that in the world of agriculture AI still continues. The use of different terminology in the animal and human spheres suggests a need to distance the two practices.

B. The Coming of Artificial Reproductive Technologies (ARTs)

The announcement of the birth of the first child conceived by *in vitro* fertilisation (IVF) in July 1978 in the UK made headlines around the world. Much of the reaction was negative—a step too far, an unnecessary and offensive technological intrusion into a private and personal realm, a deviation from normal sexual intercourse, a separation of the 'unitive and procreative' aspects of sex, and for many feminists, another patriarchal use of female bodies 'in the great technological fuck'. But the technique was able, albeit unreliably, to provide babies for some infertile couples and increasingly the press would celebrate the births of 'miracle babies'. As use of IVF spread, and was coupled with sperm, egg and embryo donation in some cases, the number of infertile couples who could have children grew.[13] In 1982 the British government set up an inquiry to consider these developments and the 'policies and safeguards that should be applied'. The Committee, chaired by the philosopher Mary Warnock, reported two years later.[14] The Warnock Committee, largely composed of medics, lawyers and social workers, was very medical in its approach: its report concerned 'infertility and its alleviation'. This included AID as well as IVF and egg donation. It recommended that the husband of a woman receiving artificial insemination should be registered as the father of the child but recognised that this would mean that if an unmarried woman was given AID the child would be legally fatherless. Significantly, they also said:

> We are fully aware that this can be criticised as legislating for a fiction since the husband of a woman who has conceived by AID will not be the genetic father of the child and the register of births has always been envisaged as a true genetic record. Nonetheless, it would in our view be consistent with the husband's assuming all parental rights and duties with regard to the child. However we are of the view that consideration should

---

[13] Today up to 2% of all babies are conceived by IVF in some countries, but the percentage is inflated because more than one egg is usually implanted and multiple births are very common.

[14] *Report of the Committee of Inquiry into Human Fertilisation and Embryology* (1984 Cmnd. 9314).

be given as a matter of urgency for making it possible for the parents in registering the birth to add 'by donation' after the man's name.[15]

The idea of a birth register being a 'true genetic record' is an odd one, as in English law there is simply a presumption that a child born to married parents is their (genetic) child. From the beginning of birth registration there will have been many children registered in the name of others than their biological parents. Furthermore, in the case of a birth to an unmarried mother a father's name may or may not be included. But the Warnock view reflects the medical perspective that so strongly frames their report.

The Warnock report led to the Human Fertilisation and Embryology Act of 1990 ('HFE Act 1990'). While the bill was before parliament there was an attempt to amend it so that the treatment of unmarried women would have been a criminal offence. This was narrowly defeated, but a compromise amendment resulting in section 13(5) was agreed:

> A woman shall not be provided with treatment services unless account has been taken of the welfare of any child who may be born as a result of the treatment (including the need of that child for a father), and of any other child who may be affected by the birth.

The Warnock report's suggestion of birth registration noting the use of donation was not followed in the legislation. Donation under the Act was anonymous (until donor anonymity was removed prospectively for gametes donated after 1 April 2005).[16] As many commentators have argued, the HFE Act 1990 attempts to underpin the nuclear family[17] and normalise 'ART families' to this model. Indeed, this can also be seen in the ways in which most heterosexual couples use ART services in relation to parentage. Two features stand out.

First, most users of ARTs have a strong preference for their own children—children conceived with their own sperm and eggs. Only when possibilities of doing this are exhausted do they turn to the use of donated gametes. This strong preference has already shaped the deployment of new technologies and may be expected to continue to do so in the future.[18]

---

[15] *Ibid*, 26.

[16] See *Human Fertilisation and Embryology Authority (HFEA) (Disclosure of Donor Information) Regulations* 2004.

[17] See Haimes, 'Gender in gamete donation', n 11 above; S Sheldon, 'Fragmenting Fatherhood: The Regulation of Reproductive Technologies' (2005) 68 *Modern L Rev* 523–53.

[18] For example, I think we may expect to see the development of techniques for the production of eggs and sperm from somatic cells for those who cannot otherwise produce gametes. The same argument may be made with regard to lesbian couples. We may note the recent request from a fertile lesbian couple to use IVF in an NHS clinic so that one of them may bear a child conceived with an egg from her partner. As one paper reported (*Independent* 18 April 2005) they wished to have 'a baby that has truly come from both of us'. Will a step down this route be a chimeric child formed through the fusion of two embryos, one from each mother? See also 'Lesbians plan IVF to create a "shared" baby', *Bionews* 25 April 2005.

A current technique that is influenced by this parental desire is ICSI—intra-cytoplasmic sperm injection. With this technique, rather than simply placing egg and sperm together in a dish for fertilisation, a single sperm is injected into the egg. The technique can be used to increase chances of fertilisation for men whose sperm lacks adequate mobility. In some cases immature sperm are extracted directly from the testes. Use of the technique means that there is a significantly larger group of sub-fertile men who can have their own children and avoid the use of donors. What is interesting about the technique is the rapidity with which it has been deployed and accepted by clinics and their patients, despite some questions about its safety and its invasiveness, illustrating the desire of couples to use their own gametes.

The second feature of ART use to be noted is that most couples who use donors do not tell their children that this is how they have been conceived.[19] They prefer normalised, 'as if' families. Clinics assist parents in choosing donors who physically resemble them so they may plausibly be seen as their own (genetic) children. For obvious reasons, this approach cannot be taken by same-sex couples and is less often used by single women. For these people there may be a continuing relationship between the mother(s), their child and the donor (or birth mother if another woman carries the pregnancy). In some cases this may be formalised in kinship terms with the donor or birth mother becoming the child's godparent or an aunt, uncle or parent.[20] Ethnographic research in clinics in the USA has described how the actors 'do kinship' in order to realign biological and social accounts.[21] So, for example, a woman who used donor eggs from a friend stressed the small percentage of pregnancy spent at the gamete and embryo stage, so minimising the biological contribution of the egg. She also pointed to a common genetic pool shared with the donor and how the bonds of friendship with her allowed her relationship to the baby to be seen as an enhancement of that friendship.

C. Donor Anonymity

As a result of government decisions, those who are born from sperm, eggs or embryos donated after 1 April 2005 will be able, when they reach 18, to seek

---

[19] ST Golombok *et al*, 'Parenting and Contemporary Reproductive Technologies' in MH Bornstein (ed), *Handbook of Parenting* (Mahwah, NJ, Erlbaum, 2002).

[20] MPM Richards, 'Future Bodies: Some History and Future Prospects for Human Genetic Selection' in A Bainham, S Day Sclater and MPM Richards (eds), *Body Lore and Laws* (Oxford, Hart Publishing, 2002).

[21] C Thompson, 'Strategic Naturalizing: Kinship in an Infertility Clinic' in S Franklin and S McKinnon (eds), *Relative Values: Reconfiguring Kinship Studies* (Durham, NC, Duke University Press, 2001).

information about the donor, including the donor's name.[22] This change follows
a long debate of arguments for and against anonymous donation which predates
the HFE Act. The Warnock report argued that there was a need to maintain the
absolute anonymity of donors because it avoided the 'invasion of the third party
into the family'.[23] It recommended that donors should have no parental rights or
duties. The Committee members were, in general, in favour of avoiding family
secrets and believed there should be more openness about the use of AID; but
they thought that this was unlikely to change without a shift in attitude towards
male infertility. Indeed, then and since, the argument that there is a need to con-
ceal male infertility has been frequently used to support anonymity.

The arguments on both sides about ending anonymity have been widely
rehearsed.[24] On one side, it is argued that children need to know their origins and
that such information may be incomplete without a name.[25] Some have argued
that children have a right to know[26] and human rights arguments seem to have
been important in the government's decision for change. On the other side, it is
asserted that social parents (and donors) should be able to keep matters secret for
a number of social, commercial and pragmatic reasons. As pointed out already,
most parents do not tell their children.[27] Where children are told they do not seem
to be particularly troubled by this and accept it. But inadvertent discovery, or
being told in adulthood, may lead to prolonged distress, anger and resentment of
the social parents' lack of honesty.[28] Part of this upset may arise from the realisation that others have intimate knowledge about them to which they have been
denied access.[29] Some of these arguments broadly parallel those that have been
used in the case of adoptive children and led to changes in practice in that field.[30]

---

[22] See *Human Fertilisation and Embryology Authority (HFEA) (Disclosure of Donor Information)
Regulations* 2004.

[23] *Report of the Committee of Inquiry into Human Fertilisation and Embryology* (1984 Cmnd 9314).
The report raised the potential hazard of consanguinity ('incest') if donor children who shared the
same donor were to meet and have children together unaware of their biological relationship. To avoid
this possibility, the use of a donor is limited and the HFE Act permits those aged 16 or over intending
to marry to ask whether they have been conceived by donation and are related.

[24] Department of Health, *Donor Information Consultation* (London, 2001); S Maclean and M
Maclean, 'Keeping Secrets in Assisted Reproduction—The Tension Between Donor Anonymity and
the Need of the Child for Information' (1996) 8 *Child and Family Law Quarterly* 243–54; K
O'Donovan, 'Who is the Father? Access to Information on Genetic Identity' in G Douglas and L Sebba
(eds), *Children's Rights and Traditional Values* (Aldershot, Ashgate, 1998).

[25] MPM Richards, 'Assisted Reproduction and Parental Relationship' in A Bainham *et al* (eds),
Children and Their Families: Contact, Rights and Welfare (Oxford, Hart Publishing, 2003); A Bainham,
Children: The Modern Law, 3rd edn (Bristol, Jordan, 2005).

[26] M Freeman, 'The New Birth Right?' (1996) 4 *International Journal of Children's Rights* 273–97.

[27] S Golombok *et al*, 'Parenting and Contemporary Reproductive Technologies', n 19 above.

[28] S Maclean and M Maclean, 'Keeping Secrets in Assisted Reproduction', n 24 above.

[29] E Blyth, 'Donor Assisted Conception and Donor Offspring Rights to Genetic Origin Information'
(1998) 6 *International Journal of Children's Rights* 237–51.

[30] D Howe and J Feast, *Adoption, Search and Reunion* (London, Children's Society, 2000).

Given that most parents who do not tell their children, do tell at least some other family members and friends there is a significant risk of inadvertent discovery—a risk increased by the easy access to paternity testing which could be used to check out suspicions.

There is one argument that has been used in this context which deserves comment. This is that knowledge of the identity of a donor is essential to a child's complete genetic identity—that a personal identity is in some way defective or incomplete without knowledge of who the donor is. This is much more specific than a more general claim that children deserve to know something of their origins—that, for example, a parent is infertile and donor gametes were used. The defective genetic identity argument is based on a premise that genetic information about both parents is in some way essential to a complete sense of personal identity. Genetic information derived from DNA can be used by comparison with a named sample of DNA to identify someone—as for example can be done with body fragments after a bomb explosion. But genetic information does not individuate people. It is not a kind of molecular essence of personhood. Monozygotic twins ('identical' twins) are clearly separate people each with their own identity despite the fact that they have identical genomes. And their personal identity is not threatened by the knowledge that their co-twin and sibling has an identical genome to themselves.

But discussions about donor children and genetic identity are often confused because the phrase 'genetic identity' is used in a number of different ways—especially to refer to genetic information and much more widely to include information about the donor and the circumstances of donation.

There are a number of different kinds of information that donor children may want to have. First, there is what we can regard of a kind of genealogical information—that they were conceived with the use of a donor and that they are not the biological child of their social father. Second, there is knowledge of the donor, as a person, who he is, information about his appearance and character and, perhaps, his family and ethnic background.[31] Importantly, there is often a keen interest in his motives for becoming a donor and the reasons for the choice of that particular donor. The point about motives has been underlined in recent discussions about the possibility of providing expenses or payment for donors. Those who are children of donation have argued strongly that donation should be altruistic and not involve any payment or provision of expenses. Some seem to regard knowing the name of a donor as important, while for others this is not a particular issue. A few wish to meet the donor. Often the motive here seems to be to learn more about the donor and fill out the information that they have, rather than necessarily seeking a continuing social relationship with them.

---

[31] The HFEA form has a space where donors can add something about themselves 'as a person'. This part of the form is not obligatory for a donor to complete and most sperm donors choose not to.

Knowledge of biological half siblings can also be important. I have spoken with some of a small group of adults who had learnt that they had been conceived through the same clinic and had used DNA testing to establish that some but not all of the group shared the same donor father. Some of those who have identified genetic half siblings had maintained social relationships with them. Donor offspring may speculate about traits they may have inherited from their biological father. In rare situations there may also be a question about an inherited disease that may have run in the donor's family.[32]

The ending of anonymity of donors remains controversial and it has a number of important implications for ART practice.[33] There are those who believe, contrary to experience elsewhere, that donors will become more difficult to obtain.[34] Others think, as the Warnock Committee did, that ending anonymity is an inappropriate intrusion into family life. But we also need to consider why the recent change in policy has come about. In the Warnock report's perspective there are three elements: the parental couple who want a child but cannot conceive one with their own gametes, the donor, and a child with a concern for genealogical truth and, perhaps, family secrets. The sperm donor provides the necessary genetic material (in the language of the HFE Act 1990). But after this he is almost entirely written out of the story—anonymised and blocked from gaining any of the rights and duties that may accrue to fathers in other situations, or indeed even from knowing whether children have been conceived with his sperm. For the couple the intrusion of the third party is to be avoided—the Archbishop's Commission's notion of adultery must be firmly laid to rest. While parliament did not accept Warnock's suggested amendment of birth certificates to note that donation had been used, the HFE Act 1990 does allow for some non-identifiable information to be available on request to the adult children of donation, but the identity of the donor remains confidential to a register held by the Human Fertilisation and Embryology Authority. But the matter of genealogical truth is left to the parents to be as open or otherwise they may choose with their children and family. Twenty years on from the Warnock report there have been some shifts in attitude. The separation of sexual activity and procreation has become more complete and attitudes toward infertility have shifted in the way that the Warnock report expected so the fact that DI has been used to create a child poses

---

[32] Under HFEA guidelines would-be donors are screened for a number of common genetic and transmittable diseases.

[33] *The Regulation of Donor-Assisted Conception* (London, Human Fertilisation and Embryology Authority, 2004).

[34] There are also suggestions that it will lead to rather different donors, fewer of the young men who seem to be largely motivated by the money they receive, and more older men who may already be fathers (R Cook, 'Donating Parenthood: Perspectives on Parenthood from Surrogacy and Gamete Donation' in A Bainham, S Day Sclater and MPM Richards (eds), *What is a Parent? A Socio-Legal Analysis* (Oxford, Hart Publishing, 1999).

less difficulty for couples. And we are more ready to acknowledge the position and needs of the children in the situation. Many parents may continue to want their 'as if' family in which biological facts of conception are glossed over but we take more seriously the need or even the right of children to know of their origins, at least when they are adults. That position is given further weight by the availability of cheap and easy DNA paternity testing. The biology of genealogy is not determined by birth registration but when push comes to shove by a DNA test result.

So the balance between the elements in the situation has shifted and we have a new compromise. Anonymity ends, but only for children at eighteen who enquire about their origins. So, only if they have learnt enough about their origins to know that there is information to be gained will children find out more. However, the signs are that this is an evolving situation and, increasingly, parents will tell their children and the situation will move towards more openness, as has been the case in adoption.

D. Genetic Truth and 'ART' Muddles

In an important article entitled 'Fragmenting Fatherhood',[35] Sally Sheldon has suggested a growing currency of a 'right to genetic truth' in the removal of donor anonymity, the Human Fertilisation and Embryology (Deceased Fathers) Act 2003, and in the development of law and practice relating to adoption and so on. But she has argued against 'the idea that a genetic vision of fatherhood is superseding other ways of grounding fatherhood': 'It has been my contention that the acceptance of a right to "genetic truth" has developed, at least in part, because of a growing belief that such knowledge is unlikely to dislodge the role of the social father.'[36]

But as we have seen at least in the case of donor anonymity this 'right to genetic truth' is highly qualified. Sheldon argues that we accept some need for children to have information because we have come to tolerate, or even value, the existence of more than one man in some kind of fatherhood role in relation to a child. In her terms, fatherhood has become 'fragmented' so children can have more than one father. Clearly, Sheldon is right saying that in an increasing numbers of situations a child may have multiple father figures. This is most obvious in post divorce families where we have moved to a situation where an existing relationship between a child and a father is expected to continue post divorce and after repartnering of the mother. Indeed, such arrangements are seen as beneficial for

---

[35] 'Fragmenting Fatherhood: The Regulation of Reproductive Technologies', n 17 above.
[36] *Ibid*, 551.

children.[37] Post divorce kinship is increasingly complex with parents and partners from previous relationships as well as wider kin all continuing to remain involved. This stands in great contrast with the clean break which was more typical of divorces of the 1950s when mothers and children were expected to cut off contact with an 'ex' to leave the coast clear for a new partner. However, whether it is the possibility of multiple father figures which has driven the move to put more stress on the access to genetic 'truth' is another matter. Rather, I would suggest that a more significant driver has been easy access to knowledge of genetic 'truth' through paternity testing.

My claim is not that genetic fatherhood is superseding other ways of grounding fatherhood, but that it may bring another kind of father into the picture, or in some situations remove one from it. As part of her discussion Sheldon presents an analysis of a recent legal case involving a mix-up of sperm in an IVF clinic. I want to revisit this case and suggest that it supports a rather different conclusion from the one that Sheldon draws. I want to argue that the judicial decision may have been determined by biological facts which could not be hidden.

In the Leeds case[38] Mr and Mrs A were treated by IVF using Mrs A's own eggs and, it was intended, Mr A's sperm. By accident Mrs A's eggs were fertilised with sperm from another couple who were receiving treatment in the same clinic. The matter came to light because when Mrs A gave birth to twins, they were both dark skinned while she and her husband were both white. A DNA paternity test showed that the genetic father was Mr B, the husband of the other woman receiving treatment in the clinic. Both the Bs are black. While it was agreed by both couples that the As should continue to bring up the twins, the couples sought a declaration of legal paternity. The court found that Mr A could not be considered the legal father. In her judgment, the President of the Family Division, Dame Elizabeth Butler-Sloss, said that although Mr A was not:

> their legal father, they will remain within a loving, stable and secure home. They also retain the great advantage of preserving the reality of their paternal identity. ... To refuse to recognise Mr B as their biological father is to distort the truth about which some day the twins will have to learn through knowledge of their paternal identity.[39]

Sheldon argues that the picture is:

> both substantially more complicated and far more interesting than simply involving a dispute about which of the two men is the 'real' father. The courts here are explicitly

---

[37] B Rogers and J Pryor, *Divorce and Separation: The Outcomes for Children* (York, Joseph Rowntree Foundation, 1998).
[38] *Leeds Teaching Hospital NHS Trust v Mr A, Mrs A and others* [2003] EWHC 259; [2003] 1 FLR 1091; [2003] 1 FCR 599.
[39] *Ibid*, paras 56 and 57.

prepared to countenance more than one father (and two parents) in the twins' lives, and to assert this as a positive, serving to foster awareness of their cultural background, and thereby enrich their familial situation.[40]

Sheldon emphasises the latitude open to the court if one accepts that children may have more than one father figure. I would emphasise another point: that despite the fact that all were agreed that Mr and Mrs A would continue to bring up the children, the court in its decision underlines the genetic 'truth' revealed by a DNA test to the extent of giving paternity to a third party. It is a pragmatic decision determined by a recognition of both social fatherhood and motherhood and genetic 'truth'.

The clinic made a mistake and used the wrong couple's sperm. And, because the sperm that was used in error came from a black man, it became obvious to the As that Mr A was very unlikely to be the genetic father. Paternity testing confirmed what was already clear from the skin colour of both couples. The option taken by most couples using DI of acting as if the social father was also the genetic father could not be used in this situation because the twins' skin colour is a giveaway. For better or for worse, the genetic father could not be written out of the picture.

Recognising Mr B as a father acknowledges the genetic truth. This judgment also follows the same pattern as can be seen in cases where married women have had affairs and there are questions about the paternity of children subsequently born. The courts now take the view that the paternity of a child is to be established by 'science' and not by legal presumption or inference and that, in most instances, the best interests of children are served by their knowing the 'truth'.[41] To this we might add that paternity is not to be determined by the intentions of the would-be parents, even though those intentions do mean that they will bring up the children, as was the case for Mr and Mrs A, and become parents.

Sheldon asks the obvious question: had the twins not been of mixed race,[42] would the Court of Appeal have decided this case in the same way? Of course we cannot know. Had the two couples been more similar in physical characteristics, the mistake might have passed unnoticed.[43] But if a paternity test had revealed paternity we may expect the same decision. However, in this case, the facts that it

---

[40] 'Fragmenting Fatherhood: The Regulation of Reproductive Technologies', n 17 above, 546.

[41] *Re H and A (Paternity: Blood Tests)* [2002] FLR 1145.

[42] Sheldon comments that there are both interesting and troubling aspects of the use of concepts such as race, culture and ethnic background in this judgement and its discussion by some commentators ('Fragmenting Fatherhood: The Regulation of Reproductive Technologies', n 17 above, 545–46.).

[43] It is possible that there are other cases where a clinic may have muddled sperm samples which have not come to light because the children are not strikingly different from what parents might expect. But given the publicity this case has received—and a similar story is soon to be a TV docu-soap—it is possible that other couples who have used fertility treatment and may feel that their children are not particularly like themselves may turn to DNA testing.

is obvious that the children have a black parent and that DNA testing has identified the genetic father would seem to be the overriding considerations for the
judgment. But importantly, in the judgment—and indeed in the couples' own
views and actions—there was no attempt to overrule or displace Mr A as the social
and day-to-day father of the twins.

Of course, Mrs A is both the genetic and gestational mother of the twins. Given
this, it would have been unthinkable to displace her as the twins' mother and so
her partner remains the social father. But there is one other point we might consider. What if it had been embryos rather than the sperm samples which had been
muddled? If both the egg and sperm had come from the Bs would the decision
have been the same? Effectively, Mrs A would have been an unwitting gestational
surrogate who had set out to have her own baby with her partner. Would the combined genetic claim of Mr and Mrs B be sufficient to change the Bs' minds? Would
they have wanted to bring up the twins? Would the As have wanted to hand them
over? And would the court have agreed to the Bs having the twins with Mrs and
Mr A perhaps having a contact order? Certainly, some would see the Bs' claims as
being much stronger in such a situation, but even then possibly not strong enough
to override the claims of a birth mother and her partner. While the intentions of
those involved in Leeds are different from our hypothetical case of muddled
embryos, we should note that under surrogacy arrangements made in the UK the
surrogate is the legal mother. However, whoever might bring up the children in
this situation, I think we can be sure that a court would have recognised that the
children should know who had provided the eggs and sperm that led to their conception.

E. DNA Testing: The 'Truth' Revealed

Until 1987, paternity and other genetic relationship testing was carried out using
blood group proteins. While such tests could rule out a potential father, they cannot identify a particular father as many individuals may have the same profile of
blood group proteins. However, DNA tests are much more specific and, apart
from cases of monozygotic twins (and other multiple births), similarities in DNA
sequences can identify a parent with an accuracy that amounts to certainty.[44]
DNA can be extracted from the white cells in a blood sample, or from cells collected from a cheek swab, but any cellular material from the body can serve—hair
roots, semen stains or the cells we may leave when we drink from a glass. The test
depends on comparing the sequences in the DNA in parts of the genome which

---

[44] Setting aside errors that can arise through muddling samples, misidentifying the origin of a sample and so on.

are highly variable from family to family. Most companies offer two kinds of testing, the regulated, court approved tests or the do-it-yourself unregulated ones. In the UK, paternity tests are regulated by government guidelines[45] which require consent from interested parties, certain technical standards and verification of the origin of the samples. Over 10,000 such tests are done each year in the UK largely for use by the Child Support Agency to determine liability to pay child support and by the Home Office to confirm family membership in immigration cases. Only a minority of tests done in the UK are carried out in the context of private paternity disputes. But these figures are only for testing done by UK-based companies working within the UK Department of Health guidelines. An unknown, but probably considerable, number of tests are done off-shore for UK residents by companies trading via the internet.

The testing of children may require a court approval, and—as noted in the previous section—in recent years there has been a shift in judicial opinion so that in most cases testing is permitted so that children may learn the 'truth' about their origins.[46] In making decisions about whether or not to permit paternity testing, courts must consider the best interests of the child. Generally, the judicial view has been that in cases where a child was living with married parents and there were questions about paternity, it was in the child's interest to refuse testing because results of this might disturb the *status quo*. But by the late 1990s when DNA paternity testing had become well-established and was widely used in the context of child support, views began to change and generally tests have been permitted to settle paternity disputes on the grounds that it would be in a child's best interest to know the truth about his or her conception.

Over the last 7 years another form of paternity testing has grown up alongside the regulated court approved testing. This is often referred to as 'peace of mind' or 'curiosity' testing by companies. This is testing where the enquirer collects samples with a kit provided by the company and sends these off for analysis. There are generally no consent requirements and, indeed, some of the companies provide detailed instructions for collection of samples in ways that avoid the knowledge of those from whom the DNA is collected or their parents. The availability and use of this kind of testing seems to have grown very rapidly and though no precise figures are available, some believe this now accounts for the greater bulk of all paternity testing. Generally this testing will involve a sample from a child and one or two putative fathers, but the companies offer many variants on this; involving various other (potential) blood relatives. One recent development has been pregnancy paternity testing. Here fetal cells are collected by amniocentesis or chorionic

---

[45] Department of Health, *Code of Practice and Guidance on Genetic Paternity Testing Services* (London, 2001); N Morling *et al*, 'Paternity Testing Commission of the International Society of Forensic Genetics: Recommendations on Genetic Investigations in Paternity Cases' (2002) 129 *Forensic Science International* 148–57.
[46] A Bainham, *Children: The Modern Law*, 3rd edn (Bristol, Jordan, 2005).

villus sampling (CVS). Both techniques are used to collect samples from a fetus during pregnancy which can be tested for abnormality. Amniocentesis involves sticking a hollow needle into the fluid in the uterus around the fetus and drawing off some of this. This amniotic fluid contains fetal cells from which DNA can be extracted in the same way as from other cells from the body. In the case of CVS a small sample of tissue is taken from the membranes which surround the fetus. These techniques carry a small risk of causing a miscarriage.[47] One might wonder why someone would want to use a technique which could put a pregnancy at risk when a paternity test could be done much more simply and safely after the birth of the child. One must assume that someone who wishes to test in pregnancy is likely to be contemplating termination of that pregnancy should the result indicate that the 'wrong' man was the father.

A lot of websites offering peace of mind testing are clearly aimed at those who are, or might be, required to pay child support. Indeed, some websites offering advice to those who may be contemplating divorce provide links to websites of paternity testing companies. Some websites carry letters from grateful clients. One UK company, for example, tells of a man who, following a test, is now set to receive a £30,000 rebate from the Child Support Agency. It is difficult to estimate the number of companies offering testing or, indeed, where all of them are based. Some companies appear to be using a number of different names and others may be agents who collect samples from customers and then send them to another company for laboratory analysis. At least one company has gone a step further and cut out the middle man. A man in Britain was recently successfully prosecuted for deception after his company had taken clients' fees but failed to send DNA samples to a laboratory. It was alleged in court that Simon Mullane simply guessed what the results of a test might be.[48]

Following the Human Tissue Act 2004 the non-consensual analysis of DNA has become a criminal offence in the UK. Section 45(1) states that:

> A person commits an offence if (a) he has any bodily material intending—(i) that any human DNA in the material be analysed without qualifying consent, and (ii) that the results of the analysis be used otherwise than for an excepted purpose.

Exempted purposes include such things as forensic or clinical use but do not include paternity testing by a putative father. This legislation is relatively recent but, as yet, there is little sign on the websites of overseas companies aimed at UK

---

[47] Recently, some companies have begun to offer 'non invasive' pregnancy paternity testing. These may use a technique which involves isolating fetal cells from a maternal blood sample. Given that fetal cells are thought to persist in a mother's circulation for a long time (on this point, see K Khosrotehrani and DW Bianchi, 'Multi-lineage Potential of Fetal Cells in Maternal Tissue: A Legacy in Reverse' (2005) 118 *Journal of Cell Science* 1559–63), doubts have been expressed about the accuracy of such tests for mothers who have been pregnant previously.

[48] BBC News, 24 September 2004. He received a three-year prison sentence.

customers that companies have thought it necessary to remind their potential UK customers of the requirements of this legislation.

F. A New Moral Order of Genetic Parentage?

Until the advent of DNA testing we did not have an evidence-trail to link sperm and eggs involved in conception to the identity of those from whom they came. A consequence of this is that legally and, indeed, socially, motherhood and fatherhood have been achieved in rather different ways. But with DNA paternity testing we can determine with near certainty whose sperm led to a conception. We have seen that in assisted reproduction and some situations of disputed paternity, DNA testing does seem to have influenced what may happen and what may be seen as the social significance of biological paternity. While socially established fatherhood may continue, more emphasis is being placed on children having knowledge of their biological origins. How widespread are these changes? Is a new moral order of genetic parentage being established? Moving beyond the field of assisted reproductive technologies, is this leading to a new moral order of paternity?

The field where DNA testing has had the most significant impact has been child support. First in the USA and then in Britain with the Child Support Act 1991 there has been legislation setting up systems for collection of child support payments which use paternity testing to determine the liability to pay. This legislation has been a major driver for the development of the paternity testing industry. Of course, liability to pay child support is not the same as parentage but undoubtedly paternity testing undertaken under the Child Support Act has had significant impact for some children. For some, it has ended a relationship with a social father who did not share DNA sequences with them, while others may have discovered a new father. But the Act may have had a wider influence in reinforcing the idea that fatherhood has a biological rather than social basis. Given that many men believe that paying child support should be linked to seeing a child, a genetic basis for fatherhood may be reinforced.

DNA paternity testing is often in the news and it is seen to play a role in the lives of the rich and famous. TV and radio 'soaps' run story lines with a 'truth' being revealed by DNA testing. And we have TV shows in which the results of testing are announced on camera. Perhaps not surprisingly given this cultural visibility, in a recent study of everyday understandings of inheritance in which participants were asked what DNA was, a significant minority said it was what was used in paternity testing.[49]

---

[49] MPM Richards and A Wilson, 'Understanding Inheritance: Kinship Connections and Genetics' (a qualitative study exploring concepts and knowledge of genetics in a group of young adults and parents, supported by the Wellcome Trust) (publication in preparation).

However, despite this visibility the marital presumption of paternity remains. A recent close analysis of state legislation in the USA[50] does show some erosion of the marital presumption which can be attributed to the availability of DNA testing. A similar trend is discernable in the UK.[51] But it is still the case in law that if a husband does not deny paternity, and no other man claims he is the father, the husband will be treated as the father whatever the biological situation may be. However, it has become easier for another man to challenge the situation and a DNA test result will usually carry the day.

The legal position of unmarried fathers has recently changed bringing a majority of them into more or less the same position with regard to their children as married fathers. Following the Adoption and Children Act 2002, automatic parental responsibility is granted to unmarried fathers if the birth of their children is registered jointly by their child's mother and themselves. As with married parents, this creates a rebuttable presumption of paternity. Research undertaken before the Adoption and Children Act[52] indicates that for many unmarried couples this change in the law simply brought the law into line with what couples had believed to be the legal situation. Many believed that as they shared parenthood and through cohabitation or 'common law marriage' they both also shared all the rights and duties of parents—just as would be the case if they had married.

However, there remains an important distinction between married and unmarried child bearing, because unmarried fathers have neither the right nor the duty to register the birth of their children. Thus, unmarried legal parentage depends on the mother registering the birth together with the father.[53] For a significant minority of children born outside marriage, the mother alone registers the birth and no father's name is recorded. We may contrast this situation with that of a donor child where it is argued that knowledge of the donor father is important to the child and there are now arrangements for such children to obtain this information when they reach adulthood. In the case of a mother-only birth registration no attempt is made to provide the child with information about the natural father—though interestingly, in the related jurisdiction of New Zealand, their Law Commission has recommended that just such procedures should be created.[54]

Of course, unmarried fathering includes a wide variety of situations and relationships between mother and father. There are those who have a continuing

---

[50] T Glennon, 'Somebody's Child: Evaluating the Erosion of the Marital Presumption of Paternity' (2000) 102 *West Virginia L Rev* 547–605.

[51] A Bainham, *Children: The Modern Law*, 3rd edn (Bristol, Jordan, 2005).

[52] R Pickford, 'Unmarried Fathers and the Law' in A Bainham, S Day Sclater and MPM Richards (eds), *What is a Parent? A Socio-Legal Analysis* (Oxford, Hart Publishing, 1999).

[53] We might also notice in this context that a mother, and a mother alone, can take the decision to terminate a pregnancy even if the father of the fetus objects to this; see E Jackson, *Regulating Reproduction: Law, Technology and Autonomy* (Oxford, Hart Publishing, 2001).

[54] New Zealand Law Commission, *New Issues in Parenthood, Report No 88* (Wellington, New Zealand, 2005).

cohabiting relationship, who plan and expect to bring up their children together and who see their parenting in the same terms as married parents. These are now treated legally in virtually the same way, via joint birth registration. However, there are many other situations. There are those who may never have had any intention on either side to conceive a child and simply had a longer or shorter lasting sexual relationship which resulted in a conception. There are women who may have wished to get pregnant but never had any intention of engaging the man they had sexual intercourse with as a co-parent of the child. In these situations—and many others that can exist—the Child Support Agency may become involved and will attempt to establish the genetic parentage of a child, regardless of the social relationship that the man concerned may, or may not, have with the mother and/or child. This is done solely to establish liability to pay for child support in cases where the mother receives state benefits. A father may also take actions to establish parentage (which may involve DNA testing) and to seek contact with his child. Legal procedures in this situation have been quite complex and have undergone a number of changes in recent years. Without going into details, the important point from my discussion here is that, as Bainham puts it:

> The reforms reflect in part the greater emphasis which is now being given throughout the law to establish the biological truth of paternity, although they also recognise that there may be circumstances in which this might not be desirable especially where to do so might be considered to be against a child's best interests.[55]

G. Conclusion

Earlier in this chapter I repeated the comment that techniques of assisted reproduction produce babies and not parents. The same may be said of sexual intercourse; it can lead to conception and (leaving aside miscarriage or termination) at the birth there will be, both socially and legally, a mother. Whether or not that child will have someone she may regard as a father will depend on the intentions and actions of the mother and the man (or men) in her life, as will legal parentage. Once we move beyond heterosexual couples who plan to have their children together, we enter a complex area of law, intended to sort out issues of parentage, parenthood and child support in the often confused social world of sex, love, relationships, parenting and kinship. As far as child support is concerned, if the state becomes involved, there is a single simple criterion for the liability to pay: biological parentage.[56] We have a reliable DNA test to determine paternity if there is

---

[55] A Bainham, *Children: The Modern Law*, 3rd edn (Bristol, Jordan, 2005) 190.
[56] Though sperm donors are exempt from this.

uncertainty or conflicting opinion. Biology rules, and in most situations, but not all, this will accord with everyday notions of social justice and relationship.

But fatherhood and parentage are much more socially complex and are not simply determined by the increasingly visible biological facts of life. As we have seen, the availability of DNA testing has begun to modify the presumption which (legally) has governed paternity within and outside marriage. When gamete donation is used to conceive children, changes in procedures have taken place so that children (at least when adult) may obtain information about their biological origins. That concern about gaining knowledge of biological origins seems, at least as yet, not to have had much influence on procedures for children conceived through sexual intercourse.

Parents, in general, want to have and rear their own (biological) children but use donation and surrogacy when this is not possible. When adult relationships end and new ones are formed, children may live with and have parental relationships with additional adults while usually retaining links to those they may regard as their 'real' parents. With relatively high divorce rates and births outside marriage, kinship networks have become more complex and varied, often with parent figures and siblings who are not first-degree biological relatives. So we may say that the biological facts of life and the genetic links that may be involved are important in family life and it is the case, at least in some situations, that the availability of DNA tests has emphasised these and has brought some changes. However, kinship and parenthood remain social institutions which are socially established.

5

The Contingency of the 'Genetic Link' in Constructions of Kinship and Inheritance—An Anthropological Perspective

ALISON SHAW

In some areas of contemporary biomedicine, doctors and patients are placing new emphasis on identifying potential genetic causes of common illnesses, for instance in seeking a patient's family history of heart disease or breast cancer. Some writers suggest that newly emerging scientific understandings of the genetics of common disorders are transforming our understandings of kinship by re-emphasising its genetic basis.[1] On the other hand, the diagnosis of syndromes associated with particular chromosomal abnormalities or gene mutations does not necessarily re-essentialise genealogical kinship, but may instead expand a person's sense of kinship with people not conventionally deemed relatives. People with a specific genetic syndrome, for instance, may regard themselves as 'brothers' and 'sisters' by virtue of their shared genetic link in the form of an unusual sequence of DNA (deoxyribonucleic acid) and its corresponding phenotypic characteristics, in this way countering conventional genealogy.[2]

These examples raise the question of what we mean by a 'genetic link'. Even within the field of genetic science, where 'genetic' refers to DNA, genetic links can be defined at different levels: they may refer to shared sequences of nucleotide

[1] K Finkler, 'The Kin in the Gene: The Medicalization of Family and Kinship in American Society' (2001) 42 *Current Anthropology* 235–63.

[2] P Rabinow, 'Artificiality and Enlightenment: From Sociobiology to Biosociality' in J Crary and S Kwinter (eds), *Incorporations* (New York, NY, Zone books, 1992); R Rapp, D Heath and K-S Taussig, 'Genealogical Dis-ease: Where Hereditary Abnormality, Biomedical Explanation, and Family Responsibility Meet' in S Franklin and S McKinnon (eds), *Relative Values: Reconfiguring Kinship Studies* (Durham, NC, Duke University Press, 2001) 384–409.

bases, to particular genes or chromosomes (or parts of them), or to entire genomes. At each level, there is the potential for DNA (as mutation, as chromosome, etc) to be put to work in processes of social classification, in generating new shared identities or constructing new differences, or in challenging or reasserting old boundaries, both within and beyond scientific discourse. These processes may operate at the level of individuals, families, ethnic groups or nations.

In other words, what matters as a genetic link and where this matters is a culturally constructed process, both within the scientific community and outside it.[3] Recent anthropological work explores how processes of defining what counts as a 'genetic link' may operate. In Euro–American kinship,[4] the dominant cultural script is that kinship is rooted in 'bio-genetic' ties. Even where there is an awareness of the distinction between biological (generally understood as genetic) and social parent, as in cases of adoption, the dominant cultural assumption is that biology and genealogy correspond, and that genetic inheritance is the medium of this correspondence. As anthropologist David Schneider puts it, for Euro–Americans, 'kinship is defined as biogenetic'.[5] In this cultural system, a genetic link refers to the ties of shared genetic substance that underpin the relationships between grandparents, parents and children, brothers and sisters, aunts and uncles. The scientific elaboration of this script is that genetic material is transferred in equal proportions via the gametes (the mother's egg and the father's sperm) to a child. The extent of a person's genetic ties with their immediate kin may then be calculated in terms of nuclear DNA.[6] In this model, parents each contribute half of their genetic material to a child: parents and siblings are 'first' degree' relatives, sharing 50% of their genetic material; grandparents, nieces and nephews, and aunts and uncles are second degree relatives, sharing 25% of their genetic material; first cousins share 12.5% of their genetic material, and so on.[7]

Yet Euro–American kinship, thus defined, is a quite particular post-Enlightenment construction.[8] Social historians have demonstrated that contemporary understandings of sexual dimorphism and reproductive physiology are

[3] S Franklin, 'Biologization Revisited: Kinship Theory in the Context of the New Biologies' in *Relative Values, ibid*, 302–25.

[4] M Strathern, 'Displacing Knowledge: Technology and its Consequences for Kinship' in I Robinson (ed), *Life and Death Under High Technology Medicine* (Manchester, MUP, 1994) 65, 69.

[5] DM Schneider, *American Kinship: A Cultural Account*, 2nd edn (Cliffs New Jersey edition Englewood, Prentice Hall, 1980) 23.

[6] Nuclear DNA is contained in every cell nucleus; it comprises 23 pairs of chromosomes (one single set is inherited from the mother, the other from the father). Each cell also contains extra-nuclear mitochondrial DNA, inherited from the mother only.

[7] This model treats 'genetic material' as a sort of abstract 'substance' without referring to its specific genetic informational content. Thus, while it is true that of the imagined 'family pool' of genetic material formed by the totality of paternal and maternal chromosomes each sibling gets 'half' and therefore, under this model, siblings share 50% of their 'genetic material', the model makes no claim about how much specific genetic informational content is shared by the siblings. [The editors].

[8] Schneider, *American Kinship*, n 5 above; DM Schneider, *A Critique of the Study of Kinship* (Ann Arbor, University of Michigan Press, 1984); Strathern, 'Displacing Knowledge', n 4 above, 70.

relatively recent developments, associated with the rise of modern biology and western science.[9] As numerous recent critiques of Euro–American kinship theory have pointed out, it is far from the case that kinship is everywhere, in all societies, defined as biogenetic.[10] One consequence of the dominance of the Euro–American model of kinship is that its assumptions—that everywhere genealogy is rooted in biology and that kinship ties, being based in 'nature', are consequently stronger than other social bonds—have been extended to and so have distorted the study of kinship in other societies.[11] The view of kinship as rooted in natural facts, broadly conceived as arising through ties of blood,[12] is a social and cultural perception that entails the 'naturalising' of kinship, that, according to recent critiques, is ultimately a means of legitimising historical and political differences by presenting them as biologically based.[13]

A potential disjunction between genetic parent (as genitor or genitrix) and a social parent has always been recognised, for instance in cases of step-parenting, adoption and non-paternity. However, the use of technologies of assisted reproduction has highlighted the ways in which biogenetic kinship is socially constructed. In cases involving donor eggs or sperm, claims to motherhood or fatherhood become grounded in the legal concept of intent rather than in genetics. Gestational surrogacy introduces a further tension in defining motherhood, by separating the 'biological' (gestating) mother from the 'genetic' mother. 'Indeed, some have suggested that shared substance [the biological substance of gestation] is a much more intimate biological connection than shared genetics, and more uniquely characteristic of motherhood, as genes are shared between many different kinds of relations.'[14] Gestational surrogacy involving donor eggs separates further gestational, genetic and social motherhood; what role do ideas about genetics and 'natural' motherhood play in defining the mother in these situations?

Intending parents using IVF involving donated eggs and gestational surrogacy provided by kin and friends may 'naturalise' kinship, in innovative ways, in order to realign biological ties with social parenthood.[15] Two intending mothers

---

[9] M Foucault, *The Order of Things: A History of the Human Sciences* (New York, NY, Vintage, 1970); T Laqueur, *Making Sex: Body and Gender From the Greeks to Freud* (Cambridge, MA, Harvard University Press, 1990).

[10] See eg Schneider, *American Kinship*, n 5 above; Schneider, *A Critique*, n 8 above; Franklin and McKinnon (eds), *Relative Values*, n 2 above.

[11] See Schneider, *ibid*, 174; Franklin and McKinnon, *ibid*, 2; C Delaney, 'The Meaning of Paternity and the Virgin Birth Debate' (1986) 21 *Man* 494–523.

[12] Schneider, *ibid*, 25.

[13] See eg C MacCormack and M Strathern (eds), *Nature, Culture and Gender* (Cambridge, CUP, 1980); S Yanagisako and C Delaney (eds), *Naturalizing Power: Essays in Feminist Cultural Analysis* (New York, NY, Routledge, 1994).

[14] C Thompson 'Strategic Naturalizing: Kinship in an Infertility Clinic' in S Franklin and S McKinnon (eds), *Relative Values*, n 2 above, 175, 178.

[15] *Ibid.*

attending a California infertility clinic chose IVF using sperm from their husbands and donor eggs from, respectively, a friend and a daughter; they chose these
donors to ensure sufficient 'genetic' (or 'racial') similarity, but gestated the pregnancies themselves to 'naturalise' their claims to motherhood.[16] In a case of gestational surrogacy, a woman named Rachel gestated a pregnancy produced by IVF
from her brother's sperm and her sister-in-law's eggs. The brother and sister-in-
law, as the intending parents, and Rachel herself emphasised the intending parents' genetic tie to the child, playing down Rachel's genetic link to the baby's father
and stressing instead her care-giving role as 'auntie Rachel'.[17] Thompson suggests
such processes are partially transforming the meaning of biological motherhood;
'it is becoming something that can be partial'.[18] At the same time, such studies
show how biological discourse continues to shape people's ideas about kinship. In
the views of couples in South East England discussing IVF, for example, it was
important that assisted parenthood remains 'true to nature's principles'.[19]

The idea of 'natural' connections between parents and children, as it is usually
understood and deployed in everyday contexts in Europe and America—without
the explicit disaggregation and reconstruction of what is 'natural' that use of IVF
demands—usually incorporates notions of biological but non-genetic relatedness, such as, for instance, the link between a mother and child that is the product of gestation or breastfeeding. It may also include notions of relatedness to
members of a particular ethnic group, even where a precise genealogical connection cannot be traced. Indeed, it is on such ideas that people draw to 're-naturalise'
kinship in situations involving assisted reproduction, such as those Thompson
describes. In other words, the particular scientific formulation of 'genetic' connection constituted through the generative template of nuclear DNA inherited, in
equal amounts, from one's parents, is only one way of conceptualising 'natural' or
'biological' relatedness and the acquisition or inheritance of human traits, and
even then is frequently partial.

Establishing kinship usually also involves long term care and nurturance in
processes that may establish powerful emotional connections between parents
and children. Such processes may be independent of genetic, and to varying
degrees, biological links. A person's non-corporeal or physical characteristics may
be thought of as being 'passed on' in families by both biological and social means,
the result of being 'born and bred'.[20] Parents raising children not biologically their
own may stress the importance of cultural inheritance[21] or the emotional ties of

---

[16] *Ibid.*

[17] *Ibid*, 182–5.

[18] *Ibid*, 176.

[19] E Hirsch, 'Negotiated Limits: Interviews in South-East England' in J Edwards *et al* (eds), *Technologies of Procreation: Kinship in the Age of Assisted Conception* (Manchester, MUP, 1993) 69.

[20] J Edwards, *Born and Bred: Idioms of Kinship and New Reproductive Technologies in England* (Oxford, OUP, 2000).

[21] Hirsch, 'Negotiated Limits', n 19 above.

kinship[22] in so doing challenging the taken-for-granted assumption of the importance of biology for kinship. The use of biology may be strategic, to 'naturalise' assisted kinship,[23] or idiomatic, providing a way of describing the process of transnational adoption.[24] The importance of biology may only be stressed if it is questioned; otherwise parents may regard the emotional connections between parents and children that result from nurture and upbringing as more central in constituting kinship.[25]

Some writers have hypothesised that, broadly, the type of kinship system in which people live will shape their understandings of how inheritance is understood and the transmission of 'biological substance' across the generations.[26] In so-called patrilineal societies, where social and political identity and ancestry is constructed in the male line, it may follow that the male's contribution to a child is deemed crucial and the female's is considered unimportant; the reverse may be true in matrilineal societies where ancestry through females is socially and politically crucial. This point was famously illustrated by the so-called 'virgin birth' debate in matrilineal Melanesia over whether fathers have *any* physiological connection with their children. Drawing on his experience of fieldwork in the Trobriand islands, where informants' emphasised the mother's role in gestation and breastfeeding,[27] Malinowski asserted that Trobriand islanders claimed to be ignorant of physiological paternity: 'The mother makes the child out of her blood',[28] and 'without doubt or reserve, ... the child is of the same substance of its mother'.[29] For them, Malinowski argued, biology was not the basis of social paternity. Heated debate ensued on whether Trobriand fathers were *really* ignorant of physical paternity.[30]

Subsequent scholars of Melanesia have emphasised how reproduction, for Trobriand islanders, is a cultural process to ensure the long-term reproduction of

[22] S Howell, 'Self Conscious Kinship: Some Contested Values in Norwegian Transnational Adoption' in S Franklin and S McKinnon (eds), *Relative Values*, n 2 above, 203–3.

[23] Thompson, 'Strategic Naturalizing', n 14 above.

[24] Howell, 'Self Conscious Kinship', n 22 above.

[25] Hirsch, 'Negotiated Limits', n 19 above.

[26] Eg MPM Richards and M Ponder, 'Lay Understandings of Genetics: A Test of an Hypothesis' (1996) 33 *Journal of Medical Genetics* 1032–36; B Meiser *et al*, 'Cultural Aspects of Cancer Genetics: Setting a Research Agenda' (2001) 38 *Journal of Medical Genetics* 425, 426.

[27] B Malinowski, *The Sexual Life of Savages* (New York, NY, Brace World Inc Harcourt, 1929).

[28] *Ibid*, 3.

[29] *Ibid*, 3.

[30] Edmund Leach denounced the anthropological view that Trobriand islanders were ignorant: E Leach, 'Virgin Birth', Proceedings of the Royal Anthropological Institute (1967) 39–49, reprinted in E Leach, *The Structural Study of Myth* (London, Jonathan Cape, 1969); Spiro's reply in M Spiro, 'Virgin Birth, Parthenogenesis and Physiological Paternity: An Essay in Cultural Interpretation' (1968) 3 *Man* 242–62, offered an alternative, psychoanalytical, interpretation of the avowed denial of the relationship between sexual intercourse and pregnancy; for a full discussion of the content and context of the debate see S Franklin, *Embodied Progress: A Cultural Account of Assisted Conception* (London, Routledge, 1997) 17–72.

the matriline.[31] Conception is perceived as resulting from the entry of ancestral spirits into a woman's body, the fetus forming from ancestral spirit combined with maternal blood.[32] 'This does not imply the mother is the genitrix, however, for it is the ancestor which supplies the generative agency'.[33] Both mother and father contribute, in different ways, to the nurturing of the child in the womb and after birth, but neither can be thought of as making an equal 'generative' contribution equivalent to the biomedical notion of genetic substance.[34] 'This [Trobriand] view of reproduction as inseparable from the total social context in which the child's identity is given meaning and value demonstrates the limitations of the cellular model of conception against which the Trobriander's views of procreation have long been pointlessly compared.'[35] For the Trobrianders, links between parents and children are thus not 'naturalised' in terms of bodily substance as they tend to be in the West.

In people's ideas of what constitutes connections across the generations, bodily substances such as blood or breast milk are often important but do not universally correspond to the currently prevailing biomedical idea of genetic substance (as DNA, genes or chromosomes) being transferred in equal amounts, via the gametes, from the mother and the father to create a child. Moreover, while the western biomedical idea is that genetic substance is, by and large, immutable, elsewhere the substances that link parents, children and other kin may be perceived as inherently malleable.[36] In addition, as noted above for Euro–American kinship, connections between parents and children usually include non-biological elements such as nurture, emotion and sociality. 'Ties of substance and the nature of bodily constitution may be determined by non-procreative factors such as nurture, the intervention of ancestral spirits or even the nature of the land where one is (to be) buried: bio- without the genetics, and created but not necessarily procreated.'[37]

In short, kinship is not necessarily or in any uniform way thought of as constituted in biogenetic facts, and bodily substance may be non-genetically produced. A view of kinship as rooted in genetics, or, more generally, in biology, is, thus contingent on a prior perception of biology as important.

---

[31] A Weiner, *Women of Value, Men of Renown: New Perspectives in Trobriand Exchange* (Austin, University of Texas Press, 1976); see also M Strathern, *The Gender of the Gift* (Berkeley, University of California Press, 1988) 235–38.

[32] Weiner, *ibid.*

[33] Franklin, *Embodied Progress*, n 30 above. See also J Carsten, 'Substantivism, Antisubstantivism, and Anti Antisubstantivism' in Franklin and McKinnon (eds), *Relative Values*, n 2 above, 29–53.

[34] See also Franklin, *ibid*, 60–61.

[35] Franklin, *ibid*, 61.

[36] See Carsten, 'Substantivism', n 33 above, for a discussion of the different meanings and uses of 'substance' in writings about American, Melanesian and Indian kinship, where substance is, respectively, immutable, fluid and partible, or an analogy for something else.

[37] Strathern, 'Displacing Knowledge', n 4 above, 68.

In what follows, I extend slightly the discussion of the contingency of genetic understandings of kinship by presenting material describing British Pakistani understandings of inheritance and inherited illness. My material is drawn from fieldwork with British Pakistani families attending a UK genetics clinic.[38] I show how ideas about patrilineal inheritance derived from the South Asian context offer a cultural template for understanding inheritance and relatedness seemingly at odds with the western model of an equal genetic contribution from both parents. However, I also present material on everyday understandings of kinship and inheritance that undermines the contrast between the South Asian 'patrilineal' and the western 'bilateral' system of kinship, and questions the idea that a social or structural model of patrilineal kinship will necessarily, or in any simple way, determine how people of Pakistani heritage understand inheritance in the particular context of familial illness.

A. Patrilineal Kinship in a South Asian Context

In Pakistan, as in the Middle East, North Africa, and many other parts of South Asia, a family identity is formally thought of as constructed through male ancestry. Across South Asia, a child's physical and intellectual qualities are regarded as being transmitted across generations from father to child.[39] A belief in many parts of India is that ancestors are reborn in the form of children. According to some ancient Hindu legal codes and scriptures, a man's life is made permanent through the agency of his son.[40] Gujarati musicians in the UK believe that their musicality was passed down over the generations through the 'blood' of their male ancestors,[41] while for Pakistanis, in Britain and in Pakistan, identity as a member of a *biradārī* or kinship group is transmitted through men by means of 'blood' (*khūn*).[42]

The view that the father's blood is 'stronger' and so more central to a child's social identity than the mother's blood has a number of implications. British

---

[38] This project 'A study of the impact of genetic risk information on families of Pakistani origin referred for genetic counselling', was supported by a grant from the Wellcome Trust UK. The names of all participants have been changed.

[39] M Bock and A Rao (eds), *Culture, Kinship and Procreation: Concepts of Kinship in South Asian Practice* (Oxford, Berghahn Books, 2000) 6.

[40] A Bharadwaj, 'Why Adoption is Not an Option in India: The Visibility of Infertility, the Secrecy of Donor Insemination' (2003) 56 *Social Science and Medicine* 1867–80.

[41] J Baily, 'Born in Music: The Khalifa Muslim Community in Britain', paper read at the 32rd World Conference of the International Council for Traditional Music, Berlin, 16–22 June 1993, cited in Bock and Rao (eds), *Culture, Kinship and Procreation*, n 39 above, 6.

[42] P Jeffery, *Frogs in a Well: Indian Women in Purdah* (London, Zed Press, 1979) 10; H Donnan, *Marriage among Muslims: Preference and Choice in Northern Pakistan* (Delhi, Hindustan Publishing Corp, 1988) 88; A Shaw, *Kinship and Continuity: Pakistani Families in Britain* (London, Routledge, 2000) 212.

Pakistanis usually marry within the kinship group, and the children of a woman who marries 'out' are viewed as belonging to their father's *birādari*.[43] Adoption is generally frowned upon unless it occurs among close kin,[44] for otherwise 'the child would not be of the same blood'.[45] Semen is the means of this intergenerational transmission and is regarded as very strong, highly concentrated blood; some maintain that one drop of semen is equivalent to one hundred drops of blood, and the strength of the semen determines a child's sex.[46]

These views have implications for British South Asian attitudes to the use of donated eggs and sperm in *in vitro* fertilisation (IVF). For many South Asians, the use of donated gametes is generally objectionable or viewed as an option of 'last resort', but if gamete donation is considered, the use of donated eggs is marginally more acceptable than the use of donated sperm. The reasoning is that since the sperm exerts a stronger influence on a child's identity than the egg and is the means through which a family line is transmitted, egg donation may be less threatening to family stability than sperm donation.[47] A similar attitude is reported from Egypt, where third-party gamete donation is unacceptable, because it is *harām* (forbidden) in Islam and interferes with patrilineality.[48] One husband commented, 'If the sperm and the egg are not from the husband and the wife, there won't be *nasab* [blood relations]. He won't be my son ... I want my own son!', while his wife commented, 'Especially the man must know that it is his own son. Unlike the woman who is carrying it, the man needs to have one of his own body'.[49]

Ideas about the potency of the male contribution to the formation of a child are frequently expressed through the 'seed and soil' analogy widespread across parts of South Asia and the Middle East.[50] As Bock and Rao write of the South Asian ethnographic literature: 'what is stressed by author after author is that generally in South Asia ....women are held to play a passive role in the creative process'.[51] The metaphor

---

[43] Shaw, *ibid*, 184–85 and 212–13.

[44] M Fischer and W Lyon, 'Marriage Strategies in Lahore: Projections of Model Marriage on Social Practice' in Bock and Rao (eds), *Culture, Kinship and Procreation*, n 39 above, 297, 316–19.

[45] Shaw, *Kinship and Continuity*, n 42 above, 217.

[46] Shaw, *ibid*, 218.

[47] L Culley *et al*, *A study of the Provision of Infertility Services to South Asian Communities: Final Report (Abridged Version)* (Leicester, De Montfort University, 2004) 16; see also Bharadwaj, 'Why adoption is not an option in India', n 40 above. British Muslim couples considering gamete donation also have to negotiate Islamic medical ethics in which the use of donated gametes is *harām* (forbidden); see AR Gatrad and A Sheikh, 'Medical Ethics and Islam: Principles and Practice' (2001) 84 *Archives of Disease in Childhood* 72–5. For a discussion of social and ethical issues and concerns about confidentiality in infertility service provision for South Asians, see Culley *et al*, *ibid*, 15–16.

[48] MC Inhorn, *Local Babies, Global Science: Gender, Religion and In Vitro Fertilization in Egypt* (London, Routledge, 2003).

[49] Inhorn, *ibid*, 110.

[50] C Delaney, *The Seed and the Soil: Gender and Cosmology in Turkish Village Society* (Berkeley, CA, University of California Press, 1991).

[51] *Culture, Kinship and Procreation*, n 39 above, 7.

of the male 'seed' (*bij*) and the female 'earth' (*zamīn*)[52] features in numerous ethnographic reports from 'almost all over northern and central India, and in some parts of eastern India'.[53] Indeed, the metaphor finds justification in a Quranic verse: 'Your wives are as a tilth unto you, so approach your tilth when or how ye will'.[54]

The views just described are cultural 'blueprints' in that they describe relatively formalised sets of ideas on which people may draw in everyday situations, in understanding illness, for instance, or in assessing options with regards to infertility treatment. They are not, however, the only ideas on which people draw; nor are they rigid guides to understanding behaviour in any particular context. In relation to use of donated sperm, for example, an assessment of circumstance, need and medical implications may result in a couple reassessing their initial rejection of the idea of sperm donation.

Tahira and Tariq are a British Pakistani couple who had lost three infants from recessive genetic disease. They were considering gamete donation in their quest for an unaffected child. Tahira initially expressed discomfort with the idea of sperm donation because of the sexual implications; she said, 'I don't like the idea of being given sperm from another man'. She had an alternative suggestion, 'I told my husband he should return to Pakistan, take a second wife, and when she gives birth he should bring the child to England and give it to me.' This suggestion was, in effect, a form of non-medical egg donation and gestational surrogacy within a culturally-acceptable idiom.[55] Tariq, however, was also uncomfortable with the sexuality implied by this suggestion. 'I could not do that', he said. Both husband and wife seemed equally uncomfortable with the idea of sperm donation for an additional reason: the fact that the donor might claim paternity. They told me, 'We don't want someone turning up at the door and saying "that is my child"'. Eventually, though, after further discussion of the protocol of both sperm and egg donation and reassurance that the resultant child would legally belong to them, Tahira and Tariq eventually opted to seek donor sperm, matched for ethnic background, because sperm donation is simpler, less invasive and thus less risky as a medical technique than egg donation.

1. Everyday Understandings of Procreation and Inheritance

Although for British Pakistanis the dominant idiom of kinship stresses patrilineality and the male contribution, my research participants' everyday understandings

---

[52] L Dube, 'Seed and Earth: The Symbolism of Biological Reproduction and Sexual Relations of Production' in L Dube (ed), *Visibility and Power: Essays on Women in Society and Development* (Oxford, OUP, 1986).

[53] Bock and Rao (eds), *Culture, Kinship and Procreation*, n 39 above.

[54] Sura 2 verse 223, A Yusuf Ali, *The Holy Qur'an: Text, Translation and Commentary* (Leicester, The Islamic Foundation, 1975) 88.

[55] Polygamy is acceptable in Pakistan, under Islamic law. It is also a South Asian cultural expectation for a man to take a second wife in cases of infertility.

of procreation and inheritance revealed a more complex set of ideas. Recognition of a male and female contribution to a child was usually expressed through the observation of patterns of intergenerational resemblances within the family. Sometimes people noted patterns of same-sex intergenerational resemblances, saying that a daughter resembles her mother, or a son is like his father.[56] More frequently, parents described characteristics as having been transferred from either parent to a child, regardless of sex. Jamilah, who is 32 years old, has lived in England for 13 years and is originally from rural Mirpur in Azad Kashmir, described her son as: 'dark, like my husband [but] he talks like me and eats like me ... [whereas] my daughter is fair like me, but ... has her Dad's eyes .... And her hair is not like mine, it is thin and silky, like her father's sister's hair.' Characteristics such as having blue-grey eyes, having pale skin, or only giving birth to boys were described as traits that 'skip' a generation, showing up not in children but in grandchildren, on the basis of observed patterns of intergenerational resemblances within the family.

Strikingly, these everyday theories about inheritance—about same-sex resemblances, traits passing from either parent to a child, and characteristics 'skipping a generation'—are paralleled in English everyday understandings of inheritance, such as those reported among members of the Women's Institute.[57] This suggests that differences in the formal structures of kinship—in this case, in the bilaterality of English, European and American kinship in comparison with the patrilineality of South Asian kinship—do not, or do not necessarily, govern people's everyday understandings of connection through inheritance.

A further parallel with evidence from a range of other cultural contexts lies in the emphasis given to 'blood' in people's understandings of the mechanisms of inheritance.[58] In her impression of Malay ideas about the constitution of the body and of relations of kinship, Carsten was particularly struck by the centrality of ideas about blood.[59] The women with whom I discussed the mechanisms of conception always spoke of blood (*khūn*) as the medium, or dominant metaphor, for the inheritance of what in biomedical terms would be 'genetic' substance. Jamilah considered that 'a baby is made from the blood of the father and this mixes with blood from the mother'. Conversely, the idea of blood 'not mixing' often featured in women's accounts of fetal abnormality and unsuccessful pregnancy. As reported in studies involving people of other ethnicities[60] my informants sometimes substituted the terminology of genetics for the concept of 'blood' as the mechanism

---

[56] See also Fischer and Lyon, 'Marriage strategies in Lahore', n 44 above, 306.

[57] Richards and Ponder, 'Lay Understandings of Genetics', n 26 above; MPM Richards, 'Families, Kinship and Genetics' in T Marteau and MPM Richards (eds), *The Troubled Helix: Social and Psychological Implications of the New Human Genetics* (Cambridge, CUP, 1996).

[58] See eg Carsten, 'Substantivism', n 33 above.

[59] *Ibid*, 46.

[60] See *eg* Richards and Ponder, 'Lay Understandings of Genetics', n 26 above.

of inheritance. Sayeeda, who is 22 years old and was educated to high-school level in Pakistan, has a family history of a chromosomal anomaly. She described conception by saying 'the chromosomes from the mother and father mix together and the baby starts'. Several other women used the word 'gene' rather than 'blood' when discussing conception, explaining unsuccessful pregnancies as ones when 'the genes did not match'.

In these accounts, blood was sometimes described as if it was a stable substance of fixed quality, many people mentioning their blood groups, for instance, as aspects of their identity. On the other hand, the quality of the blood, its thickness and thinness, and whether it was 'bad' or 'good', was also described in ways that suggested something that could be altered. Such ideas also prevail in English everyday understandings of the ability of aspirin to 'thin' the blood and so prevent cardiovascular disease. Carsten makes a similar point that among the Malay people, blood had, in part, a 'given' quality, but was also, partly, mutable or transferable.[61] Several of my research participants, speaking of genes as 'in the blood', used the word 'gene' synonymously with the Urdu/Panjabi word *jarasīm*, which means germ, thus implying that a gene is an infective agent. One grandfather of a child with a clinically-identified recessive genetic condition perceived the risk of genetic disorders to be a new phenomenon, linked with the British environment.[62] One mother of a child with a recessive condition, who is, by clinical definition, herself a healthy carrier of the particular mutation (an 'obligate carrier') asked for a genetic test to ascertain if the gene was still in her blood or had, by now, left her body. Tariq, an obligate carrier of two recessive mutations, wondered whether he might have acquired these mutations as the result of a snake bite in childhood; if this was the case, he thought that 'changing' his blood by transfusion might change his carrier status and remove his reproductive risk. Blood, in these usages, thus did not correspond to the idea of a generative contribution through the male and female gametes.

My informants rarely used technical terms other than blood, genes or chromosomes to describe the male and the female contribution to a child. Several women expressed surprise when I used either the 'proper' Urdu word for sperm, *madd-e-taulīd*, literally 'material of procreation' or the more colloquial *mani* or *mazi*, sometimes adding that it is shameful for women to speak about such things. When they did refer to the male contribution, women would usually use the euphemism *pāni*, (water) or *mard ka pāni* (water from the man), rather than the 'proper' Urdu or colloquial Panjabi terms.[63]

---

[61] Carsten, 'Substantivism', n 33 above.

[62] See A Shaw, 'Attitudes to Genetic Diagnosis and the Use of Medical Technologies in Pregnancy: Some British Pakistani Perspectives' in M Unnithan-Kumar (ed), *Reproductive Agency, Medicine and the State: Cultural Transformations in Childbearing* (New York, Berghahn Books, 2004) 25–57.

[63] For discussion of the implications of everyday knowledge for translating information about genetics into Urdu, see A Shaw and M Ahmed, 'Translating Genetics Leaflets into Languages Other than English: Lessons from an Assessment of Urdu Materials' (2004) 13 *Journal of Genetic Counselling* 321–42.

Women generally located the female contribution to a child within the uterus (*bachchā dāni*—literally 'child receptacle'), and were unfamiliar with the formal Urdu word for ovum (*beze*) and generally unclear about what the female contribution comprised. When I asked, 'what comes from the mother to make a baby?' Jamilah, perhaps feeling that her knowledge of biomedical science was being tested, replied, 'I think the woman has eggs, yes, that is the word you use here', adding, 'I think it contains blood but it might contain something else'. Amira, 45 years old with 4 children, who came to Britain in 1980 from a village in Jhelum district in Pakistan, explained: 'People don't talk about these things before marriage. It is shameful to talk about these things. Even after marriage, you don't find out what the words are. It is the same for a girl and for a boy. But here in England, for our children, it is different; now they learn from school, and they know all the words.'

On the other hand, despite the emphasis on shared blood in patrilinal connections, and the apparent haziness about what exactly the male and female generative contribution comprises, all the women I spoke with stressed the importance of the mother's body in nurturing the fetus. Khalida is 24 years old, has been in Britain for four years and was educated to the equivalent of GCSE level in Pakistan. She forcefully countered my suggestion that a man contributes more to the formation of a child. She was speaking in Urdu, and I was struck by her use of the English term 'gamete' to describe male and female substance, a term I had not used previously in our conversation:

> We had a teacher who told us that the gametes from which a child is made come equally from the father and mother. She said it is not that the father's contribution is greater. In fact the mother's contribution is greater. She told us this is because for nine months the child grows in the mother's body; it does not grow in a man's body. For nine months the mother does not have periods, and the blood that would have come out in that time goes into the baby. The mother's health and the food she eats in pregnancy are also very important for how the baby develops. For these reasons, the baby gets more from the mother than from the father. When our teacher told us this, we felt shame that she was talking about such things. We looked down and hid our faces. She told [us] we should not feel shame. She said she was telling us because one day it would be useful for us to know this.

While the emphasis here is on the baby's physical health, this comment has features in common with English women's views of the importance of nurturing the child in the womb[64] and of the American women for whom the biological link created by gestation can naturalise motherhood in the absence of a direct genetic link.[65] A similar view was expressed by two 20–year old cousins, who are also

---

[64] J Edwards *et al* (eds), *Technologies of Procreation: Kinship in the Age of Assisted Conception* (Manchester, MUP, 1993) 59.

[65] Thompson, 'Strategic Naturalizing', n 14 above.

sisters-in-law: Shameem, who was born and raised in the UK, and Salma, who was born and raised in Pakistan. I asked Shameem if she thought what a child inherits from its mother and what it inherits from its father is the same, or whether a child inherits more from the mother or from the father: 'More from the mother, for sure. That's obvious. The father, he just has to do something once, that's all he has to do, then he can forget about it. [She and Salma laugh]. Then the rest is up to the mother. Much more is up to the mother.'

Despite the formal structure of patrilineal kinship, the idea at work here seems rather similar to that expressed by Malinowski's Trobriand informants who claim 'the mother makes the child out of her blood', namely, the importance of physiological connection between mother and child that is created by gestation. I pressed her, asking, 'So a child is more closely related to the mother than the father?' 'Yes', she replied, 'much closer. Of course the child is related to the father, but not so much'. Salma replied to the same question in Urdu, stressing that a child gets more from the mother (*zyadatar māṅ se mylta hay*). She said she did not know what exactly the child gets, but it is 'something like it gets from the father, and then more'.

From the material presented so far, it seems that while ideas about 'blood' are important to Pakistani ideas of kinship and inheritance they do not necessarily reflect a 'one-sided' patrilineal model, because a male and female contribution to a child is recognised, expressed, for instance, as the 'mixing' of paternal and maternal blood so that the baby 'starts'. Moreover, understandings of the parental contributions of bodily substance to a child include, in addition to 'blood' from the mother and father, a notion of maternal blood nourishing the child in the womb. Indeed, from this perspective, the maternal contribution of generative substance and physiological nurturance equals or exceeds the paternal. The idea that the mother's body crucially influences a baby's development is emphasised in widely-held beliefs about appropriate behaviour and correct diet[66] reinforced by antenatal health messages from medical professionals. Consequently, women themselves may attribute infant miscarriage, stillbirth, death or disability to faults in the mother's behaviour, diet or fluid intake during pregnancy, even when doctors insist that the mortality or morbidity in question has a 'genetic' cause. In these accounts, ideas about the role of 'blood' as reproductive substance and in nourishing the fetus/child do not necessarily correspond in any precise way to a 'genetic' link as it is understood in genetic science, even where the words 'gene' or 'chromosome' rather than 'blood' are used. For my informants, as for many other users of genetics services, the idea of male or female gametes as complimentary blueprints for infant development, produced by the germ-line cells in the ovaries and testes (and separated early on in embryonic development from the somatic cells) is often unfamiliar. Both clients and clinicians may employ 'genetic' vocabulary, but may do so with mutually inconsistent meanings.

---

[66] Shaw, *Kinship and Continuity*, n 42 above.

2. The Discourse of Genetic Risk

Early on in my research, I learnt that for many of my study participants the term 'genetic' had an additional meaning, that is possibly quite specific to British Pakistanis. One father of a child with learning difficulties told me that to him genetics meant 'illnesses you get when you marry in the family'. When I asked how he knew this, he told me, 'an Asian lady came to our house and said my son was like this because I am married in the family'. A young mother with a family history of a recessive genetic disorder told me that she was fearful of attending the genetics clinic because she expected the doctors would criticise her for being married to a first cousin. These comments reflect the public discourse of parental consanguinity and genetic risk that has focused on British Pakistanis since the 1980s.

Cousin marriages have come to be frowned upon, on biological or evolutionary grounds in Euro–American culture since the late 19th century.[67] Since then, epidemiological research has demonstrated an association between parental consanguinity and an elevated risk of recessively inherited disorders.[68] In the UK, a prospective study of nearly 5000 babies in Birmingham, England, from all ethnic groups, showed higher rates of infant mortality and morbidity among Pakistanis. Within the Pakistani sample, infant mortality and morbidity was three times higher among the offspring of consanguineous couples (who comprised 69% of the Pakistani sample) compared with the non-consanguineous Pakistani couples.[69] The authors demonstrated that this excess was mainly due to rare recessive disorders. Following the publication of the Birmingham study, the risks of cousin marriage have been reported in the UK news media at intervals over the past 10 years in ways that emphasise the risks of cousin marriage.

Most of my study participants were aware of this discourse but were generally sceptical of it as a 'popular' explanation of adverse birth outcome, offering alternative explanations for their child's disorder that recognised spiritual and environmental causes of illness and disability (such as accidents and infections) and the perceived additional risks associated with the British environment.[70] They

---

[67] See M Ottenheimer, *Forbidden Relatives: The American Myth of Cousin Marriage* (Chicago, 1996). See also A Shaw, *Family, Community and Genetic Risk: British Pakistani Experiences* (New York, NY, Berghahn Books, forthcoming).

[68] A Bittles, *Empirical Estimates of the Global Prevalence of Consanguineous Marriage in Contemporary Societies* (Stanford, CA, Morrison Institute Population and Resources Studies, Stanford University, 1989). Recessive disorders are associated with inheriting two copies of an identical mutation. Cousins are more likely to inherit an identical mutation because they have a pair of grandparents in common, one of whom might pass identical copies of a mutation to their children and grandchildren.

[69] S Bundey and H Alam, 'A Five-Year Prospective Study of the Health of Children in Different Ethnic Groups, with Particular Reference to the Effect of Inbreeding' (1993) 1 *European Journal of Human Genetics* 206–19.

[70] For details see Shaw, 'Attitudes to Genetic Diagnosis', n 62 above.

frequently made the accurate lay epidemiological observation that 'many Pakistanis marry cousins and don't have disabled children' and that 'English people don't marry cousins and they have disabled children'. Media reports rarely stress that while the probability of adverse birth outcome in the child of a consanguineous couple is double that for a non-consanguineous couple, and three times higher if there is a history of consanguineous marriage in the family, in terms of birth incidence it remains relatively low, at between 2 and 6%. This leaves a 94% chance of having an unaffected child.[71]

3. Encountering Clinical Knowledge

Most of my study participants attended the genetics clinic in the hope of a treatment or a cure for their child, rather than for specifically genetic advice (but see the case of Mariam and Mukhtar discussed below). Often the 'clinical script' of recessive inheritance, with its equal male and female contribution of reproductive substance, sat uneasily alongside family theories of the causes of a child's problems. On various occasions, after attending clinical appointments with them, clinic attendees would ask me to explain again what the doctors had told them. On one such occasion, a Pakistan-born mother of a child diagnosed with a recessive disorder interrupted my explanation of recessive inheritance by asking, 'Are you saying, the material from the father and mother is equal? Does the father not give more?' On another occasion, a woman with whom I was discussing a leaflet on recessive inheritance, asked me, 'So the baby gets material from both sides—so it has to come from the mother and from the father? I thought it just came from the father. I had never known that'. In the context of a discussion of marriage arrangements, a woman who had lost three children in infancy to a recessive disorder told me she thought it would be safer to marry her daughter to a maternal rather than to a paternal relative, saying 'if the fathers of the boy and [the girl] are brothers, there is the most danger'. These incidents reflect the cultural idea that a 'genetic' link from father is stronger than from mother, and thus that the children of sisters less likely to have the 'same blood' than the children of brothers.

Such ideas, however, are not necessarily fixed and can be challenged by experience. Mariam and Mukhtar are first cousins. Mariam's mother is Mukhtar's father's sister. The couple attended the clinic seeking carrier testing because of a family history of Congenital Adrenal Hyperplasia (CAH), a recessive condition involving a mutation that affects the production of steroid hormones. In girls, it is associated with masculinisation of the genitals at birth, and, if it is untreated, can cause masculinisation at puberty. In Mariam and Mukhtar's family history

[71] A Shaw, *The Impact of Genetic Risk on UK Pakistani Families* (2003), available online at http://www.wellcome.ac.uk/en/genome/geneticsandsociety/hg14f005.html.

there were two affected children, a niece and nephew, the son and daughter of one of Mariam's sisters and one of Mukhtar's brothers,[72] who are thus, from a clinical perspective, 'obligate carriers' (each carrying a single copy of the mutation). None of Mukhtar's and Mariam's other married brothers and sisters had children with this condition. The only other reported family history, probably unrelated to the CAH, was a congenital deformity in the form of an unusually-shaped nose in the daughter of one of Mukhtar's brothers and in a son and a daughter of another of his brothers. On the basis of the family history, the clinicians calculated a probabilistic risk (of $^1/_9$) that Mariam and Mukhtar will each themselves be carriers. Since the mutation for CAH has been identified, the clinicians also took blood samples for a DNA carrier test. The results, a couple of months later, showed that Mukhtar is carrier and Mariam is not.

18 months later, Mariam told me that she had not understood that both parents must be carriers for a child to be affected with a recessive condition:

> We thought my husband's family were carriers of CAH through the men. My sister is married to my husband's older brother, two of her children have CAH. My husband's two younger brothers each have children with a congenital nose defect. It was in my husband's family—because this is where the problems are. This is why I thought any children I have with my husband might also be at risk.

Nevertheless, her theory was entirely consistent with the incidence of CAH in the family. Then something happened that transformed her understanding. One of Mariam's sisters, who had until then one unaffected son, gave birth to a baby girl with CAH. For Mariam, 'This was a total shock. It was not even in our dreams that she or her husband could be carriers'. Since this new baby's father is Mariam's sister's maternal first cousin, her mother's sister's son, Mariam and her sisters had not thought that there was any genetic risk; they had understood that the condition could only arise in a descendant, *through men*, of their mother's brother, not in the descendants of any of their mother's sisters:

> My sister [the one with the affected baby] always said it was in our husbands' family, not on our side of family. We thought it was only our uncle [Mariam's Mum's brother and also her father-in-law] who had passed it on to his sons, and one of them had passed it on to my niece and nephew. We thought it went through the men, in the male line. Now I now know that this wrong. We did not realise that there has to be a wife who is a carrier for the kids to have got it. ... It was such a shock. The stress has been incredible—realising it is in our side of the family too, not just in my husband's side. ... People always say, not in our family. Originally, we thought only my husband is a carrier—and that he

---

[72] This pattern of a brother and sister being married to a sister and brother, which is in effect, the exchange of opposite-sex siblings, is not uncommon; it is also regarded as socially and emotionally risky in that a rift in one marriage can have a direct effect on the other.

got it from his father, my Mum's brother. We did not think that my Mum could be a carrier too—or her sisters. But now we know she is, she must be, and she has passed it on to us, and we are carriers—at least, two of my sisters are—they must be, because they both have affected children. My sister, the one with the affected baby, is gutted. She has not even told my Mum that there is something wrong.

B. The Problematic Presumption of Genetic Links

The dominant Euro–American academic and professional view of kinship as founded upon and rationalised by natural biogenetic facts,[73] and based on the principle of bilateral descent through both the father and the mother, has prevailed since the Enlightenment.[74] In this chapter, I have attempted to illustrate how this view of kinship is not universal, but is contingent on a particular construction of biology, and of biology as important. While the current interest in the new reproductive technologies and in the genetic basis of illness has in some contexts placed a premium on genetic understandings of kinship and inheritance, recent anthropological explorations of the meaning of kinship in everyday European and American family life show that primacy is not always accorded to genetic ties.[75] At the same time, cultural processes are often simultaneously at work in establishing kinship as 'natural', in keeping with the dominant cultural script.

My presentation of British Pakistani case material in the context of genetics clinic attendance illustrates some of the connections invoked by the idea of biological links, against a background of South Asian kinship. These ideas do not necessarily correspond to 'genetic links' as understood by clinicians. British Pakistani ideas about what 'genetic' refers to may also be influenced by the particular social and political context of the epidemiological and popular discourses of genetic risk. Yet the emphasis on 'blood' in Pakistani understandings of reproduction and genetic disorder also includes notions of both fixity and mutability that are shared across a wide range of other cultural contexts.[76] A focus on notions of blood, as substance, might, therefore, destabilise assumptions about how cross-cultural differences in kinship structures are maintained.[77] Further, while ideas about patrilineal inheritance may shape clients' initial understandings of the

---

[73] Schneider, *American Kinship*, n 5 above.
[74] Strathern, 'Displacing Knowledge', n 4 above.
[75] Hirsch, 'Negotiated Limits', n 19 above; Howell, 'Self Conscious Kinship', n 22 above; Thompson, 'Strategic Naturalizing', n 14 above.
[76] Edwards *et al*, *Technologies of Procreation*, n 64 above; see also Carsten, 'Substantivism', n 33 above.
[77] Carsten, *ibid*.

inheritance of genetic illness, at least where these correspond to the pattern of illness within the family, these may also be challenged by experience. To conclude, then, the social ascription of relevance or irrelevance to a 'genetic link' cannot always be predicted in advance, and will depend, in part, on prior understandings of the connections between parents, children and siblings, and of what constitutes kinship, ethnicity and ancestry. This is so even in contexts in which concerns to establish parenthood or to establish the genetic basis of illness are routine.

6

Regulating the Science and Therapeutic Application of Human Embryo Research: Managing the Tension between Biomedical Creativity and Public Concern

MARTIN H JOHNSON*

Much is made of the distinction between reproductive and recreational sex and the impact that science has had on their separation. However, science is a 'Johnny come lately' in this regard. The separation of sex and reproduction by social and individual interventions has occurred for as long as humans have realised, however imperfectly, that there was a connection between sexual intercourse and babies. Indeed, in evolutionary terms, the 'recreational' pleasures of orgasm have provided for mammals the main behavioural driver of coition and thereby secondarily of reproduction. Orgasm is widely observed in mammals and genital stimulation is widespread and, in many animals including higher primates, is often non-reproductive.[1] The extensive social regulation of sexual expression and activities seen in most societies attempts to harness these powerful sexual recreational urges to desirable economic, reproductive and religious ends.

What *has* changed over the past century, and in particular the last 20 years, is a more effective and varied capacity to separate birth from coition.[2] Initially, this

* I thank Kerry Petersen for constructive advice and discussion, and Antje du Bois-Pedain and JR Spencer for the opportunity to take part in a stimulating meeting.

[1] See A Dixson, *Primate Sexuality: Comparative Studies of the Prosimians, Monkeys, Apes and Human Beings* (Oxford, OUP, 1998); and B Bagemihl, *Biological Exuberance: Animal Homosexuality and Natural Diversity* (New York, NY, St Martin's Press, 1999).

[2] See MH Johnson and B Everitt, *Essential Reproduction* (Oxford, Blackwell Science, 2000).

new scientific knowledge and understanding about human reproduction focused on controlling reproduction through more effective birth control (sex without babies or recreation without reproduction), but latterly reproduction without recreation (babies without sex) has also become an option. The type and number of babies, the time in the parents' lives at which they are born and the range of parents responsible for producing them can be controlled. The genetic selection of early embryos *in vitro* is possible,[3] and interventions by clinicians are the main cause of multiparity (multiple births).[4] Medical assistance enables post-menopausal women to give birth,[5] and gay and lesbian couples, as well as women on their own, to become parents.[6] Scientists now distinguish between four categories of parenthood (genetic, coital, uterine or gestational, and post-natal), each contributing to the establishment of an individual's identity and each susceptible to biomedical intervention.[7] The discoveries of science have thus forced a major re-evaluation of social attitudes to reproduction, sexual expression, parenthood and the nature of families.

These remarkable achievements of biomedicine were hard won. They often occurred in the teeth of professional hostility or scorn, as well as social disapproval.[8] The early pioneers studying human sexuality and reproduction were at best regarded as freakish oddballs, at worse as intellectually shallow perverts, and even in the 1960s medical students learnt more about the reproduction of rats and mice than about humans. Infertility and sexuality were barely mentioned publicly until the late 1960s, and sexual and reproductive activities were only respectably conducted within the confines of marriage, and then often uncomfortably. Even in the late 1970s and 80s, when the prospect of *in vitro* fertilisation became a reality, there was almost uniform social and professional hostility, and within the past few years a similar level of hostility has greeted prospects of lesbian motherhood, surrogacy, reproductive cloning and embryonic stem cell research. If history is a reliable guide, these too will come to be more acceptable when society has had

---

[3] See P Braude *et al*, 'Preimplantation Genetic Diagnosis' (2002) 3 *Nature Reviews Genetics* 941.

[4] See American Society for Reproductive Medicine, *Multiple Pregnancy Associated with Infertility Therapy: Practice Committee Report 2002* (Birmingham, 2002); and A Pinborg, A Loft and A Andersen, 'Neonatal Outcome in a Danish National Cohort of 8602 Children Born After *In Vitro* Fertilization or Intracytoplasmic Sperm Injection: The Role of Twin Pregnancy' (2004) 83 *Acta Obstetrica Gynecologica Scandinavia* 1071.

[5] G Pennings, 'Postmenopausal Women and the Right of Access to Oocyte Donation' (2001) 18 *Journal of Applied Philosophy* 171.

[6] F MacCallum and S Golombok, 'Children Raised in Fatherless Families from Infancy: A Follow-up of Children of Lesbian and Single Heterosexual Mothers at Early Adolescence' (2004) 45 *Journal of Child Psychology and Psychiatry* 1407.

[7] MH Johnson, 'A Biomedical Perspective on Parenthood' in A Bainham, S Day Sclater and MPM Richards (eds), *What is a Parent? A Socio-Legal Analysis* (Oxford, Hart Publishing, 1999) 47.

[8] See RL Gardner and MH Johnson, 'Robert Edwards' (1991) 6 *Human Reproduction* iii; M Ashwood-Smith, 'Robert Edwards at 55' (2002) 4 *Reproductive Biomedicine* 2 (Supp 1); and M Mulkay, *The Embryo Research Debate: Science and the Politics of Reproduction* (Cambridge, CUP, 1997).

time to reflect on them and engage with them at more than a visceral level—indeed there is already evidence that this is happening.[9]

There are two reasons to pause and ponder on this consistent history of the social rejection of biomedical interventions in human reproduction followed by reflection and then positive engagement. First, if biomedicine is prevented by precipitate social rejection from being creative and inventive, the space for public reflection and positive engagement is unlikely to be generated and much will be lost. Second, the intensity of the immediate visceral resistance to almost all of the work done over the past century on human reproduction and sexuality should give biomedical scientists and doctors undertaking challenging new research cause for serious reflection as to how best to take the public and the establishment with them. Both these points are central to any consideration of the history, the practice and the future of regimes to regulate the development and use of novel biomedical approaches to human reproduction and sexuality. For this to be a productive regulatory process, both the biomedical community and society in general must engage responsibly when considering the freedoms to be given or taken and the responsibilities to be imposed on or carried by biomedical science. In this regard, history shows us that the biomedical community must shoulder the main burden for ensuring responsible discussion. Recent examples of somewhat intemperate criticism from within the biomedical community by prominent scientists[10] are unhelpful to reasonable debate, and serve to promote potentially damaging opportunities for those doctrinally wedded to regressive pre-scientific beliefs.

It is with the central dilemma of this potential for conflict between the creativity and inventiveness of biomedical scientists and doctors[11] and the responsible acknowledgement by them of the wider social interest and how best to meet it that this chapter is concerned.

A. Models of Regulation

Several studies have considered the purpose of regulation and features of different regulatory systems.[12] The perspective of the biomedical scientist is, however,

---

[9] K Calman, 'Evolutionary Ethics: Can Values Change' (2004) 30 *Journal of Medical Ethics* 366.

[10] J Buxton, 'UK Fertility Expert Blasts HFEA' *BioNews* 2004.

[11] I use the term 'biomedical scientist and doctor' without differentiation between the two since from the outset there has been no clear boundary between scientists and doctors in this field with regard to creativity and innovation in both research and application—see for example the creative partnership of Edwards (scientist) and Steptoe (doctor) that resulted in the birth of Louise Brown.

[12] See D Morgan, 'Regulating Reproductive Technologies: Ten Years Down the Tube' in J Gunning (ed), *Assisted Conception: Research, Ethics and Law* (Aldershot, Ashgate, 2000) 175; R Lee and D Morgan, *Human Fertilisation and Embryology: Regulating the Reproductive Revolution* (London, Blackstone, 2001); E Jackson, *Regulating Reproduction: Law, Technology and Autonomy* (Oxford, Hart Publishing, 2001); and T Caulfield, L Knowles and E Meslin, 'Law and Policy in the Era of Reproductive Genetics' (2004) 30 *Journal of Medical Ethics* 414.

distinctive. In an earlier study, I have compared the beneficial and adverse features of different types of regulatory regimes from the point of view of a biomedical scientist,[13] and I summarise key points here.

Non-regulated regimes are characterised by a free market in ideas and services with the expectation that only useful discoveries and new treatments will flourish and survive, and that patients as consumers are able to decide for themselves. These regimes provide an appealing 'evolutionary' model. Their main advantages from a biomedical perspective consist in the freedoms they preserve: to use one's own judgment, to challenge taboos and perceived wisdoms, and to earn and benefit from one's own creativity. Such regimes usually ensure that a variety of therapies remain on offer and avoid reproductive tourism by biomedical scientists, doctors and patients, which reduces patient risk. Civil and contract law, including insurance law, and 'peer pressure' provide a modicum of 'regulation'. But these regimes also have significant disadvantages because they rely on ethical choices made by individual scientists and doctors rather than on a 'social ethic' which informs an official regulatory scheme, and so the range of available treatment options may be narrowed as well as expanded. Controls are also reactive and compensatory rather than proactive and preventative, and often lead to apparently inconsistent and piecemeal case law where biomedical scientists and doctors are uncertain of their legal position and hence feel unprotected. Mavericks can damage the profession as a whole, and bad reactive statute law can follow.

A second option, peer self-regulated regimes, ranges from professional societies through peer-based accrediting bodies to statutorily-based regulation via a professional body, which may or may not include non-professional members as well. Such regimes provide professional guidance and standards and thereby offer legal protection to those who comply with the guidance which is given. The rules are made by people who have the professional expertise to 'understand' that which is being regulated. Peer self-regulation protects the interests and status of the profession and encourages professional responsibility by not disempowering professionals. But the approach comes with its own problems. The professional perspective is exaggerated over others, and can give undue weight to a conservative senior elite in a hierarchical profession: what junior professionals, and indeed patients, desire can be more 'radical'. Often such bodies are secretive, ineffective at explanation and education, and not seen to be generally accountable. Peer self-regulation can also raise public suspicion by being, or appearing to be, lenient on professional misconduct.

The third option, external regulation, ranges from regimes which merely protect consumer choice to comprehensive prohibitory or permissive statutory regulation of activities. Through the legislative process, they incorporate a wider range

---

[13] MH Johnson, 'The Art of Regulation and the Regulation of ART: The Impact of Regulation on Research and Clinical Practice' (2002) 9 *Journal of Law and Medicine* 399.

of pertinent perspectives, including potentially a social perspective. The framework they provide can be consensual rather than confrontational, and they make the legal position clear(er) in advance. They also provide opportunities for public education and consultation. The main concerns of the profession against external regulation are that it can inhibit creativity and slow the pace of change. If heavy handed, it can poison relationships between professionals and regulators and so polarise society. It can also lead to over-bureaucratisation and can intrude into inappropriate areas and disempower professionals.

Yet, my main conclusion from this earlier analysis was that the creative and novel therapeutic work of biomedical scientists and doctors *should* be subject to limited and carefully defined independent regulation. The available evidence does not suggest that the profession can do a sufficiently good job of self-regulation to be entrusted with it entirely.[14] Practical and intellectual arguments also favour an external regulatory body representing more than just professional peers. At the heart of this argument is the fact that biomedical scientists and doctors are themselves part of a wider and diverse community and cannot arrogate to themselves exclusive powers of decision over matters, the outcome of which affects others profoundly. Whilst acknowledging that there are domains in which scientists and doctors must properly be pre-eminent and authoritative, and so must be encouraged to exercise a fair degree of autonomy responsibly, it is also clear that there are other domains in which the biomedical voice is just one of many competing and valid claims to be heard. Biomedical scientists and doctors have been shown as often as not by history to be 'wrong' about novelty. It is in the best interests of the biomedical profession to understand and accept the complex objectives of a regulatory framework, and to engage constructively in an attempt to produce a framework for regulation that optimises the outcome for all, including themselves. Unless they do so, they are likely to forfeit respect and lose influence in the debates and decisions about regulation, as has been seen elsewhere in Europe. Indeed, as the next section illustrates, it was precisely because biomedical scientists and doctors participated in the public debate in this manner in the UK that we have a relatively progressive regulatory system that honours and protects individuality in both professionals and patients, whilst assessing the social and ethical impact of new research and therapies.

B. Key Features of a Regulatory Regime

Implicit in any regulatory structure is an underlying philosophy, which informs the regulatory and legal framework and thereby defines a set of objectives

---

[14] See for a recent example in a different context J Smith, *Shipman Inquiry: Fifth Report—Safeguarding Patients: Lessons from the Past—Proposals for the Future* (Norwich, HMSO, 2004).

for regulatory practice. The philosophy may not be explicit and indeed, when analysed carefully, may be confused or fragmented. For example, a society's 'philosophy of the status of the human embryo' may lead to different codifications in law. Thus, for instance, the view that the embryo is an individual life and deserves complete protection has influenced legislation in Austria (1992), Italy (2004), Germany (1990), Norway (1987) and France (1994 and 1997). The position that the embryo deserves respect as a potential human being governs the legislative approaches in the UK (1990), Hungary (1997), Spain (1988 and 1997), Sweden (1991), Denmark (1997) and Australia (Federal law of 2002). Draft legislation in Taiwan reflects the conviction that the embryo is the conduit for generational continuity, and that the validity of that continuity must be protected. Lastly, it is possible to say that in countries in which 'the market' is allowed to regulate artificial reproductive technologies (ARTs) the embryo is to that extent seen as part of a commercial transaction (see, for instance, Italy pre–2004 and some jurisdictions within the United States of America today).[15] How we view the embryo influences strongly how we treat it and what types of assisted reproductive services can and cannot be offered, as well as what research is allowed. The biomedical community offers one cultural view of the embryo's status among several, even within a single society, and so this point illustrates nicely why a single sub-community cannot reasonably expect to have the sole voice in the form that regulation takes. It is for this reason that the biomedical community must make clear its philosophy of, for example, the status of the embryo, and why it holds this philosophy. It must also explain the practical consequences for the profession, for patients and for society that flow from that status and how these consequences differ from those that flow from alternative ways of thinking. This constructive engagement in a dialogue leading to regulation will maximise the chance of benefit for all. It also focuses on outcomes and thus reinforces an objective-driven regulatory regime. If the objectives are unclear or not stated, then how can the likely impact and actual effectiveness be ascertained and how can changes to the implementation (or even the legal structure) of the regulatory regime be proposed?

The debate within the United Kingdom between 1984 and 1990 illustrates vividly how an objective-driven regulatory regime with an explicit underlying philosophy was at least approximated during the development of the Human Fertilisation and Embryology Act (HFE Act) 1990. Over this period, the British biomedical community engaged with parliamentarians, women's groups, patients' groups, disability groups and charities, the churches, the press and society at large

---

[15] This necessarily somewhat cursory overview relies in part on information compiled by J Gunning, 'Overview: Legislative Approaches' in J Gunning (ed), *Assisted Conception: Research, Ethics and Law* (Aldershot, Ashgate, 2000); and on K Petersen *et al*, 'Assisted Reproductive Technologies: Professional and Legal Restrictions in Australian Clinics' (2005) 12 *Journal of Law and Medicine* 373.

to foster an increasingly informed discussion about both the status of the human embryo and the arguments for and against permitting research on it. It was a unique and highly effective dialogue that changed public and parliamentary opinion from overwhelming hostility to embryo research to broad approval.[16] The discussion was fundamentally about the 'philosophy of the embryo's status' and the practical consequences that flowed from different philosophies. The HFE Act was drafted in the light of this discussion: at its core is the special status of the embryo as a 'genetic entity' or, as the Act describes it, 'genetic material'.[17]

From the philosophy comes the framework for regulation, in which are embedded the objectives of regulation. In the HFE Act, the objectives went beyond the immediate philosophical driver of regulation (the status of the embryo) to incorporate and codify a broader set of social values relating, for example, to how the doctor-patient relationship is currently conceptualised, the prevailing economic and social values (broadly consumerist and individualised), and the diversity of moral and religious beliefs. The types of objectives that might form part of a regulatory regime include:

1. *Protecting the at-risk interests of existing stake-holders: patients, family members, professional health care workers and scientists;*
2. *Protecting the at-risk interests of potential individuals: embryos and/or the children who may result from treatment;*
3. *Protecting human rights and defining responsibilities;*
4. *Expressing a public morality;*
5. *Imposing a morality or view, whether governmental or sectional interest such as a religious, social or professional group;*
6. *Protecting creativity and inventiveness;*
7. *Educating and leading;*
8. *Promoting fair and effective economic activity;*
9. *Balancing management of individual and social harm against protection of personal privacy and individuality.*

This list should not be viewed as exhaustive. The objectives listed in points 1, 3, 5, 6, 7 and 8 are of particular interest to biomedical scientists and doctors as professionals (rather than as citizens). Clearly, the philosophical, political, religious and social framework of any society will determine which objectives are selected and

---

[16] J Gunning and V English, Human In-Vitro Fertilization: A Case Study in the Regulation of Medical Innovation (Ashgate, 1993); and M Mulkay, The Embryo Research Debate: Science and the Politics of Reproduction (Cambridge, CUP, 1997).

[17] See further MH Johnson, 'A Biomedical Perspective on Parenthood' in A Bainham, S Day Sclater and MPM Richards (eds), *What is a Parent? A Socio-Legal Analysis* (Oxford, Hart Publishing, 1999) 47.

given weight. Even within a society there may be conflicting objectives.[18] For example, although the relationship between doctors and patients might be idealised as a partnership in which interests coincide, the reality is often different. There may be financial conflicts, the doctor is prey to other pressures such as performance league tables, some patients are more concerned about having babies regardless of the risks of multiple births while the doctor's concern may be to prevent multiple births (the reverse may apply in less scrupulous clinics with an eye on pregnancy rates!). Likewise, the potential interests of babies-to-be and of mothers may conflict with those of embryos used for research.[19] However, an explicit acknowledgement of objective-driven regulation deriving from an explicitly articulated philosophy will hopefully make for a more transparent and perhaps better legislative regime.

C. What Should Biomedical Scientists and Doctors Expect of Regulation?

If we accept the need for a regulatory regime that clearly articulates its objectives against which the effectiveness of its provisions can be measured, what are key objectives for the biomedical community? I offer some suggestions.[20]

First, an external regulatory body should not intrude unnecessarily into the day-to-day regulation of professional practice and standards, which is properly the province of professional peer-mediated self-regulation. Biomedical professionals should not feel disempowered by legislation, but should undertake this self-regulatory role under general regulatory oversight with a light touch. Only where *novel* research or therapeutic procedures are involved, is there a major and more detailed role for external regulators, and even then that role should be tempered with professional expertise. I have argued elsewhere[21] that, in this regard in the UK, the HFEA has perhaps usurped roles that might better be assumed by

---

[18] MH Johnson, 'The Art of Regulation and the Regulation of ART: The Impact of Regulation on Research and Clinical Practice' (2002) 9 *Journal of Law and Medicine* 399; MH Johnson, 'Should the Use of Assisted Reproduction Techniques Be Deregulated? The UK Experience: Options for Change' (1998) 13 *Human Reproduction* 1769; and L Cannold and L Gillam, 'Regulation, Consultation and Divergent Community Views: The Case of Access to ART by Lesbian and Single Women' (2002) 9 *Journal of Law and Medicine* 498.

[19] P Braude, V Bolton and MH Johnson, 'The Use of Human Pre-embryos for Infertility Research' in CIBA Foundation (ed), *Human Embryo Research Yes or No?* (London, CIBA Foundation, 1986) 63.

[20] See for more detailed discussion MH Johnson, 'The Art of Regulation and the Regulation of ART: The Impact of Regulation on Research and Clinical Practice' (2002) 9 *Journal of Law and Medicine* 399; and MH Johnson, 'Should the Use of Assisted Reproduction Techniques be Deregulated? The UK Experience: Options for Change' (1998) 13 *Human Reproduction* 1769.

[21] MH Johnson, 'The Art of Regulation and the Regulation of ART: The Impact of Regulation on Research and Clinical Practice' (2002) 9 *Journal of Law and Medicine* 399.

professional bodies, notwithstanding their reluctance or professed structural inability to assume such roles.

Second, external regulatory powers should be fundamentally permissive and flexible through licensing rather than rigid through prohibition. In this way, the regulator (and the courts where decisions are challenged) can engage in dialogue rather than confrontation and can be responsive to social and technical change. In this regard the HFE Act is broadly effective.

Finally, regulatory powers should contain clear provisions that allow imaginative scientists, doctors and others to make the case for change and should enable them to collect the evidence required to make that case convincingly. The regulatory regime should also involve biomedical scientists and doctors in the decision-making process. This the HFE Act does, although often biomedical scientists and doctors fail to engage as constructively as they might.

A possible template for a biomedically friendly procedure for innovation can be set out as follows:

The first stage should be to allow biomedical scientists and doctors to collect the evidence to make the case for new treatments. This will include quantitative data on safety, reliability and side effects. It will allow research on appropriate animal embryo models and on human embryos, *eg* therapeutic as distinct from reproductive cloning.[22]

The second stage involves biomedical scientists and doctors in any decision to allow research on human embryos and any decision to apply new research findings in treatment. Their involvement is essential for both steps because of the informed judgment they bring to the quality of supporting data presented. Their involvement is likely be more dominant in the first than in the second step, because the wider social and ethical arguments involved in any decision whether and how to apply new research findings in treatment need wider input. However, their views on safety and side effects are especially important. In essence, they should be well placed to ascertain whether those of their peers advocating new treatments have a realistic appreciation of the risks and benefits, are aware of and alert to any dangers, and have proposed reasonable contingency plans should dangers emerge during application.

The third stage involves the introduction of new treatments (and in some cases new research) under regulatory scrutiny. This may, for example, involve case-by-case reports back, and/or restriction of treatments to certain sub-groups of patients (such as by age or reproductive history).

The fourth stage consists of ensuring the longer term assessment of major new types of treatment in the form of prospective clinical trials with long term follow-up and regular review.

---

[22] MH Johnson, 'Cloning Humans?' (1997) 19 *BioEssays* 737.

This template resembles the flow-chart developed during the implementation of the HFE Act by the HFEA. The Act itself, as we saw above, was a product of dialogue, indeed the HFEA was a development of an earlier non-statutory body that had been set up voluntarily in 1984 by the Medical Research Council and the Royal College of Obstetricians and Gynaecologists.[23] For all these reasons, the Act is among the most biomedically congenial and innovation-friendly of statutory regulatory regimes and so provides a useful bench-mark for critical evaluation in light of experience.

D. Criticisms of an Enlightened Regulatory Process

The Human Fertilisation and Embryology Act has proved to be remarkably robust and capable of dealing directly or through validation in the courts with many changes and innovations. However, there *are* criticisms from all sides, including some very vocal critics among the biomedical community. Indeed, currently there is much discussion about the need to change the Act, focused in part through the House of Commons Select Committee of Science and Technology,[24] but also initiated by the HFEA itself, both in-house and collaboratively, with, for example, the Medical Research Council[25] or with government in the context of the revised proposals for administration of the Human Tissue Act 2004. However, even among some of its strongest critics, which are relatively few in number, there is an acknowledgement of the value of the HFEA to professionals as well as to patients. It is also important for professionals to remember just how much public communication and discussion was required over a six year period during the gestation of the HFE Act. The biomedical community must be prepared to re-engage in that level of discussion and public education, if any changes made to primary legislation are not to be more oppressive than helpful. Here I select two examples from the HFE Act where change in its application and perhaps in primary legislation may be warranted: the time and nature of the evidence base, and the amount of paperwork generated by the activities of the HFEA.

1. Time and the Nature of the Evidence Base

While it is often argued that the procedure for assessing innovative work outlined above slows innovation, this claim needs self-critical evaluation by the biomedical

---

[23] For a history of the origins of the HFEA, see J Gunning and V English, *Human In-Vitro Fertilization: A Case Study in the Regulation of Medical Innovation* (Aldershot, Ashgate, 1993).

[24] Hansard Society, *Online Consultation on Human Reproductive Technologies and the Law* (London, House of Commons Science and Technology Select Committee, 2004).

[25] Medical Research Council, *Assisted Reproduction: A Safe, Sound Future* (London, Medical Research Council, 2004).

community. The process of gaining approval for novel research or therapy is evidence-based, and the collection of evidence takes time, as does a risk-based evaluation of the evidence by the regulatory body. In a non-regulated jurisdiction, it is often argued, hunches or serendipity can be followed up faster and, if they work, can be applied more rapidly. This argument is based on two fallacies: that there is a clear single biomedical outcome by which to assess whether or not an innovation has 'worked' and that case histories provide adequate evidence of something having 'worked'. The whole purpose of evidence base and risk assessment is to deal with each of these fallacies. If biomedical scientists and doctors are on top of their brief, they should have no trouble convincing peers and regulators that they have sufficient data (from the literature, observation, experimentation on animal and/or on human embryos) on efficacy, safety and side-effects to proceed to controlled application. After all, the regulatory body could be considered effectively to be in the position of a patient, asking to be well informed before giving consent to treat. However, one objection to this analogy of the regulatory body as 'patient' is that it sets the risk threshold inappropriately, imposing an unrealistic burden of proof on the biomedical applicant. There are two aspects to risk threshold setting: level and scope.

(a) The Risk Assessment Threshold

Concerns about the level of risk assessment arise when the biomedical scientists and doctors consider their evidence to be sound and clearly presented, but the regulator does not. It is almost certainly going to be the case that a regulatory body will be better informed and under less pressure than most patients, and thus better able to give genuine 'consent' to treat or study. My own experience as a member of the HFEA and as a referee of proposals is that most delays arise from incomplete or poorly evidenced proposals, which therefore shuttle back and forth from regulator to applicant. This shuttling process can itself be informative and help to raise best practice standards. However, there is a potential problem with the application of the HFE Act here, since of biomedical scientists and doctors requesting a licence to develop and apply novel treatments it expects:

> that embryos will not be used for treatment where there are reasonable grounds for believing that procedures to which the embryos themselves have been subject carry an actual or a reasonable theoretical risk of harm to their development, *or a theoretical risk of harm to their developmental potential*. Treatment centres are expected to satisfy the HFEA that sufficient scientific evidence is available to establish that procedures used *do not prejudice the developmental potential of embryos* (emphasis added).[26]

---

[26] Human Fertilisation and Embryology Authority, *Code of Practice*, 6th edn (London, Human Fertilisation and Embryology Authority, 2004) s 8.5.

There are likely to be few if any situations in which there is total certainty about either the development or the potential of an embryo produced by or exposed to new procedures. So, interpreted literally, this requirement would prevent all novel treatments. Clearly, since this has not happened, a strict interpretation has not been applied by the HFEA and risk has been interpreted probabilistically. A judicious mix of reasonable evidence, reasonable judgment, informed consent, careful monitoring, and a clinical action plan should problems arise has sufficed. Nonetheless, this interpretation relies on a common agreement as to what is reasonable. Ultimately, the test of reasonableness can be made in the courts through legal challenge of an HFEA decision. Several such challenges have been made, and the HFEA has been shown to be remarkably robust in its decision-making.[27]

(b) The Scope of Risk Assessment

Concerns about the scope of risk assessment differ from threshold issues, since here it is the extent, not the level, of risk assessment applied by the regulator that is contested. The biomedical scientist or doctor may focus on clinical and scientific risk. But the regulator also has to take account of legal uncertainty (does the biomedical request lie within its regulatory powers and thus the law?), ethical doubt (are there issues that go beyond the direct use in the submitted case, in which the case for the directly interested parties may seem clear cut), and social concerns (will the public and/or parliament accept a decision to proceed such that the regulatory body, regime and indeed profession retain public confidence?). Each of these can also be conceived of as risks. Whilst risk assessment on biomedical evidence can and should be quantitative, social, legal and ethical 'risk assessment' is more qualitative and conditional, so there is a real concern here about how risk is determined. But it is precisely because of the less quantitative, and thus more difficult, nature of these risks that the final decisions have been moved from the doctor or scientist to the regulator. The recent cases involving applications to the HFEA for tissue typing of embryos by preimplantation genetic diagnosis (PGD) illustrate these complexities.

Where an existing child has a fatal genetic condition that can only be 'treated' by a graft, an application to test embryos for both the genetic condition (select only non-affected) and histocompatibility status (select only histo-compatible) was accepted by the HFEA. The ethical justification for this decision is reported in the HFEA's records.[28] Subsequently, the legal justification for this decision was

---

[27] Anon, 'Posthumous Fathers to Gain Legal Recognition' *BioNews* 2003; Anon, 'Court Rules that Embryos Cannot Be Used Without Consent' *BioNews* 2003, and Anon, 'Man Continues Paternity Challenge for IVF Child' *BioNews* 2004.

[28] Human Fertilisation and Embryology Authority, *A Summary of the One Hundred and Thirteenth Meeting of the Human Fertilisation and Embryology Authority* (London, Human Fertilisation and Embryology Authority, 2001).

also clarified, namely that the first test lay clearly within the law (paragraph 1(3) of Schedule 2 of the HFE Act) and that no further risk of harm to the biopsied embryo would arise from performing a second test on the biopsy sample.[29] Thus, ethical, legal and technical risks were assessed and the application passed on all three.

An application was also received for histocompatibility testing only, and was declined initially. The main reason for this decision appeared to be that such a procedure would run contrary to the welfare of the child provision.[30] The apparent reasoning behind this conclusion was clarified subsequently.[31] It was argued that the dangers of the PGD technique itself constituted an uncertain biomedical risk to the selected embryo that was not for the benefit of *that* embryo but only for that of a third party. By 2004, the HFEA reviewed the evidence base and concluded that this risk was no longer significant. It therefore agreed to license histocompatibility testing only. It is unclear whether in 2001 the legal risk (procedure not within the HFEA's powers?) was also considered too high, on the grounds that the PGD procedure was not 'necessary for the provision of treatment services' and was of questionable 'desirability' (Section 13 and Schedule 2 of the Act). However, legal doubts in 2001 were at least provisionally resolved by 2004, for, in the interim, a ruling by the Court of Appeal on a case brought against the HFEA by Comment on Reproductive Ethics (CORE) confirmed that it was within the powers of the HFEA to license PGD for tissue-typing.[32] Thus, both legally and biomedically, the risk assessments were positive by 2004.

It is not entirely clear whether in 2001 the ethical risk was considered too high, and a range of opinions on this matter has been published.[33] A particularly potent issue for the press and public opinion (social risk) was that a precedent was being set, which might lead to 'designer babies', for example pressure for sex selection for a female embryo in order to provide the existing two sons with a sister. A clue as

---

[29] Human Fertilisation and Embryology Authority, *Preimplantation Tissue Typing* (London, Human Fertilisation and Embryology Authority, 2004).

[30] Human Fertilisation and Embryology Authority, *A Summary of the One Hundred and Thirteenth Meeting of the Human Fertilisation and Embryology Authority* (London, Human Fertilisation and Embryology Authority, 2001).

[31] Human Fertilisation and Embryology Authority, *Preimplantation Tissue Typing* (London, Human Fertilisation and Embryology Authority, 2004).

[32] *R (on the application of Quintavalle) v HFEA* [2002] EWHC Admin 2785; [2004] EWCA Civ 667. The House of Lords has subsequently confirmed this ruling in *Quintavalle (on behalf of Comment on Reproductive Ethics) v HFEA* [2005] UKHL 28.

[33] J Savulescu, 'Procreative Beneficence: Why We Should Select the Best' (2001) 15 *Bioethics* 413, G Pennings, R Schots and I Liebaers, 'Ethical Considerations on Preimplantation Genetic Diagnosis for HLA Typing to Match a Future Child as a Donor of Haematopoietic Stem Cells to a Sibling' (2002) 17 *Human Reproduction* 534, M Katz, L Fitzgerald, A Bankier, J Savulescu and D Cram, 'Issues and Concerns of Couples Presenting for Preimplantation Genetic Diagnosis (PGD)' (2002) 22 *Prenatal Diagnosis* 1117, and J Robertson, 'Extending Preimplantation Genetic Diagnosis: The Ethical Debate: Ethical Issues in New Uses of Preimplantation Genetic Diagnosis' (2003) 18 *Human Reproduction* 465.

to how the ethical risk was addressed is evident in the conditional nature of the decision given by the HFEA,[34] specifying that use of PGD exclusively for tissue typing would only be licensed as a last resort and because there was a sick child who could not be helped in any other way. Thus was the ethical hurdle cleared, although whether the ethical basis for this highly qualified decision was adequate is still being debated actively.[35]

This case study illustrates how complex the regulatory process can be. It can leave biomedical scientists and doctors (and their patients) frustrated—in this case for three years—compared with less regulated clinicians overseas (as in the USA for this example, where PGD for tissue typing went ahead more rapidly). On balance, however, the HFEA has been doing the statutory task asked of it, which is to undertake risk assessments for its decisions that cannot be based exclusively on biomedical information. Occasional frustration in the biomedical community may be understandable, but not on current evidence excusable, in view of the thorough airing of issues that occurs during the process, and the level of legal and professional protection given to both patients and practitioners. In the process, the public and the press are informed and have an opportunity to reflect on the issues raised, and so a measure of social acceptance is gained. This is important. If parliament and/or the public sense that they are being pushed too far too fast by science they may dig in their heels in ways that seem unreasonable to science—as exemplified by the backlash against MMR vaccination and genetically modified crops in the UK. Scientists and doctors who advocate the demolition of the HFEA would do well to ponder on the possible consequences—the briefest look at the debris surrounding other scientifically controversial issues should convince them that the regulation of ART shines like a beacon of enlightenment in comparison.

2. Useless Bureaucracy?

Regulation generates paper. It must do. The critical question is: who benefits from this paper and the labour that goes into compiling, verifying and auditing data and completing forms? Too often, paper trails appear to be there to cover the back of the regulator in case of complaint or problem, so that they can show that they are performing the duties required of them. This can easily become a sterile and

---

[34] Human Fertilisation and Embryology Authority, *Preimplantation Tissue Typing* (London, Human Fertilisation and Embryology Authority, 2004).

[35] See MH Johnson, 'A Moral Case Study for Discussion: Designer Babies and Tissue Typing' (2004) 9 Re*productive Biomedicine* 372; and responses by M Sousa and A Barros, 'A Moral Case Study for Discussion: Designer Babies and Tissue Typing', E Dahl, 'Babies by Design: A Response to Martin Johnson's Moral Case Study on Tissue Typing', and M Ludwig, 'Martin Johnson's Moral Case Study: A Reply', all (2004) 9 Re*productive Biomedicine* available online at http://www.rbmonline.com/4DCGI/Article/Detail?38%091%09=%201565%09.

defensive exercise loathed by all. In addition, there is now enormous pressure for a more regulated culture in UK medicine, largely because the profession has not self-regulated successfully and so has suffered a variety of embarrassing scandals, to which it has often not responded either honestly or effectively. Thus, clinicians have reasonable concerns that their activities are now subjected to multiple forms of regulation and audit, and this burden must be rationalised to prevent duplication. Some may argue that the HFEA's powers should be *extended* so that it is the single regulatory body for this area of medicine, not just one of several. The proposed transfer to the HFEA of responsibility for administering the Human Tissue Act 2004 is an example of this rationalisation of regulatory bodies.

However, regulators should do more than rationalise. They really do need to show unambiguously that the data collected are needed and that benefits accrue from its collection. These benefits should be visible to clinicians and their patients. For example, as a result of all the form filling that is being carried out, the HFEA has a massive and unique database. Paradoxically, the provisions regarding the confidentiality of the data mean that access to it is limited by law. The law (or its interpretation) needs to be changed, consistent with the protection of sensitive information, so as to make the data more readily available and linkable in an anonymised form to other databases.

Related to this point is the lack of provision for prospective clinical trials and follow-up that the HFEA would be well placed to initiate. It is clearly not the major role of a regulatory body to engage in or to commission research. However, the HFEA might work better than it does with other professional bodies such as the Medical Research Council to promote and further such studies. Not only would this be useful, it would ensure that as regulator it was well informed and it would in the eyes of biomedical scientists and doctors provide an independent reason for the compilation of data, namely that this information was going to be useful clinically as well as legally or bureaucratically.

E. Conclusion

Regulation has many advantages for biomedical science. It can be easy for biomedical scientists and doctors to overlook these when complaining about the less congenial or more frustrating aspects of regulation. Overall, however, any regulatory regime is bound to be a compromise between competing concerns. In the UK, we have pioneered a legislative form of regulation which is relatively, but not perfectly, biomedically friendly. Some of the reasons underlying this relatively benign outcome have been summarised in this paper. Central to a successful outcome was the historical willingness of the biomedical community to engage openly and constructively in debates at all levels of society. If hostile social attitudes (the gut reaction or 'yuck factor') to the novel are to be addressed and a more informed and reflective social attitude developed, biomedical scientists and doctors must continue to do the ground work and earn confidence and respect for themselves and their regulators. Without this groundwork, both risk forfeiting public confidence and prejudicing the protection to be creative and innovative that they currently enjoy. Simply carping at the regulator will, in the end, not work in their favour but will rebound against them. History has a strong clear message: the public can be trusted to reach sensible conclusions if communicated with clearly; the public rapidly sniffs out self-serving and partisan special pleading; and the public may take its time in arriving at a conclusion. It is a measure of the effectiveness of the HFE Act that, within the current legislation, imperfections can be addressed and that, in the climate in which we operate, there is a will to address them.

7

Defining Parenthood*

BONNIE STEINBOCK

Advances in reproductive medicine require us to rethink concepts previously taken for granted, including the notion of parenthood. On the one hand, it has always been possible to distinguish between reproduction and rearing, the biological aspect and the social component of parenthood. Adoption and fostering of children are nothing new, and neither are disputes over custody. On the other hand, assisted reproductive technology (ART) compounds the potential for complication. A child can have five different parents: the genetic father, who provides the sperm; the genetic mother, who provides the egg; a surrogate who is not genetically related to the child she carries and bears; and the intended rearing parents who have no biological connection to the child. Indeed, the notion of 'genetic mother' can be even further divided. Using a technique known as egg cell nuclear transfer, the nucleus containing most of the DNA can be taken from one woman and transplanted into an enucleated egg cell from another woman.[1] The new egg cell has the nuclear DNA from one woman, while its ooplasm, containing mitochondrial DNA, comes from another woman. The resulting child has genetic material from two different women, and thus potentially up to six contenders for

* Reprinted with minor changes from (2005) 13 *International Journal of Children's Rights* 265–88. The editors of this collection thank the author and the editors of the International Journal of Children's Rights for their friendly permission to reprint Professor Steinbock's earlier publication here.

[1] D Grady, 'Doctors Using Hybrid Egg to Tackle Infertility in Older Women' *New York Times*, 10 October 1998, A16. A different technique, which also results in children receiving genes from two different women, transplants ooplasm from donor eggs into the eggs of women whose infertility is due to ooplasmic defects (see JA Barritt *et al*, (2001) 16 *Human Reproduction* 513). The technique was developed by Dr Jamie Grifo in the United States, but none of his patients became pregnant. Dr Grifo gave his findings to doctors in China after regulations imposed by the Food and Drug Administration in 2001 made it too difficult to continue the research in the United States. In 2003 Chinese doctors were able to make an infertile woman pregnant with the technique, although the pregnancy ended when the woman went into premature labor and the twin fetuses she was carrying died. See D Grady, 'Pregnancy Created Using Egg Nucleus of Infertile Woman' *New York Times*, 14 October 2003, A1.

the role of parent. Sometimes this multiplication of parents results in custody disputes, and courts have had to decide who are the 'real' parents.

A. Surrogate Motherhood Cases[2]

In the famous *Baby M* case,[3] biological parentage was not at issue. William Stern was the child's biological father, and Mary Beth Whitehead her biological mother. Rather, the issue was whether signing a surrogacy agreement deprived Ms Whitehead of the status of 'mother', even though she carried and gave birth to her own genetic child. In another well-known case, *Johnson v Calvert*,[4] the biology was more complicated because the surrogate, Anna Johnson, gestated an embryo created by the Calverts. Ms Johnson was the gestational mother, but Ms Calvert was the genetic mother. The California Supreme Court did not rule that one sort of connection is stronger than the other as regards claims to custody. Rather, it held that when there are two mothers, the one who intended to 'bring about the birth of a child that she intended to raise as her own ... is the natural mother under California law.'[5]

However, the intended rearing parents might not have either a genetic or a gestational connection to the child. This was so in a widely reported California case, *In Re Buzzanca*,[6] in which the couple had used sperm donation, egg donation, and a surrogate in their attempt to have a child. The Buzzancas ended up in court because John Buzzanca divorced his wife before the child, Jaycee, was born and then refused to pay child support, arguing that the resulting child was not a child of the marriage. The trial court agreed with his biological interpretation and held that Jaycee Buzzanca had *no* legal parents. John Buzzanca did not owe child support because he was not the father. Luanne Buzzanca, who had cared for the child from birth, was a 'temporary custodial person', and would have to adopt her to become her legal mother.

Commenting on the decision, columnist Ellen Goodman writes:

> Now, from all reports, the toddler is being lovingly cared for by that temporary custodial person she illegally calls 'mommy'. But as the case goes to appeal, I am trying to

---

[2] Some writers object to the term 'surrogate motherhood' on the ground that 'referring to the women who have carried a fetus to term and delivered a child as surrogates slights their status as mothers, and prejudices the discussion of disputes concerning parental status' (JL Nelson and HL Nelson, 'Reproductive Technologies, VI Contract Pregnancy' in SG Post, *The Encyclopedia of Bioethics*, 3rd edn (London, Macmillan, 2003). I take the point but use the term 'surrogate mother' because it is more familiar than 'contract birthgiver'.

[3] *In the Matter of Baby M* 109 NJ 396 (1988).

[4] *Johnson v Calvert* 851 P 2d 776 (1993).

[5] *Ibid*.

[6] *In Re Buzzanca* 61 Cal App 72 (4th Cir), Cl Rptr 2d 280.

imagine how a judge, who is supposed to act in the best interests of the child, could leave a child without any parent at all. How could the same judge rule that the man responsible for a child's creation, had no responsibility for her support?[7]

Common sense, Goodman suggests, tells us that: 'John Buzzanca is as responsible for the existence of Jaycee as any man who ever created a child the lo-tech way. Perhaps more so, since he did so intentionally.'[8]

If this is right—and I think it is—it suggests that being a parent is about more than reproduction in the narrow genetic sense.

The California appeals court agreed. It overturned the decision, holding that the intent to parent made John and Luanne the lawful parents of Jaycee. The court wrote: 'Let us get right to the point: Jaycee never would have been born had not Luanne and John both agreed to have a fertilized egg implanted in a surrogate.'[9]

It rejected John Buzzanca's contention that he had no parental responsibility for the child by analogising the case to one in which a woman is artificially inseminated:

If a husband who consents to artificial insemination [under California law] ... is 'treated in law' as the father of the child by virtue of his consent, there is no reason the result should be any different in the case of a married couple who consent to in vitro fertilization by unknown donors and subsequent implantation into a woman who is, as a surrogate, willing to carry the embryo to term for them.[10]

Luanne Buzzanca was given legal custody of Jaycee, while the matter of child support was remanded.

1. Lesbian Mothers

In a very recent case, the San Francisco Court of Appeals ruled that the genetic mother of twins born to her lesbian partner has no parental rights because she signed a waiver of parental rights at the time of donating her eggs.[11] KM and EG began living together in March 1994 and registered as domestic partners in San Francisco in October 1994. Long before their relationship began, EG had been exploring ways to have a child on her own. She underwent 12 rounds of artificial insemination, but did not become pregnant. Attempts at IVF using EG's eggs and donor sperm failed because EG was unable to produce enough eggs. At that point, EG's fertility doctor suggested that she might like to try IVF using KM's eggs. EG

---

[7] E Goodman, 'The Disturbing Case of a High-tech Orphan' *Boston Globe*, 14 December 1997, D7.
[8] *Ibid.*
[9] *In Re Buzzanca* 61 Cal App 1410 (4th Cir), 1412.
[10] *Ibid*, 1418.
[11] *KM v EG*, A101754, No CV 020777 (Cal Ct Appl (1st Cir) App Dist, 5 October 2004).

was reluctant to do so because the couple's relationship was still new. Moreover, a mutual friend of theirs was then involved in a child custody dispute with her lesbian partner, something EG wanted to avoid. Eventually, however, EG overcame her misgivings, and asked KM to donate her eggs, provided that KM would be a 'real donor' and EG would be the only legal mother. The possibility of a future adoption by KM was discussed, but the women agreed that this should not happen for at least 5 years when the relationship was proven stable and permanent.

The consent forms KM signed explicitly provide that the egg donor must waive any right and relinquish any claim to any offspring resulting from the donated eggs. After meeting with a psychological counsellor, KM and EG discussed what they would disclose publicly about the parentage of a child formed from KM's donated eggs. They agreed to tell the child eventually that KM was the genetic mother, but that EG would decide when. They also agreed not to tell other people about KM's role and to reveal only that EG was the mother.

In April 1995, KM underwent the egg retrieval procedure, her eggs were fertilised with sperm from an anonymous donor, and four of the resulting embryos were implanted in EG's uterus. EG gave birth to twin girls on 7 December 1995. Soon afterwards, EG asked KM to marry her and on Christmas Day the couple exchanged rings. For the next 5 years, they all lived as a family unit, with both women caring for and raising the girls.

In 2000, KM became insistent that she wanted to adopt the girls, but EG had misgivings. They separated in March 2001, and EG filed a notice of termination of the domestic partnership. They got back together in July, but in August 2001, EG moved to Massachusetts with the girls. In February 2002, KM filed a new petition to establish a parental relationship. She also sought joint custody. In response, EG filed a motion to quash and dismiss the petition on the ground that KM lacked standing to assert parentage.

At trial, KM testified that she and EG had planned to have children together from the very beginning. She denied that there had been any agreement that EG would be the sole legal mother. She admitted signing the ovum donation consent form, but claimed that she had not understood the legal implications, and treated it as merely a matter of form necessary to proceed with the egg donation. She never intended to relinquish her parental rights, she alleged, and thought that the language of the donor form would not apply to her because she knew the recipient.

The trial court did not buy KM's story. It found that KM relinquished her claim to parentage when she knowingly, voluntarily, and intelligently signed the ovum donor consent form. Further, the court found substantial evidence that the parties had agreed that EG would be the sole legal parent. Accordingly, the court ruled that KM lacked standing and granted EG's motion to quash and dismiss the petition.

The court of appeal upheld the trial court's decision, although it disagreed with its ruling that KM lacked standing to bring the action to determine parentage under the Uniform Parentage Act (UPA). As the genetic mother, KM qualified as an 'interested party' for purposes of obtaining a judicial declaration of her status as a parent. However, KM's claim to be a legal parent was rejected. Following *Johnson*, the court said that when there are two biological mothers, the legal mother is the one who 'from the outset intended to be the child's mother.' In subsequent cases, appellate courts have construed the *Johnson* test to mean that the intent to be the parent is the 'tie-breaker' when two women have equal claims.[12]

The court explicitly declined to consider the parental role played by KM, saying that the appellate courts have consistently held that the domestic partner of a child's natural mother does not qualify as a parent under the UPA despite the parental role the partner played.[13] Nor was the court willing to consider the interests of the children, who had established a loving relationship with KM. It noted that in *Johnson*, the Supreme Court expressly rejected the assertion that parentage can be based on the best interests of the child: '[S]uch an approach raises the repugnant spectre of governmental interference in matters implicating our most fundamental notions of privacy, and confuses concepts of parentage and custody. Logically, the determination of parentage must precede, and should not be dictated by, eventual custody decisions.'[14] Basing parentage on a best interests standard would put at risk the rights of any natural parent who entered into a relationship and encouraged the formation of parental bonds between the children and the new partner.

Thus, *KM v EG* reaffirms the approach taken in *Johnson*. Ordinarily, the 'natural' parent is the legal parent, but where there are two biological mothers, it is the initial intent to parent that matters, not the parental role, and not the best interest of the child. The appellate court also rejected the assumption of the trial court that under California law there could be two legal mothers: 'As we understand *Johnson*, although genetic consanguinity gives a woman a colorable claim of maternity, the biological connection does not ripen into parentage unless the evidence establishes that the genetic mother intended to raise the child as her own.'[15]

But what if both women had intended to raise the children together? The court did not address this issue, because this was not the situation in this case. It is virtually certain, however, that such a case will arise, if one is not already making its way through the courts. It seems likely that in a case where there are two biological mothers, who intended to raise the children together, the California courts will have to recognise both as legal parents.

---

[12] *Ibid*, citing *Robert B v Susan B* 109 Cal App 1115 (4th Cir); see also *In Re Marriage of Buzzanca* 61 Cal App 1410 (4th Cir, 1998), 1421–22.

[13] See *Nancy S* 228 Cal App 3d 836.

[14] *Johnson* 5 Cal 93 (4th Cir), n 10.

[15] *KM v EG*, A101754, No CV 020777 (Cal Ct Appl (1st Cir) App Dist, 5 October 2004).

The *Baby M, Johnson, Buzzanca* and *KM* cases all involved collaborative reproduction[16] in which one of the contracting parties had a change of mind after the
initial agreement was made, and either sought to establish or, in the case of Mr
Buzzanca, to disavow, parental rights and responsibilities after the child's birth.
However, disputes over parentage and custody are not occasioned solely by con-
tractual relations and a subsequent change of mind; sometimes medical error
leads to competing parental claims.[17]

2. Switched Embryos

Perry-Rogers v Fasano[18] was a case in which medical error led to implanting the
wrong embryos into a woman, causing an 'accidental surrogacy'. In April 1998, two
couples began an IVF programme. Embryos created by Deborah Perry-Rogers and
Robert Rogers were mistakenly implanted in the uterus of Donna Fasano, along with
embryos created by Donna and Richard Fasano. On 28 May 1998 both couples were
notified of the mistake and of the need for DNA and amniocentesis tests. The
Rogerses attempted to contact the Fasanos, but the Fasanos did not respond. Nor did
Mrs Fasano undergo any testing to find out the genetic identity of the babies she was
carrying. However, the truth became obvious on 29 December 1998, when she gave
birth to two male infants, one white and one black. In April 1999, DNA testing was
conducted, and the results established that the Rogerses were the genetic parents of
the black child, now known as Akeil Richard Rogers. However, according to Ms
Perry-Rogers, the Fasanos agreed to relinquish custody of Akeil only upon the exe-
cution of a written statement, which entitled the Fasanos to future visitation with
Akeil. Ms Perry-Rogers stated that during the period between Akeil's birth on 29
December 1998 and 10 May 1999 the Fasanos permitted her only two brief visits
with Akeil, and that she felt compelled to sign the agreement in order to gain custody
of her son. The visitation agreement provided for visits one full weekend per month,
one weekend day each month, one week each summer, and alternating holidays. The
agreement also contained a liquidated damages clause, providing that a violation of
the Fasanos' visitation rights under the agreement would entitle them to $200,000.

The legal situation became unbelievably complex, with numerous applications,
orders, and counter-orders. The upshot was that the Rogerses were named Akeil's
legal and biological parents, and given sole and exclusive custody, while the

---

[16] The term 'collaborative reproduction' was coined by John Robertson, who defines it as 'those situations in which someone other than one's partner provides the gametes or gestation necessary for
reproduction, such as occurs with sperm, egg, or embryo donation, or surrogate motherhood' (JA
Robertson, *Children of Choice: Freedom and the New Reproductive Technologies* (Princeton, NJ,
Princeton University Press, 1994) 119).

[17] See *Leeds Teaching Hospital NHS Trust v Mr A, Mrs A and others* [2003] EWHC 259; [2003] 1 FLR
1091.

[18] *Perry-Rogers v Fasano* 715 NYS 2d 19 (NY App Div, 2000).

Fasanos were given visitation with Akeil every other weekend. The Rogerses then challenged the visitation order, which led the Fasanos to appeal the order giving the Rogerses custody of the child.

The Rogerses maintained that the Fasanos had no basis for a legal claim to Akeil, because they were 'genetic strangers' to him. The court rejected their argument, saying: 'In recognition of current reproductive technology, the term "genetic stranger" alone can no longer be enough to end a discussion of this issue. Additional considerations may be relevant for an initial threshold analysis of who is, or may be, a "parent".'[19]

The court declined to accept the 'broad premise' that in *every* case the genetic parents would necessarily win against a gestational surrogate who claimed parental rights. It acknowledged that there might be cases in which there could be more than one 'natural mother'; for example, a lesbian couple who had agreed from the outset to create and raise a child together. The Fasanos had not sought custody, but if they had, the court noted parenthetically, application of the 'intent' analysis employed in *Johnson v Calvert* would, in its view, require that custody be awarded to the Rogerses: 'It was they who purposefully arranged for their genetic material to be taken and used in order to attempt to create their own child, whom they intended to rear.'[20] The court's decision in favour of the Rogerses, however, was not based on an 'intent' analysis, but rather on the fact that the Rogerses' embryo was implanted in the 'gestational mother' by mistake, and the Fasanos knew of the error not long after it occurred. Therefore:

> [T]he happenstance of their nominal parenthood over plaintiffs' child should have been treated as a mistake to be corrected as soon as possible, before development of a parental relationship. It bears more similarity to a mix-up at the time of a hospital's discharge of two newborn infants, which should simply be corrected at once, than to one where a gestational mother has arguably the same rights to claim parentage as the genetic mother.[21]

The court held that the Fasanos were not entitled to a full evidentiary 'best interests' hearing to determine whether a psychological bond exists that should not be abruptly severed. Any bonding on the part of Akeil to his gestational mother and her family, the court held: '... was the direct result of defendants' failure to take timely action upon being informed of the clinic's admitted error. Defendants cannot be permitted to purposefully act in such a way as to create a bond, and then rely upon it for their assertion of rights to which they would not otherwise be entitled.'[22]

---

[19] *Ibid*.
[20] *Perry-Rogers v Fasano* 276 AD 2d 67, 73.
[21] *Ibid*, 75.
[22] *Ibid*, 76.

There is little doubt that the Fasanos behaved badly. First they ignored the attempts of the Rogerses to contact them, probably because they did not want to acknowledge that any mistake had been made. Next, when the mistake could not be ignored, given the race of Akeil, the Fasanos extracted from Deborah Perry-Rogers, in exchange for custody of her own child, a visitation agreement that no court would have issued or upheld. Small wonder that the Rogerses wanted the Fasanos out of their family and their lives! In light of the Fasanos' shoddy treatment of the Rogerses, the decision to deny them visitation rights seems eminently reasonable.

However, the analogy on which the court based its decision—a mix-up of newborns in the hospital—is deeply flawed. A woman who learns that she has taken the wrong baby home can give it back to its rightful parents before a 'parental relationship' develops. What exactly was Donna Fasano supposed to have done when she learned she was carrying someone else's baby? Obviously, she could not return the mistakenly implanted embryo. Should she have promised the Rogerses that she would not form a gestational bond with their son, and that she would hand the baby over to them at birth? Admittedly, this is what surrogates are supposed to do (and what they not always do successfully, as the *Baby M* case dramatically shows); but at least surrogates can decide whether they want to carry a child for 9 months and never regard it as their own before they contract to gestate someone else's child for money. Donna Fasano did not make that decision. She carried the Rogerses' child, at additional risk to her own health and that of her own biological child, without any compensation, because she had no other realistic choice. It seems most unfair to blame her for not correcting the mistake as soon as she learned of it.

Courts make rulings based on the facts of the case, rather than on hypothetical situations. Nevertheless, we may wonder how the court would have decided the issue of visitation, if the Fasanos had behaved honourably. Suppose that they had not ignored the attempts of the Rogerses to contact them, had undergone prenatal genetic testing, and had acknowledged the mistake from the outset. Suppose further that Mrs Fasano was willing to correct the mistake by relinquishing the Rogers baby to his parents upon his birth. But then suppose that the experience of gestation and birth had a profound and unexpected psychological effect on Mrs Fasano. She might be unable to think of Akeil as just 'someone else's child', but as her own baby and the twin brother of her other child. In this imaginary scenario, Mrs Fasano does nothing blameworthy. In fact, our moral opinion of her is likely to be higher than our opinion of a woman who finds it easy to give up a child she has carried and given birth to. If the Fasanos had done nothing wrong, would they have been entitled to visitation rights, or perhaps even joint custody?

All the above cases make it clear that courts are increasingly required to make Solomonic decisions regarding the parental rights and responsibilities of those involved in artificial reproduction. The *Buzzanca* court issued a plea to the legislature 'to sort out the parent[al] rights and responsibilities of those involved in artificial reproduction', saying:

> No matter what one thinks of artificial insemination, traditional and gestational surrogacy (in all its permutations), and—as now appears in the not-too-distant future, cloning and even gene splicing—courts are still going to be faced with the problem of determining legal parentage. A child cannot be ignored. Even if all means of artificial reproduction were outlawed with draconian criminal penalties visited on the doctors and parties involved, courts will still be called upon to decide who the lawful parents really are and who—other than the taxpayers—is obligated to provide maintenance and support for the child. These cases will not go away.[23]

In deciding who the lawful parents really are, courts must ask themselves, 'What makes someone a parent?' As one writer has put it: 'What exactly makes a child "ours"? The DNA we contribute or the time and love? The womb or the sweat equity?'[24] Let us turn to this question.

B. Bases of Parenthood

Mary Shanley extracts four major positions concerning the question of what should give someone a claim to be recognised as a legal parent.[25]

1. Genetic link between the adult and offspring: '[T]his position would make it reasonable to give parental rights to a biological lesbian mother, while denying them to her partner, and to allow gamete donors to seek legal recognition of their parenthood.'[26]

This standard makes biology the most important factor, but biological connection is not identical with genetic connection, as the switched embryo and gestational surrogate cases make clear. What if two women have a claim to be the biological mothers? This leads to the next criterion:

2. Contract or 'intent-based parenthood':[27] '[T]his position would make it possible for a caregiver who was genetically unrelated to a child to assume parental status by agreement or contract.'[28]

---

[23] *Ibid*, 1428–29.
[24] E Goodman, 'In This Test of Family Values, The Answer is Love, not Science' *Boston Globe*, 9 August 1998, E7.
[25] ML Shanley, *Making Babies, Making Families* (Boston, MA, Beacon Press, 2001).
[26] *Ibid*, 129–30.
[27] See, for example, MM Shultz, 'Reproductive Technology and Intent-based Parenthood: An Opportunity for Gender Neutrality' (1990) 2 *Wisconsin L Rev* 297.
[28] ML Shanley, *Making Babies, Making Families* (Boston, MA, Beacon Press, 2001) 130.

3. Social role or parenting. This position is likely to favour the parental claims of adoptive parents over biological parents, and to recognise the parental claims of non-biological caregivers like lesbian co-mothers.[29]

4. Best interest of the child. This position focuses not on the adults' rights, but the child's needs. This gives it a moral significance that is missing in the other three viewpoints. As Mary Shanley explains it:

> The strength of the best interest standard is that it places the child at the center of the analysis and allows (indeed invites) a particularized ruling in the light of the specific facts of a given child's situation. It distinguishes the grievances adults have with one another from their respective abilities to provide for and nurture a child. The best interest standard directs attention not to adults' self-ownership, intent, or action, but to how best to provide a particular child with physical sustenance and psychological nurture.[30]

The best interest of the child has great intuitive appeal since it moves away from the presumption that children are property, to be parcelled out to their rightful owners. However, a best interest standard has its own difficulties. How do we determine where the best interests of children lie? Should we assume that, in the absence of neglect or abuse, children are better off with a biological parent? Or is it more important that children have two parents rather than one? How important is it that their parents be married? Clearly, our views about what is in the best interests of children are going to be affected, perhaps determined, by a host of moral, social, and political views.

While such questions are often raised in the context of artificial reproduction, they can occur in a variety of situations. One situation that has required courts to think long and hard about the components of parenthood are cases in which unwed fathers challenge adoptions to which they have not consented. In thinking about the puzzles raised by ART, it may be helpful to examine these cases, and the principles courts have developed to balance the claims of biology and rearing.

C. Unwed Father Cases

The cases known as 'unwed father cases' or 'thwarted father cases' provide a vehicle for understanding the different components of parenthood. We can begin with one of the more famous ones, the case of Baby Girl Clausen,[31] or Baby Jessica, as the media dubbed her.

---

[29] See, for example, *VC v MJB* 163 NJ 200; 748 A 2d 539 (2000): 'Once a third party has been determined to be a psychological parent to a child, he or she stands in parity with the legal parent, and custody and visitation issues are to be determined on a best interests standard.'

[30] ML Shanley, *Making Babies, Making Families* (Boston, MA, Beacon Press, 2001) 135–36.

[31] *In the Interest of BGC* 496 NW 2d 239.

The nation watched in dismay as 'Baby Jessica' was dragged, sobbing, from the arms of the woman she knew as 'mommy', and returned to her biological parents. The story began in Iowa in 1990 when Cara Clausen, 28 and unmarried, discovered she was pregnant. Cara had just broken up with her boyfriend, Daniel Schmidt, and started dating Scott Seefeldt, so it was Scott's name she put on the birth certificate when her daughter was born.[32] Two days after giving birth on 8 February 1991, Cara waived her parental rights, as did Scott, allowing Roberta and Jan DeBoer, a Michigan couple, who had learned about Cara through an Iowa friend, to take custody of Jessica and begin the process of adopting her. Six days after the birth, Cara regretted her decision and sought to regain custody of her daughter.[33] She began by informing Dan Schmidt, whom she had never told she was pregnant, that she believed he was the father of her child. She went to a support-group meeting of Concerned United Birthparents and heard other mothers' stories of the sorrow they felt at giving up their babies. On 6 March 1991, when Jessica was not yet one month old, Cara filed a request to revoke her consent to custody, confessing to the court that she had lied about the identity of the biological father. Shortly thereafter, Daniel filed an affidavit of paternity, and a petition to vacate the termination of paternal rights and to intervene in the adoption. An Iowa court voided the entire adoption, and the DeBoers were ordered to hand Jessica over. Because Daniel's consent to the adoption had never been obtained, his parental rights could not be terminated absent a showing of abandonment or unfitness, neither of which was established.

The DeBoers decided to fight for Jessica. They argued that Dan was not a fit parent, pointing out that he had had two other children out of wedlock whom he had failed to support and with whom he had only sporadic contact. The Iowa Supreme Court agreed with the DeBoers that they were undoubtedly the better parents, and Jessica would be better off with them.[34] Nevertheless, the court declined to take a 'best interests' approach and ordered custody of the baby to be transferred to Daniel:

> As tempting as it is to resolve this highly emotional issue with one's heart, we do not have the unbridled discretion of a Solomon. Ours is a system of law, and adoptions are solely creatures of statute. As the district court noted, without established procedures to guide courts in such matters, they would 'be engaged in uncontrolled social engineering.' This is not permitted under our law; 'courts are not free to take children from parents simply by deciding another home appears more advantageous.' *In Re Burney,* 259 NW 2d 322, 324 (Iowa 1977).[35]

[32] N Gibbs, 'In Whose Best Interest?' *Time,* 19 July 1993, 46.
[33] DL Forman, 'Unwed Fathers and Adoption: A Theoretical Analysis in Context' (1993–94) 72 *Texas L Rev* 967, 968.
[34] *In the Interest of BGC* 496 NW 2d 239.
[35] *Ibid,* 4.

The DeBoers refused to comply and instead filed a petition in their home state, Michigan, asking that the Michigan court refuse to give full faith and credit to the Iowa decree, since the Iowa court failed to make a 'best interest' determination regarding custody between the biological father and the prospective adoptive parents with whom child had lived almost since birth. By the time the case was over, it had been through five courts, including the United States Supreme Court, Dan and Cara had married and had another child, and Jessica was $2^1/_2$ years old.

An overwhelming majority of the public believed the courts erred in returning Jessica to the Schmidts, taking her from the only parents she had ever known. Harvard law professor Elizabeth Bartholet, author of *Family Bonds: Adoption and the Politics of Parenting*,[36] and an adoptive mother herself, considers it 'outrageous' that the only issue the courts considered was whether Dan Schmidt's rights were appropriately terminated.[37] In an op-ed piece entitled 'Blood Parents vs Real Parents', she writes: 'Dan Schmidt, who hasn't been part of Jessica's life since the sexual act that resulted in her conception over 3 years ago, is termed the "real" or "natural" parent and given an absolute right to claim his genetic product.'[38]

Bartholet regards the DeBoers as the real parents: they were the ones who cared for, loved, and raised Jessica. She regards Dan Schmidt as an interloper into that family unit, a mere 'sperm impregnator',[39] someone who has no significant connection to Jessica. Bartholet's dismissal of genetic connection as a basis for parenthood is shared by many adoptive parents. As one of them put it to me, 'Why should being a parent depend on who screwed whom?' Yet surely genetic connection counts for something. It certainly counts for 'financial fatherhood'. States uniformly require men not married to child's mother to pay child support so long as they are proved to be the biological father. The obligation to pay child support is not alleviated by the fact that the woman misled the man into thinking that she was using birth control.[40] In fact, even being the victim of statutory rape does not alleviate child support obligations. The Kansas Supreme Court upheld a child support order on a 13–year-old boy who, at the age of 12, had a sexual relationship with his 17–year-old babysitter.[41] Other courts have held the same, saying

---

[36] (Boston, MA, Beacon Press, 1999).

[37] N Gibbs, 'In Whose Best Interest?' *Time*, 19 July 1993, 46, 49.

[38] E Bartholet, 'Blood Parents vs Real Parents' *New York Times*, 13 July 1993, A19.

[39] 'Sperm impregnator' was the term used by an adoptive couple to refer to the birth father in *Terraszas v Riggs (In Re Riggs)* 612 SW 2d 461 (Tenn Ct App, 1980) 466; cited in Forman, 'Unwed Fathers and Adoption', above n 33, 980.

[40] An Albuquerque man objected to paying child support after his ex-girlfriend became pregnant because, according to him, she purposely stopped taking birth control pills without telling him. He sued her for breach of contract, fraud, and conversion of property: his sperm. The New Mexico Supreme Court declined to hear the case, giving Kellie Smith her third and final legal victory. See S Sandlin, 'Mom Wins Again in Stolen-sperm Case' *Albuquerque Journal*, 26 April 2001.

[41] *State ex rel Hermesmann v Seyer* 847 P 2d 1273 (Kan, 1993); cited in Forman, 'Unwed Fathers and Adoption', above n 33, 989.

that 'public policy strongly favors legitimization and protection of children' and holding that 'wrongful conduct of one of the parents does not in any way alter the parental obligation to support the child.'[42] Biological fatherhood thus imposes parental obligations, but is it a basis for parental rights?

1. Common Law and Unwed Fathers

Under common law, the father of a child was identified by his relation to the child's mother. If she was his wife, the child was 'his' and he exercised exclusive custodial authority. If she was not his wife, the child was 'filius nullius', a child of no one.

Because unwed fathers had no responsibility for, or rights to, non-marital children, the common law gave all the decision-making power about adoption to the child's mother, which some feminists think is the way it ought to be. However, common law was hardly feminist. It was profoundly patriarchal, and designed to protect men's authority over their wives and marital children, while protecting them from the claims of non-marital children. The husband's authority over his wife at common law was far-reaching. Her legal personality was subsumed in that of her husband. She couldn't enter into contracts or be sued or engage in legal transactions without her husband. He owned outright her moveable property and had control of (though he could not alienate) her real estate: 'So complete was the husband's custodial authority that during his lifetime he had the power to convey his parental rights to a third person without the mother's consent, and could name someone other than the mother to be the child's guardian after his death.'[43]

Common law did not protect the interests of women or children, and ironically, in the modern era, it has not protected the interests of men either, insofar as they have attempted to have a say in the raising of their children when they have not married their mothers.

In part, the common law conception of fatherhood is a result of the difficulty in past eras of ascertaining paternity. As the saying goes, 'Mama's baby, papa's maybe'. Today, of course, the biological father can be determined with near certitude. The question, then, is why have the courts not based paternal rights on genes alone, as they have tended to base paternal responsibilities? The answer, I think, is a recognition that genes alone do not, and should not, determine legal paternity. At stake are more than the interests or rights of biological fathers, but also the interests of children, women, and existing families.

---

[42] *Mercer County Dep't of Social Servs Ex Re Imogene T v Alf M* 589 NYS 2d 288 (Fam Ct, 1992) 289; cited in Forman *ibid*, n 149.

[43] ML Shanley, 'Unwed Fathers' Rights, Adoption, and Sex Equality: Gender Neutrality and the Perpetuation of Patriarchy' (1995) 95 *Columbia L Rev* 60, 68.

The legal status of unwed fathers began to change in 1972, when in a series of cases, the Supreme Court held that while biological fatherhood by itself does not confer parental rights, biological connection does give unwed fathers the opportunity to establish a parental role. The first case in which the Supreme Court considered custodial rights of unwed fathers was *Stanley v Illinois*.[44] Mr Stanley had lived with his three biological children and their mother intermittently for 18 years. When she died, Illinois declared the children wards of the state and placed them with court-appointed guardians without hearing as to Stanley's fitness as a parent. Stanley protested, arguing that Illinois law denied him equal protection of the laws since neither unwed mothers, nor married fathers or mothers, could be deprived of custody of their children unless shown to be unfit. Illinois argued that Stanley's fitness was irrelevant because an unwed father was not a 'parent'; an unwed biological father was presumed unfit because he had not married the mother.

The Supreme Court rejected Illinois's argument. It held that the failure to provide a hearing on parental fitness violated the Equal Protection Clause of the Fourteenth Amendment, because it treated Stanley differently from married fathers and unmarried mothers, and it violated the Due Process Clause because it deprived Stanley of a fundamental liberty interest (that of a man in the children he has sired and raised) without a hearing.[45]

Chief Justice Burger disagreed. He held, dissenting, that Stanley's right to equal protection was not violated because there are relevant distinctions between biological fatherhood and biological motherhood. Not only are fathers harder to identify but, more importantly, the biological link between mother and child has social significance: 'The biological role of the mother in carrying and nursing an infant creates stronger bonds between her and the child than the bonds resulting from the male's often casual encounter.'[46]

In other words, gestational connection makes for a stronger claim to parental rights than genetics alone. Why should this be the case? One answer is 'sweat equity': the mother's biological role involves a lot more work than the father's, because it includes 9 months of gestation, labour, and birth. Another answer alludes to the prenatal bonding between mother and child. Not only does separating the child from its mother impose emotional harms on the woman; it also deprives the child of a mother it has already come to know. Recent research indicates that the fetus, late in gestation, is aware of its mother's heartbeat and respiration, recognises her voice, and shortly after birth has memorised her smell. A third answer, which in some ways combines the first two, considers gestation as a kind of rearing, which includes both work and psychological bonds.

---

[44] *Stanley v Illinois* 405 US 645 (1972).

[45] *Ibid*, 657–58. See also ML Shanley's discussion in 'Unwed Fathers' Rights, Adoption, and Sex Equality', n 43 above.

[46] *Stanley v Illinois* 405 US 645 (1972) 665–66 (Burger CJ, dissenting).

Burger's argument that states may justifiably deprive unwed fathers of the right to consent to adoption, because fatherhood is different from motherhood, is not based only on the fact that mothers gestate. In addition, he argued that most unwed mothers exhibit concern for their offspring either permanently or at least until safely placed for adoption, while unwed fathers rarely burden either the mother or the child with their attentions or loyalties: 'Centuries of human experience buttress this view of the realities of human conditions and suggest that unwed mothers of illegitimate children are generally more dependable protectors of their children than are unwed fathers.'[47]

Burger rejected the majority's characterisation of Stanley as a good father, noting that after the death of the children's mother, Stanley transferred the care of the children to another couple. He made no efforts to be recognised as the father until the state became aware that no adult had any legal obligation for the support of the children. At that time, Stanley made himself known, but only, according to Burger, because he feared losing welfare payments if others were named guardians of the children.

As in many of these cases, there are different versions of the stories, and the differences make a difference. But even if Burger was right that Stanley was not, in fact, a good father, that is no reason to deny Stanley the chance to prove otherwise, still less is it a reason to assume that all unmarried fathers are unfit. The state presumed that Peter Stanley was an unfit father, simply because he was not married to the children's mother. That presumption, I maintain, is unfair not only to Stanley and other unwed fathers, but also to their children.

Both *Stanley* and *Baby Jessica* can be faulted for an exclusive focus on the rights of the biological father; both left out a crucial element, namely, the welfare of the children. On the face of it, depriving children of the man they consider to be their father, and putting them into foster care, hardly can be in their interest. Their welfare is as important as, if not more important than, whether Stanley was denied equal protection.

2. Are Rights the Problem?

A number of commentators argue that 'rights talk' distorts the issues in these kinds of cases.[48] Some object to rights talk generally,[49] especially when notions like family and parenthood are involved.[50] These critics argue that a rights-based

---

[47] *Ibid.*

[48] See, for example, WA Fitzgerald, 'Maturity, Difference, and Mystery: Children's Perspectives and the Law' (1994) 36 *Arizona L Rev* 11; and M Minow, *Making All the Difference: Inclusion, Exclusion, and American Law* (Ithaca, NY, Cornell University Press, 1990).

[49] MA Glendon, *Rights Talk: The Impoverishment of Political Discourse* (New York, NY, Free Press, 1991).

[50] See TA Murray, *The Worth of a Child* (Berkeley, CA, University of California Press, 1996).

conception is grounded in notions of exchange and individual rights and implicitly encourages parental possessiveness and self-centredness. Some do not reject rights altogether.[51] They acknowledge that appeals to rights can provide effective tools for protecting vulnerable individuals, including children. Nevertheless, they remain suspicious of the ways in which rights talk can distort matters. Katharine Bartlett writes: 'Legal disputes over parenthood are an example of how the presentation of claims in terms of individual rights may force controversies into a framework that misstates the harm to be avoided and undermines the values we should promote.'[52]

In my view, this is an over-simplification. The problem is not framing the issue in terms of competing individual rights, but rather that the rights of children are too often given short shrift. There are a number of reasons for this. Historically, of course, children were treated virtually as property. Moreover, constitutional rights, such as equal protection and due process, have very little to do with the rights that children have to loving parents and a stable family. Constrained to analyse cases in these terms, it is little wonder that custody decisions often have nothing to say about the impact on the child. Rejecting this approach, one commentator writes:

> Children are not chattels in which adults have rights. Children 'belong' to no one but themselves. Parental rights doctrines should be seen as a way of protecting the child's right to parental relationships free from unwarranted intrusion by the state or third parties. To the extent that a recognition of parental rights would be adverse to the child's interests, the parental rights must give way to the child's best interests.[53]

An important element of a best interest analysis would be the rearing role a biological parent has played, since children are likely to be psychologically damaged if deprived of someone who has played an important role in their upbringing. In cases after *Stanley*, the courts have begun to acknowledge the importance of rearing, drawing distinctions between unwed biological fathers who were involved in raising the children and those who were not.

In *Quilloin v Walcott*,[54] the Court determined that an adoption could take place without an unwed father's consent where he had 'never shouldered any significant responsibility with respect to the daily supervision, education, protection, or care of the child',[55] did not now seek custody, and where adoption did no more than

---

[51] KT Bartlett, 'Re-expressing Parenthood' (1988) 98 *Yale Law Journal* 293. See also Minow, *Making All the Difference*, above n 48, 303–04.

[52] Bartlett *ibid*, 295–96.

[53] J Leach Richards, 'Redefining Parenthood: Parental Rights Versus Child Rights' (1994) 40 *Wayne L Rev* 1227, 1271–72.

[54] *Quilloin v Walcott* 434 US 246 (1978).

[55] *Ibid*, 256.

legally recognise the existing living situation of the child and a family unit already in existence. In *Lehr v Robertson*,[56] an unwed father objected against the adoption of his biological daughter by her step-father, claiming that he had a liberty interest in a relationship with his child and that the state's failure to provide him notice of her pending adoption violated equal protection because it required the consent of the biological mother but not the biological father for adoption. The Court rejected Lehr's claim. According to the Court, it is only when an unwed father demonstrates a full commitment to the responsibilities of parenthood by participating in the rearing of his child that his interest in personal contact with the child acquires substantial protection under the Due Process clause. He must act as a father toward his child. The biological connection by itself does not merit constitutional protection, but merely provides the man with a unique 'opportunity' to develop a relationship with his child. One commentator remarks: 'The advent of this "biology plus" formula led many to conclude that the Court had ushered in a new era recognizing the rights of fathers based on the parent-child relationship.'[57]

Nevertheless, it is important to recognise that the 'biology plus' formula focused on the father's right to the child, not on what would be best for the child.

The most recent unwed father case decided by the Supreme Court is *Michael H v Gerald D*.[58] The novel factor in this case is that the child, Victoria, was conceived through an adulterous relationship between Michael H and Carole, who was married to Gerald D. Carole continued to live with Gerald throughout the pregnancy and for five months after the child's birth, and Gerald believed the child was his. During the next three years, although Gerald and Carole remained married, she and the child lived sporadically with Gerald, Michael, and others. When Victoria was 3 years old, Carole reconciled with Gerald. They had two more children together. Both Gerald and Carole opposed Michael's petition to establish his paternity. Although Michael engaged in some social parenting and at times held himself out as a parent, Gerald appears to have been the predominant social parent.

Scalia's plurality opinion views the case as pitting a marital father's rights against those of an 'adulterous natural father', who traditionally has never merited rights. Some commentators object to Scalia's analysis as overly moralistic and conservative. However, it can be argued that children should be protected from third parties whose intervention threatens the integrity of their families. Once again, the problem with the analysis is not Scalia's defence of the marital family against an outsider, but rather that the opinion does not focus on, or even consider, Victoria's interests. The decision stressed Gerald's status as exclusive rights-bearer according to history and tradition, rather than the importance of his parental role to the family and to Victoria. Barbara Woodhouse comments:

---

[56] *Lehr v Robertson* 463 US 248 (1983).
[57] *Ibid.*
[58] *Michael H v Gerald D* 491 US 110 (1989).

If the law were to adopt a child's perspective, however, the question would not be whether each of the daddies in Michael H has the right to Victoria's company, but whether two daddies are better than one. ... If parental rights flow from children's needs, as I have argued, then the right of the biological father is defeated not by the right of the marital father but by the fact that the child already has a father who, not unimportantly, is the mother's mate and the father of the child's siblings. The child not only does not need but might be harmed by acquiring a competing father.[59]

Although I agree with Woodhouse that the focus should be on the child's interests, this case exposes some of the difficulties with a best-interests standard. Woodhouse suggests that a child may be harmed by having two daddies. In contrast, Alta Charo suggests that perhaps 'you can never have too many parents to love you.'[60] Who is right?

D. The Best Interest of the Child

The 'best interest of the child' standard is clearly an improvement over the outdated patriarchal, possessive model of children as property. Nevertheless, the best-interest-approach is not without problems. It is often criticised as vague, difficult to apply, and reflective of social prejudices (although it can equally be used to refute a socially conservative approach).[61] Some decided cases certainly give cause for concern that a best interest standard may be used against poor and working class people, as well as members of a racial minority.[62] However, that is not an argument against the best-interest standard, but against its misuse. Surely, love and caring *are* more important than material goods when determining a child's best interest. But even when best interest is based on the right values, it remains extremely difficult to determine. For example, how should we weigh the value of remaining with one's biological or 'birth' family against remaining with parents to whom one has become psychologically attached? On the one hand, there is

---

[59] BB Woodhouse, 'Hatching the Egg: A Child-centered Perspective on Parents' Rights' (1993) 14 *Cardozo L Rev* 1746, 1858.

[60] RA Charo, 'And Baby Makes Three—Or Four, or Five, or Six: Redefining the Family After the Reprotech Revolution' (1992–93) 7 *Wisconsin's Women's Law Journal* 1, 23.

[61] *Ibid*. Charo argues that the refusal to recognise non-traditional families, and the fact that multiple adults sometimes play important roles in children's lives, can be harmful to children.

[62] In an unreported case, a Chinese child who had been placed with foster parents on what the birth parents understood was a temporary basis was not returned to her birth parents despite the fact that there was no evidence that the birth parents were unable to care for their child. For the discussion of the case in the press, see A Hart, 'Chinese Parents Not Tricked, Judge Says in Custody Case' *New York Times*, 13 May 2004, A16, and A Jacobs, 'Chinese and American Cultures Clash in Custody Battle for Girl, 5' *New York Times*, 2 March 2004, A14.

considerable evidence that adopted children often seek information about or contact with their birth families, suggesting that birth families do matter. On the other hand, the ties between adopted children and their parents can be just as strong as those between biological parents and children. How can we possibly know what will be best for the child? According to news reports, Baby Jessica—now Anna Jacqueline Schmidt—has made a happy adjustment to her new life. So, is she better off now, and how can we know?

Or consider a young unmarried woman who becomes pregnant. She wants what's best for her child. Should she attempt to raise him by herself, or give him up for adoption? People have extremely strong views on the topic, but I do not think that the evidence is decisive, one way or the other. What I am suggesting is that there may not be a 'best interest of the child', or at least not a discoverable one. If the child stays with his mother, he will become one sort of person, with one set of interests. If he is adopted, he will very likely become another, with entirely different interests. We cannot decide which choice will serve *his* best interests, as the interests themselves will change, depending on the family and the environment in which he grows up.

But if we cannot know what is in the child's best interest, at least we can try to minimise the harm to children. Prolonged custody battles, such as occurred in the Baby Jessica case, clearly are harmful to children. For this, the DeBoers must take much of the responsibility. It was the DeBoers who appealed each decision, dragging out the legal proceedings until Jessica was two-and-a-half. I think it is ironic that the basis of their claim that the Michigan court should not uphold the decision of the Iowa courts was that those courts did not consider the best interests of the child. Can their decision to continue the fight for Jessica, given its shaky legal basis, be reasonably seen as in her best interests?

The Baby Jessica case provokes allusions to the biblical story of King Solomon who had to decide which of two women was a baby's real mother. As a child, I never understood why his offer to cut the baby in half demonstrated his wisdom; why would even a phony mother want half a dead baby? Yet the story has relevance for us because it shows how adults, bent on parenthood, can put their own needs first, to the detriment of the child. Psychologist Gerald Koocher says that Jessica became a pawn.

> The sad thing is that each set of adults has their own agenda. The DeBoers want and need a child, and she's it. And the Schmidts, she's their flesh and blood, and they want to hold on to her.[63]

This may not be entirely fair to the DeBoers, who undoubtedly fell in love with Jessica (or 'bonded', to use the psychological terminology) as soon as they took her

---

[63] Quoted in D Terry, 'Tug-of-War Ends as Child Is Moved' *New York Times*, 3 August 1993, A13.

home. She was not just 'a child' to them, even at the beginning. Nevertheless, for her sake, they should have returned her to her biological parents when she was a tiny infant, before she became attached to them.

Deborah Forman says, correctly, I think, that the Baby Jessica case was a disaster, but 'it was caused less by the decision to protect an unwed father's rights than by procedural problems with the case.'[64] These procedural problems would be greatly reduced if the law on adoption did not vary from state to state. This would eliminate the temptation to 'forum-shop', as the DeBoers did. Another welcome change would be a reasonable waiting period before an adoption is final, as is the law in the United Kingdom. I suggest one month, on the ground that a woman who is still post-partum should not be asked to make an irrevocable decision about giving up her child.

The Uniform Adoption Act (UAA) requires, as a general rule, that both parents must consent to their child's adoption. However, it distinguishes the men who manifest parenting behaviour and have therefore earned the right to withhold consent from a proposed adoption from the men who fail to perform parental duties and may therefore be denied the right to veto a proposed adoption.[65] The Act pays special attention to 'thwarted fathers' who have been prevented by the misdeeds of others from functioning as parents. A thwarted father who wants to block a proposed adoption of a child must prove a compelling reason for not having performed parental duties. Even if this is the case, he will not succeed if there is clear and convincing evidence that it would be detrimental to the child to deny the adoption. The Act makes decisions about adoption and custody focus on the needs and welfare of the child, not simply on the rights of adults.

E. Conclusion

Are there lessons from the unwed father cases for understanding parenthood in the context of artificial reproduction? Clearly there are important differences. For example, the notion of intent, so central to sorting out parenthood in the collaborative reproduction cases plays virtually no role in the adoption cases. Nevertheless, a theme common to both situations in the importance of parenting, of being a parent, that is, caring for and loving a child. However, the importance of parenting is not that it entitles a person to rights in the child. Rather, parenting is important because of its crucial importance in the life of a child. The potential

---

[64] Forman, 'Unwed Fathers and Adoption', above n 33, 970.

[65] The Uniform Adoption Act (UAA) was promulgated in 1994 by the National Conference of Commissioners on Uniform State Laws (NCCUSL), but has not become state law in many US jurisdictions. For further information see http://encyclopedia.adoption.com/entry/Uniform-Adoption-Act-UAA/363/1.html.

dangers of a best-interest approach can be avoided if best interest is understood in terms of psychological well-being, not material wealth.

The thwarted father cases are among the most troubling. The presumption that children belong with, and are better off with, their natural, biological parents is a reasonable one. Moreover, the fathers in these cases were undeniably wronged. Through no fault of their own they were deprived of the opportunity to play a parental role. However, if we focus on the child's best interests, then we will not take a child from the only parents she has ever known in order to do justice to her biological father. Whatever benefit to the child would come from knowing her biological parents, it is outweighed by the psychological damage resulting from taking her from the people she regards as her parents. Thus, it is inconsistent with a child-centred approach.

The San Francisco Court of Appeals based its decision in *KM v EG* entirely on the agreement between the two women that EG would be the sole legal mother, and on the egg donor form KM signed, waiving all parental rights. The court acknowledged that the children would be harmed by being deprived of someone who had been a part of their family all their lives, but said that the children's welfare could be considered only *after* parenthood is determined. KM's genetic connection to the twins might have given her a claim to be a parent, if she had intended from the outset to be a rearing parent. Since she had waived her parental rights, and agreed that only EG was the legal mother, KM's claim to be their mother was rejected. Therefore the best interests of the children were irrelevant and could not be considered.

The test of intent-based parenthood, established in *Johnson* and followed in *KM*, is a reasonable way of protecting those who contract with egg donors and surrogates from subsequent claims to offspring. However, this case was not comparable to the normal case of egg donation, where the donor has *only* a genetic connection and plays no parental role. KM was not just an egg donor; she was EG's lover, a family member, and a co-parent. It is hardly surprising that KM came to regard as her own children the twins she helped to create and to raise. She can hardly be blamed for trying to stop EG from taking them away. The psychological counsellor they saw should have foreseen that this arrangement was a disaster waiting to happen, and have strongly advised them against it.

The refusal to consider KM a parent stems from the fact that this was a lesbian couple. If the couple had been heterosexual, the man who fathered the twins (whether coitally or by artificial insemination), and who participated in their rearing, would certainly have been recognised as the twins' legal father, no matter what their agreement or what forms he signed. And if the children's father were married to EG, there would be absolutely no question that he was the natural, biological, and legal father. Though EG asked KM to marry her, and they exchanged rings, the marriage was merely symbolic, without legal force. If they were legally married, KM would have had the same rights as a member of any other divorced couple. This is another reason in favour of same-sex marriage, as it would protect the interests of children when their parents separate.

In the normal case, where the gamete donor plays no parental role, intent is the correct basis for determining parenthood. But once a biological parent is given the opportunity to play a parental role, that role, and its impact on the children, cannot be ignored. As Alta Charo puts it:

> Perhaps it is time to take a great leap in family law ... . Once a parent enters into a child's life, whether by virtue of genes, gestation, or declaration, there is an unbreakable bond of psychology and history between the two. ... In an age when courts have been forced to manage the untidy families created by divorce and remarriage it is simply not enough to argue that it will be difficult to organize a regime of family law that accommodates the permanency of both contractual and biological (both genetic and gestational) ties. And having admitted already that step-parents and grandparents are indeed real family members, what legitimate obstacle remains to accepting the adults who enter family arrangements via group marriage or homosexual marriage? Surely we can be creative enough to create a new category, somewhere between custodial parent and legal stranger, that captures these relationships.[66]

It may be objected that too many parents will be confusing and stressful for children. But I suspect that children are more likely to be damaged by the feeling that they have been abandoned by those who have played a parental role than by having multiple individuals who wish to remain in their lives, in some form or other. The insistence that children can have only one mother and one father is not necessarily in their best interests. However, this is an empirical question, and each case needs to be looked at on the merits. Woodhouse is probably right that the child's interests in *Lehr v Robertson* are not served by the intrusion of her mother's ex-lover into their family.

Winston Churchill once said that 'democracy is the worst form of government, except all those other forms that have been tried from time to time.'[67] Given the difficulties and potential pitfalls, the same might be said of a best interest approach to determining parenthood. The correct approach is not to give up on a best-interests approach, but to try to minimise its pitfalls. In the words of the *Buzzanca* court: 'A child cannot be ignored.'

---

[66] Charo, 'And Baby Makes Three—Or Four, or Five, or Six', above n 61, 22.
[67] *Hansard*, 11 November 1947, col 206, cited in T Augarde (ed), *The Oxford Dictionary of Modern Quotations* (Oxford, OUP, 1991) 55.

Part III

Reproductive Autonomy and Parenthood

8

Parenting by Being; Parenting by Doing—In Search of Principles for Founding Families

JUDITH MASSON

Three interrelated concepts are used to define the position of parents *vis-a-vis* their children: Being a parent, having parental responsibility and having Article 8 rights under the European Convention on Human Rights,[1] *ie,* the right to respect for family life, for the relationship with your child. These overlap. Some parents have all three, but some biological and legal fathers (for example a man who has fathered a child as the result of a brief sexual encounter) have only the status of parent without any associated rights. Also, non-parents can have rights to family life and/or parental responsibility, but their parental responsibility is narrower than that of a parent, usually ends when the child reaches age 16 and is automatically revoked if the child becomes subject to a care order. On this basis those who are 'social' but not 'legal' parents may appear 'second class'—at least in comparison with those who are *both* legal *and* social parents.

Being a parent gives only limited rights—inheritance rights,[2] the right to apply to the court for any order concerning the child, and the right to be consulted if the child is looked after by a local authority.[3] It also imposes a duty to provide financial support.[4] But it is an enduring status, ending only through death or the child's

---

[1] Convention for the Protection of Human Rights and Fundamental Freedoms, ETS No 5, adopted on 4 November 1950 and entered into force on 3 September 1953.

[2] The Family Law Reform Act 1969 extended inheritance rights to fathers of children born outside marriage. Children necessarily die intestate; the parent's legal right to inherit is unrelated to the care they have provided: *Bouette v Rose* [2000] Ch 662.

[3] Children Act 1989, ss 10(4), 22(4)(b).

[4] Child Support Act 1991, s 1 and under various earlier matrimonial family proceedings and social security statutes. The common law duty was largely unenforceable.

adoption. *Parental responsibility* gives rights to make decisions about the child— including appointing a guardian or consenting to the child's adoption. For mothers (and fathers married to the child's mother) parental responsibility is an essential and integral element to being a parent. But for unmarried fathers it is *additional*, acquired only after the child's birth, by the joint action of father and mother or a court order, and is also revocable by the court.[5] *Family life,* the basis of Article 8 rights, depends on 'the real existence in practice of close personal ties'[6] between the parties. The need for real relationships may preclude the existence of 'family life' between people related by blood or marriage. However, the European Court of Human Rights has stated that:

> the notion of 'the family' ... is not confined solely to marriage-based relationships and may encompass other *de facto* 'family' where the parties are living together outside marriage. A child born out of such a relationship is *ipso iure* part of that 'family' unit from the moment of the birth and by the very fact of it. There thus exists between the child and his parents a bond amounting to family life even if at the time of the birth his or her parents are no longer cohabiting or their relationship has then ended.[7]

Article 8 brings positive as well as negative obligations;[8] the state must facilitate the development of family life between the parties, not merely refrain from interfering with it.

This chapter seeks to explore the law and policy behind the identification and recognition of these three sets of rights within various different families, including those created through assisted conception and adoption, within or without marriage. Particularly, it examines the extent to which decisions about parental status and rights relate to what we do or who we are. *Parenting by doing* acknowledges the reality of looking after children by recognising adult–child relationships. *Parenting by being* reflects a wish to identify for the child and the state people with responsibility for the child, regardless of the practical role they are playing or want to play in the child's life. In order to do this, the chapter examines the distinctions made between different people who may play a parenting role and the different processes applied to those who seek to become parents through fertility or adoption services.

Presently, the legal relations which a man has with a child born to his partner differ greatly depending on his biological connection, or absence of it, to that child, the relationship he has with the child's mother (married or not) and the

---

[5] Children Act 1989, ss 3, 4.

[6] The Commission in *K v UK* (1987) 50 D & R 199.

[7] *Keegan v Ireland* Series A no 290 (1994) 18 EHRR 342, para 44; see also *X, Y and Z v UK* Reports of Judgments and Decisions 1997–I [1997] 2 FLR 892, 900 where the mother's transsexual partner who had acted as 'father' to the child since birth had established the necessary ties.

[8] *X and Y v the Netherlands* Series A no 91(1986) 8 EHRR 235, para 23.

context (if one may put it like this) of the child's creation (through sexual relations, or through medically assisted reproduction). The same is true for the same-sex partners of women giving birth to a child. Increasingly, the distinctions on which these differentiations in treatment rest become fragile, and their outcomes more difficult to justify.

It is thus unsurprising that the legal framework for family life is undergoing substantial transformation, necessitating a reconsideration of the basis for recognising or not recognising parenting and the consequences of parenthood. Since 2005, the Adoption and Children Act 2002 permits unmarried couples (heterosexual or same-sex) to adopt children jointly and thus to become (co-)parents.[9] The Act also facilitates adoption by step-parents by enabling step-parents to acquire the status of parent by adoption without a need either to be married to the parent or for the parent to adopt their own child.[10] In addition, the Civil Partnership Act 2004 enables same-sex couples to have a recognised relationship with identical legal consequences to marriage. Civil partnership thus gives obligations in respect of children but neither the rights nor status of parenthood even where both partners were treated together to achieve a pregnancy.[11] The law and practice of assisted reproduction is also under review.[12] Rules developed to protect or privilege marriage will look out of place, or even discriminatory, when same-sex unions and unmarried parenting are recognised. Similarly, the creation by law of heterosexual families where the adults have duties to children, but not towards each other, and the more limited protection if the relationship breaks down which that entails, raises questions about the extent the state is safeguarding child welfare in the new arrangements it has approved. This chapter seeks to find a coherent approach to recognising parents which focuses on their children's welfare.[13]

---

[9] Adoption and Children Act 2002, ss 50, 144(4).

[10] Adoption and Children Act 2002, s 52(2). Where the step-parent is married or in a civil partnership, he or she will be able to obtain parental responsibility by agreement with the child's parents (Adoption and Children Act, s 112, adding s 4A to the Children Act 1989; subject to amendment for civil partnerships).

[11] The Human Fertilisation and Embryology Authority commented on the differential treatment of civil partners and husbands or unmarried partners in its response to the DTI Women and Equality Unit, *Consultation on Civil Partnership* (2003) paras 8–12. The government's response indicated that its intention was to maintain the distinction and treat the civil partner as the step-parent of their partner's children (DTI, Women and Equality Unit, *Responses to Civil Partnership* (2003) 29 and 40).

[12] The review is conducted by the House of Commons, Select Committee on Science and Technology Inquiry on Human Reproductive Technologies. The Department of Health stated in its written evidence that it will consider the need for changes to the Human Fertilisation and Embryology Act 1990 'to better recognise the wider range of people who seek and receive assisted reproduction treatment in the 21st century.' para 21. For further information see http://www.publications.parliament.uk/pa/cm/cmsctech.htm.

[13] In *X, Y and Z v UK* the European Court of Human Rights commented that '[t]he community as a whole has an interest in maintaining a coherent system of family law which places the best interests of the child at the forefront' [1997] 2 FLR 892, 903.

A. Parenting from Birth

The relationship between child and parent needs to be established no later than birth so that it is clear who has the right to make decisions about the child's care. The child too has an interest in the protection of this link because it offers the possibility of a unique relationship, which carries important messages about identity and belonging.[14] A status based on *being* can clearly operate from birth, as can a status based on the fact of giving birth. However, if recognition depends on practical parenting, time will be needed to demonstrate this, and there will be a period while the relationship is developing when it will not have become sufficiently established for full recognition. If the potential parent dies during this period the child may not be able to have the relationship recognised.[15] If parental responsibility does not follow automatically from the status of parent, there may similarly be a period of vulnerability for a parent or carer without parental responsibility.[16]

If sufficient ties are established for the creation of 'family life' between the adult and child, the state is under an obligation to support it: 'The State must act in a manner calculated to enable that tie to be developed and legal safeguards must be established that render possible as from the moment of birth or as soon as practical thereafter the child's integration into his family.'[17]

Since 2001, the European Court of Human Rights has been asked to consider four separate cases where babies were removed from their parents at birth.[18] On each occasion it has commented that removal of a child from the parents is a 'Draconian power' which requires the clearest justification. It appears then that family life with a parent is capable of being established at birth. This point was reinforced by Hale LJ (as she then was) when considering the rights of a mother

---

[14] Convention on the Rights of the Child, adopted by General Assembly Resolution 44/25 of 20 November 1989 and entered into force on 2 September 1990, Arts 7 and 8. For in-depth discussion, see A Bainham, 'Birthrights? The Rights and Obligations Associated with the Birth of a Child' (in this collection).

[15] For example, if the (unmarried) father dies before the birth is registered it was not possible until the introduction of the Family Law Act 1986 to have his name included on the birth certificate. The Family Law Act 1986 now allows the mother to obtain a declaration of paternity and apply for the father's name to be included. In *Haas v the Netherlands* ECHR [2004] 1 FLR 673, the alleged father's death before he formally recognised the child, and his cremation, meant that paternity could never be established.

[16] See *B v UK* [2000] 1 FLR 1 where the father could not use the Hague Convention on International Child Abduction to have the child returned to the UK because as an unmarried father he did not have 'rights of custody'. The application to the ECHR was declared inadmissible on the basis that distinctions between married and unmarried fathers are justifiable.

[17] *Kroon v the Netherlands* Series A no 297 (1994) 19 EHRR 263, para 32.

[18] *K and T v Finland* ECHR 2000–VII [2000] 2 FLR 79; *P, C and S v UK* ECHR 2002–VI [2002] 2 FLR 631; *Covezzi and Morselli v Italy*, Application no 52763/99 (unreported); *Haase v Germany* ECHR 2004-[2004] 2 FLR 39.

who rejected her child and requested adoption: 'were it otherwise, the state could always interfere without fear of contravening art 8 by removing the child the moment they were born.'[19]

The main part of this chapter is devoted to an analysis how the law presently recognises people as parents in the three different 'dimensions' highlighted at the outset, and whether such recognition should be expanded to other 'candidates for parental recognition', or conversely withheld from some who do acquire this status under the present law, in the interest of the child. But before I begin with this analysis, I need to make a general comment about the child's perspective and the need to be watchful of the way in which the interests of the child feature in debates about the legal recognition of parenthood.

There is a danger in allowing arguments by adults based on children's interests—adults may, consciously or unconsciously, seek to use children to assert claims which serve adults' positions but do not promote either children's welfare or their autonomy. It might be asserted that children have an interest in having more rather than fewer parents. This is certainly arguable. More parents may provide greater protection against the vicissitudes of life and bring potentially greater material benefits (but only if the number of children is constant!). However, in a society where almost all children have one or two parents, they may not have an interest in having more, because this will distinguish them from other children, and children frequently report that they do not want to be different. Similarly, the greater the number of parents the more possibility of dispute, and being the focus of conflict is damaging to children.[20] Children have a key interest in their parentage being undisputed. Family disputes undermine carers' ability to care, sap their financial resources and force children to divide their loyalties and sometimes their lives.[21] They also have an interest in their parentage being accepted willingly rather than imposed, and in knowing who their parents are.[22] The aim for law and law reform must be to identify the right parents for children—those whose identification as parent is most likely to secure a stable and happy upbringing for the child—and not 'as many parents as possible' for them.

---

[19] *Re B* [2001] 1 FLR 589, 599.

[20] B Rodgers and J Pryor, *Divorce and Separation: The Outcomes for Children* (York, Joseph Rowntree Foundation, 1998) 41.

[21] C Smart and B Neale, *Family Fragments?* (Cambridge, Polity, 1999); C Smart, 'Children and the Transformation of Family Law' in J Dewar and S Parker (eds), *Family Law: Processes, Practices and Pressures* (Oxford, Hart Publishing, 2003) 223, 226–32.

[22] Substantially more adoptees have sought access to their birth records than was originally expected; see R Rushbrooke *Population Trends* 104 (2001) 31. The need for those born following DI to knowledge of their genetic identity has been recognised through the (prospective) ending of donor anonymity for children conceived with gametes donated after April 2005 (see *HFEA (Disclosure of Donor Information) Regulations 2004* and statement by Melanie Johnson, Minister of Health, 21 January 2004).

B. Acquiring the Status of Parent
by Doing and by Being

1. Mothers

As far as mothers are concerned, parenting seems always to have been a matter of *doing*—giving birth to the child. Even under Roman law motherhood was established by proof of giving birth; there was a system of birth witnessing to ensure that the child was produced by the woman claiming to be the mother.[23] Recognising as mother the woman who had given birth to the child also ensured that any child had an identifiable mother from the moment of birth. Given that fatherhood (and the child's legitimacy) depended on the man's relationship to the mother, it was crucial for both that motherhood was easily and definitively proved. The common law produced what has later been termed a 'bright line'[24] rule that had the advantage of certainty.

Before the development of reproductive medicine there was no other candidate for mother. However, some cultures gave special recognition to other women who nurtured a baby, again recognising *doing*. For example, under Islamic law a woman who has breast-fed a child has a special status.[25] The possibility of egg (or embryo) donation created another possible candidate—the genetic mother—but the gestational link was seen as a better basis for maternity because it provided certainty from the moment of birth.[26] Recognising the gestational mother rather than the genetic mother also served to discourage surrogacy. As the mother, the woman who has given birth to the child has a claim to care for the child that is superior to that of any other woman.

2. Fathers

Historically, the common law presumption that the mother's husband was the child's father avoided the difficulty of establishing paternity and the severe stigma of illegitimacy. There was no alternative; not until the late 20th century could genetic paternity be established reliably through scientific tests. The presumption

---

[23] Justinian XXV, iv i 10, cited in S Cretney, J Masson and R Bailey-Harris, *Principles of Family Law*, 7th edn (London, Sweet & Maxwell, 2003) 523.

[24] Evidence of the Head of Section with responsibility for policy on assisted reproduction, Department of Health in *Evans v Amicus Healthcare Ltd; Hadley v Midlands Fertility Services Ltd* [2004] 1 FLR 67 (FD) para 187.

[25] C Hamilton (tr), *The Hedaya* (Lahore, Premier Book House, 1957) at xiii; SS Ali, *Gender and Human Rights in Islam and International Law: Equal Before Allah, Unequal Before Man?* (Dordrecht Kluwer, 2000) 154–57.

[26] *Report of the Committee of Inquiry into Human Fertilisation and Embryology* (Cmd 9314, 1984), para 6.6–6.8 (the 'Warnock Report').

was not absolute, but a high standard of proof was required; so, effectively, *being* the mother's husband made the man the father of her child. If the child was born outside marriage, the fact of procreation was irrelevant because the common law made no provision for recognising the relationships of a *filius nullius*.

These ways of establishing parentage ensured that, for any child born within marriage, the identity of both the child's parents was determinable once pregnancy was confirmed and known from the moment of birth.

The development of donor insemination from the 1940s did not lead to consideration of the issue of the paternity of the children that resulted until 1960.[27] The common law presumption served to provide a father; and the stigma of infertility, combined with a practice of mixing the husband's sperm with the donor's which allowed men to believe the child was genetically theirs, operated as strong discouragement to any husband who might want to reject the child. The Feversham Committee, established to consider donor insemination in humans 'viewed the practice of AID with something approaching repugnance'[28] and in order to discourage it, specifically recommended that the laws relating to paternity and birth registration should not be amended.[29] There was no legislation; children conceived by donor insemination were illegitimate even though the mother's husband consented; they were 'children of the family' and so the husband was liable to maintain them. Adoption was the only process whereby the husband could become the child's father but registration of the husband as the father appears to have been common practice.[30]

Techniques for paternity testing, particularly the discovery of a method of matching DNA samples, made it possible to establish genetic paternity. Basing the status of the father on his relationship with the mother was no longer tenable; scientific discovery had made the presumption readily rebuttable. Not only was it possible to disprove that the husband was the father, another man could be proved, positively, to be the father. Paternity *by being* shifted its focus from the establishing the man's relationship with the mother to establishing a genetic relationship with the child. In practice, the relationship with the mother remained crucial. The majority of children are still born within marriage, and evidence of paternity is found on the birth certificate where inclusion of the man's name requires proof of marriage, the agreement of the mother or a court order establishing paternity.[31]

---

[27] *Report of the Departmental Committee on Human Artificial Insemination* (Cmd 1105, 1960) (the 'Feversham Report').

[28] S Cretney, *Family Law in the Twentieth Century: A History* (Oxford, OUP, 2003) 542.

[29] (1960 Cmd 1105) (the 'Feversham Report') para 187.

[30] M Barton, 'AID as an Alternative to Adoption' in Association of British Adoption Agencies, *Child Adoption* (1977) 168–71 notes that to use adoption would be 'to defeat the purpose of the whole operation—the completion of a normal family with no possibility of the offspring questioning his origin'.

[31] Births and Deaths Registration Act 1953, s 10.

Donor insemination was reconsidered by the Law Commission in its *Report on Illegitimacy*.[32] Following its recommendations, provision was included in the Family Law Reform Act 1987 that where a child was born as a result of donor insemination the mother's husband would be the child's father unless 'he proved that he did not consent' to her insemination.[33] Following the recommendations of the Warnock Committee, the Human Fertilisation and Embryology Act (HFE Act) 1990 extended paternity to cover other methods of assisted reproduction,[34] enabling the law to keep pace with scientific and clinical developments. More problematically and controversially, the Act also allowed for non-genetic paternity where unmarried couples were 'treated together' in a licensed clinic.[35] Thus the status of father was given to a man who had neither a legal relationship with the mother nor a genetic relationship with the child and could not be readily identified when the child was born.[36] Such a man was not a parent because of who he was, but it was not clear what he had to do to become a parent.[37]

3. Adoptive Parents

In contrast, parental status acquired through adoption has always been a matter of *doing*, transferring responsibility for a child from the original (birth) parent to the adopter(s). English law was reluctant to provide for adoption,[38] and when it did so it did not confer the same status on adoptive parents as on birth parents, nor remove all the rights from birth parents.[39] A key factor in legalising adoption was the acceptance that people who cared for children ought to have this relationship recognised and protected. Those wishing to become adoptive parents had to arrange to have a child placed with them, obtain the consent of the mother[40] and

---

[32] Law Commission No 118, *Illegitimacy* (1982) Pt XII. This approach was endorsed in the Warnock Report (Cmd 9314, 1984) para 4.17.

[33] Section 27. Contrast the position of the mother's husband with the arguments in relation to organ donation where 'presumed consent is no consent'.

[34] HFE Act 1990, s 28(2).

[35] HFE Act 1990, s 28(3).

[36] The HFEA *Code of Practice*, 6th edn (London, Human Fertilisation and Embryology Authority, 2004) does not require this man's consent to the woman's treatment but 'Centres are expected to try to obtain written acknowledgement' from the couple that they are being treated together (para 6.36).

[37] *Re Q (Parental Order)* [1996] 1 FLR 369, 372, per Johnson J.

[38] Two government committees and three bills were required to secure legislation, some 50 years after the adoption legislation in New Zealand (see N Lowe, 'English Adoption Law: Past, Present and Future' in S Katz, J Eekelaar and M MacLean (eds), *Cross Currents: Family Policy in the United States and England* (Oxford, OUP, 2000) 307.

[39] Adoption Act 1926, s 5 did not provide for inheritance rights between parents and adoptive children, nor end those rights within the birth family. It was not until 1949 that children acquired inheritance rights in the adoptive family, Adoption Act 1949, s 9. This did not (and never has) applied to titles of honour.

[40] In almost all cases children were illegitimate and therefore had no recognised father.

apply to the court for an adoption order. The court had to be satisfied that adoption would promote the child's welfare—a matter assessed with the assistance of a guardian *ad litem*.[41] In practice, many early adoptions were not legalised by a court order. Adopters sought to preserve their secrecy and sacrificed the formal status in order to prevent the mother from finding out the child's whereabouts.[42]

Initially, adoption practice was largely unregulated, but concern for child protection and adoption agencies' interests in strengthening their position combined to require adoption agencies to register with the local authority and to exclude unregistered agencies from placing children for adoption. Parents could still place their children directly, or through an intermediary such as a doctor; practices which were only outlawed in 1976. Professionalisation of adoption services also increased the emphasis on preparation for adoption, and on supervision of adoptive placements by the local authority or the adoption agency. Adoption orders could only be made in favour of applicants who had cared for children for a probationary period. If the child was not placed by an agency (and was not related to the applicant) a longer probationary period was required. Prolonging the probationary period also strengthened the adopters' position if the parent sought to withdraw their consent, because courts were willing to find that parents who wished to disrupt the *de facto* relationship between adopter and child were unreasonable, and to dispense with their consent on this basis.[43]

Although adoption has always operated as a method for relieving infertility, agencies increasingly emphasised the child's need for a family. And as the number of babies available for adoption declined, home-finding for older 'hard to place' children, most of whom have been the subject of child protection proceedings, developed. This change in the focus of adoption from healthy babies to children with special needs also necessitated agencies taking more positive steps to recruit adopters, to prepare them to become parents and to support them after the adoption order had been made. Over time, despite concerns about a shortage of adopters for children (not babies), those wanting to adopt have had to do more and more to establish that they are able to be a parent. Now both agency practice in adoption and the legal process of obtaining the order underline that, for adopters, becoming a parent is about engaging in a process through which their demonstrated ability to parent a child effectively is ultimately recognised.

---

[41] But, according to S Cretney, *Family Law in the Twentieth Century: A History* (Oxford, OUP, 2003) 603, their responsibilities were not regarded as very onerous.

[42] *Ibid*, 605.

[43] Adoption Act 1976, s 16(2)(b); *Re W (A Minor)* [1984] FLR 880 (CA).

Although would-be adopters have from time to time claimed 'a right to become a parent', this has been consistently rejected by those making adoption policy,[44] the domestic courts[45] and the European Court of Human Rights.[46] Restrictions on who could obtain an adoption order (married couples or single or separated individuals) constrained agency practice. But in the 1990s, some agencies became willing to consider non-traditional families. Unmarried couples (heterosexual or same-sex) who could not adopt jointly were considered, as were single people who could adopt alone. Agencies focused on the child's needs and the quality of care that would be provided. Where the carers were an unmarried couple, applications to court were made for adoption by one of the adults with a joint residence order to them both. Both adults thus had parental responsibility for the child but only one was a legal parent.[47] Most of the differences between the parent and non-parent could be dealt with by making wills, naming guardians and providing for inheritance. However, the arrangement left the child without any right of support from the non-parent, and imposed on the adults no obligations to each other, which could protect the child in the event of a break-down of their relationship.

The Adoption and Children Bill, as originally drafted, would have retained this approach although it provided for unmarried couples to have a lesser status as a child's *special guardians*.[48] The government considered that adoption should not be opened to unmarried couples until there was provision for a formal legal sta-tus establishing a legal relationship (outside marriage) for such couples. However, adoption agencies successfully campaigned for the marriage requirement to be removed for adopting couples. In doing so, they established the possibility of adoption for both heterosexual and same-sex couples. This was the most contro-versial and hardest fought aspect of the legislation, with the House of Lords repeatedly rejecting the Commons amendment. Two key arguments strengthened the hands of the reformers. The first was evidence from the British Agencies for

[44] Jacqui Smith, Minister of State, Department of Health, *Hansard*, Commons vol 392, col 96 (Commons consideration of Lords amendments to Adoption and Children Bill) 4 November 2002. Reports have only recognised would-be adopter's rights to 'courtesy and sensitivity' (*Adoption: The Future* (Cmd 2288, 1993)) or 'a clear and thorough assessment' (*Adoption: A New Approach* (Cmd 5017, 2000) paras 6.1, 6.18).

[45] Adoption agencies have a statutory right (and duty) to remove children from prospective adopters in specific circumstances. Judicial review has occasionally been granted against decisions by adoption agencies to remove children from prospective adopters on the basis that proper consideration has not been given to the issue, eg *R v Devon CC, ex parte O* [1997] 2 FLR 388.

[46] *Frette v France* ECHR 2002–I [2003] 2 FLR 9.

[47] See *Re W (Homosexual Adopter)* [1997] 2 FLR 406.

[48] Children Act 1989, s 14A-G (added by Adoption and Children Act 2002).

Adoption and Fostering (BAAF)[49] that there was a substantial shortage of people willing to adopt which left children in care without secure families. Far from providing children with parents, the marriage criterion demonstrably prevented children from enjoying family life. Secondly, the restrictions on adoption meant that children being cared for by couples who were willing to adopt could not enjoy the greater legal protection an adoption order provided. Eligibility criteria which prevented carers from becoming parents potentially breached the children's rights to respect for their family life under Article 8 ECHR.[50]

The 2002 Act also sought to control adoption agencies, which were repeatedly portrayed in the media as imposing unwarranted and idiotic restrictions on parenthood, for example barring smokers and the obese. Agencies, which had long been subject to regulations and guidance would be given additional guidance on assessment of adopters, and an appeals system would be established so that those who were not approved could challenge the decision.[51] In addition, when approval was given for adoption by unmarried couples, parliament imposed a condition that such couples should be in 'an enduring family relationship.'[52]

Qualification for adoptive parenthood is about capacity to care and personal qualities rather than status. These qualities are assessed through a process of preparation and approval, which may lead to the placement of a child for adoption, or the approval of foster carers to adopt a child in their care. Qualification for applicant couples no longer includes status, '*who you are in law*', and is only about the way your relationship appears to others. The adoption order provides legal endorsement for what *they are already doing*, and frees them from the control of the agency. The court retains discretion not to award parental status to would-be adopters—parenting is a necessary but not a sufficient criterion for this status. The court may refuse the order, granting residence or special guardianship instead because it considers that retention of some status by the birth parents is in the child's interests (or because it is not satisfied that the parents' objections can be overruled). Thus, whereas parenthood *by being* is automatic, parental status may be withheld from those *doing* parenting.

---

[49] This is an umbrella group for adoption and fostering agencies.

[50] See Joint Select Committee on Human Rights, 24th Report 2001–2 HC 979 (*Adoption and Children Bill 2002 as amended by the House of Lords on Report*).

[51] The Adoption and Children Act 2002, s 12 gives those refused by agencies a right to have that decision reviewed. Guidance is provided by the Department of Health on adopter preparation and assessment; see *Draft Adoption Regulations and Consultation on Guidance on Arranging Adoptions and Assessing Prospective Adopters (2004)* available at: www.dfes.gov.uk/adoption/lawandguidance/index.shtml#pubs.

[52] Adoption and Children Act 2002, s 144(4).

C. The Acquisition of Parental Responsibility by Doing and by Being

Although parental responsibility is defined as 'all the rights, duties, powers and responsibilities and authority which by law a parent of a child has',[53] this bundle of rights has long been unpacked, and obligations, particularly the duty to maintain the child financially, have been imposed without other rights. Parental responsibility was originally the power of the father over his legitimate child, indivisible from the status of parent, acquired automatically because of who he was. Mothers were eventually recognised as having the same rights, again for *being* the mother.[54]

Despite serious consideration of the case for removing all distinctions in respect of their children between married and unmarried fathers,[55] the very different relationships between such men and their children and the children's mothers has continued to justify differential treatment.[56] Initially, such fathers could only obtain parental responsibility by a court order. The courts developed a test based on the father's commitment, attachment to the child and reasons for seeking the order,[57] and applied the welfare test in these proceedings.[58] Where a father has provided financial support and maintained contact, cogent evidence is required to justify refusing the order. Indeed, the test does not appear to impose a high hurdle. The courts have accepted that it is 'overwhelmingly in the child's interests for both parents to have parental responsibility.'[59] They have allowed parental responsibility to be granted to fathers who have failed to maintain their children, even to fathers who are simultaneously barred from contact,[60] and excluded only those who have shown callous indifference or whose behaviour has damaged their children.[61] The test has effectively been reduced to one of *being and not doing bad.*

---

[53] Children Act 1989, s 3(1).

[54] Guardianship of Infants Act 1925 and Guardianship Act 1973; see S Cretney, 'What Will the Women Want Next? The Struggle for Power Within the Family 1925–1975' in S Cretney, *Law, Law Reform and the Family* (Oxford, Clarendon Press, 1998) 155.

[55] For an account of these developments see S Cretney, J Masson and R Bailey-Harris, *Principles of Family Law*, 7th edn (London, Sweet & Maxwell, 2003) 552–55. Eekelaar has also argued that parental responsibility is an unnecessary legal concept (J Eekelaar, 'Re-thinking Parental Responsibility' [2001] *Fam Law* 426).

[56] *B v UK* [2000] 1 FLR 1, 5.

[57] *Re H (Minors) (Local Authority: Parental Rights) (no 3)* [1991] Fam 151.

[58] *Re P (A Minor) (Parental Responsibility Order)* [1993] 1 FLR 578.

[59] *Re P (A Minor) (Parental Responsibility Order)* [1994] 1 FLR 578, 586 per Wilson J.

[60] *Re C and V (Contact and Parental Responsibility)* [1998] 1 FLR 392.

[61] *S v P (Contact Application: Family Assistance)* [1997] 2 FLR 277; *Re P (Parental Responsibility)* [1997] 2 FLR 722 (CA); *Re G (Domestic Violence)* [2000] 1 FLR 865.

Even before the introduction of this provision, the Law Commission expressed ambivalence about the need for court proceedings where there was agreement between the parents that the father should have parental responsibility. Only two years after the enactment of the court power, provision was made for parental responsibility agreements.[62] The courts were then faced only with cases where the mother refused to agree. The focus became justifying the maternal veto, rather than establishing that the father was *doing* enough.

Concern was also focused on the very many unmarried fathers who played an active part in their children's lives but had no parental responsibility because they were unaware of the need for an agreement or a court order.[63] The Lord Chancellor's Department consulted on reform and the new scheme was enacted.[64] The mechanism chosen, joint registration of birth, could operate both as a proxy for the mother's agreement and provide official evidence of the father's rights. In effect, acquisition of parental responsibility for fathers may be seen as a matter of *being* named on the birth certificate. The distinction between married and unmarried fathers is reduced to the right to register—the married father's name can appear without his participation but the unmarried father's name can only be included if both he and the mother register the birth jointly or paternity is established through the courts.[65]

D. The Acquisition of Parental Responsibility and Other Obligations by Non-Parents Through Doing and Through Being

The position of men who provide for a child as a member of their family without being the child's biological father has similarly changed over the last 50 years. Before the creation of the welfare state, a man who married a woman with children had obligations to maintain those children under the Poor Law.[66] This public law duty was abolished in 1948. However, the 'cohabitation rule' continued to make step-parents (married or unmarried) indirectly liable to support children in

---

[62] Children Act 1989, s 4(2).

[63] See R Pickford, *Fathers, Marriage and the Law* (York, Joseph Rowntree Foundation, 1999); A Barlow *et al*, 'Just a Piece of Paper: Marriage and Cohabitation' in A Park *et al* (eds), *British Social Attitudes, the 18th BSA Report: Public Policy, Social Ties* (London, Sage, 2001).

[64] Adoption and Children Act 2002, s 113 (adding s 4(2A) to the Children Act 1989).

[65] Births and Deaths Registration Act 1953, s 10(1).

[66] Introduced in the Poor Law (Amendment) Act 1834, see *eg* Poor Law Act 1930, s 14 and generally S Ramsey and J Masson, 'Stepparent Support of Stepchildren: A Comparative Analysis of Policies and Problems in American and English Experience' (1985) 36 *Syracuse L Rev* 659, 681.

their household by removing the right of the parent to continue to receive state benefits when she was cohabiting with someone who did not also qualify for them. This position still pertains. It now applies to same-sex couples; the Civil Partnership Act introduced the concept of living together as if civil partners for them.[67]

The Royal Commission on Marriage and Divorce 1953–55 considered much of the law of husband and wife, including family proceedings and the interests of children. Amongst its recommendations was that the divorce court should have an inquisitorial role to protect the welfare of children caught up in divorce proceedings by considering the arrangements made by the parties.[68] This responsibility could not be limited only to the children of the marriage but should cover all children living in the family. The court should also have powers to make orders relating to custody, access or maintenance for all such children. Although some who gave evidence to the Commission opposed this imposition on step-parents of a private law obligation to maintain, others appeared to want step-parents to pay, at least if they had been responsible for the break-up of the original marriage.[69]

The Matrimonial Proceedings (Children) Bill 1958 originally provided for the divorce courts to have powers only in respect of children of the marriage, but was amended to cover the children of either spouse, living with the parties who had been 'accepted' as a child of the family by the other party. This extension was seen as uncontroversial. It reflected the recommendation of the Commission and only sought to continue obligations that had been voluntarily assumed during the marriage. In other words, a step-parent who had maintained the child during the marriage could be made to continue to do so after divorce. Further amendment in 1960 made it possible to enforce this obligation during the marriage where the step-parent wilfully failed to maintain the child.[70]

The concept of *acceptance* required the man to know that the child was not his and to form a family that included the child. Neither the duration of this family unit nor the responsibility of others for the child's support were relevant to the step-parent's liability.[71] The step-parent's obligations seem to have been regarded as a natural consequence of living with the child, of *being there*. The Law Commission commented in 1967 that the step-father 'shall be regarded as having

---

[67] Social Security Contributions and Benefits Act 1992, s 137; Jobseekers' Allowance Act 1995, s 35. Amendments to these provisions are included in the Civil Partnership Act 2004, Sch 24, paras 46 and 124. The new 'cohabitation rule' will apply equally to those in civil partnerships and those in informal same-sex relationships.

[68] Cmd 9678, para 390 II.

[69] See evidence to Morton Commission cited in Ramsey and Masson, 'Stepparent Support of Stepchildren', above n 66, 690, n 172.

[70] Matrimonial Proceedings (Magistrates' Courts) Act 1960, s 1. Enforcement was also possible where the step-parent had committed a matrimonial offence. The magistrates' jurisdiction in matrimonial matters was very important at the time and used by those who did not wish or could not afford to divorce.

[71] *Snow v Snow* [1971] 3 All ER 833; [1971] 3 All ER 858 (CA).

taken the risk of having to maintain to the extent that the first husband failed to do so.'[72] In 1969, it reiterated its view that the step-father's obligations should depend on his having accepted responsibility for the child with full knowledge of the child's parentage.[73] So *being the husband* was not enough if the wife had concealed the child's parentage from him. However, following criticism from respondents, the Law Commission changed its position and recommended a new definition of 'child of the family' based on the way the child was 'treated' by the parties. The step-father's knowledge was not relevant to the existence of his liability but was to be taken into account when quantifying maintenance. It was not the child's fault that the step-father had assumed responsibility in ignorance of the child's true parentage, and the child should not be made to suffer because of this.[74] This provision was enacted in the Matrimonial Proceedings and Property Act 1970 and is now found in the Matrimonial Causes Act 1973 and the Children Act 1989. Although a test based on 'treatment' suggests that the step-parent must have *done something*, in practice this does not seem to be the case. There must have been a family but it is very difficult for the step-parent to show that he or she did not treat the child as a member of it.[75] Effectively, the wish to secure the possibility of continued financial support for step-children has resulted in a test which imposes liability on step-parents purely on the basis that they were formerly a spouse of a person caring for a child.

These private law provisions only apply to married (or formerly married) step-parents. Their origin as part of an Act designed to increase the powers of the divorce court, passed at a time when cohabitation outside marriage was stigmatised and uncommon, firmly bond them to the married family, even though they only operate when that family has broken down. There have been no attempts to extend this liability to unmarried couples, although responsibilities are imposed more widely in social security law, and rights can be acquired by a wider class of step-parents, including the unmarried or same-sex partners of the child's parent.[76]

In order to acquire a status in relation to the child, some step-fathers adopted their wife's children, a practice which until the 1970s was well-accepted and simple.[77] Step-family adoptions were the subject of less scrutiny than other adoptions

---

[72] Law Commission, Working Paper No 9, *Matrimonial and related proceedings, financial relief* (1967) para 171.

[73] The man might have married in the belief that he was the father of the child.

[74] Law Commission Report No 25, *Financial provision in matrimonial proceedings* (1969) para 28.

[75] JG Miller, *Family Property and Financial Provision*, 3rd edn (Croydon, Surrey, Tolley, 1993), cited after 2nd edn, 1983, 343–44.

[76] See *eg G v F (Contact and Shared Residence: Application for Leave)* [1998] 2 FLR 799. See also Civil Partnership Act 2004, s 72, Sch 5, para 80(2), Sch 6 para 48 for the position of same-sex partners in a civil partnership.

[77] Step-parent adoption was open to step-mothers but very rarely used by them. See J Masson *et al*, *Mine, Yours or Ours? A Study of Step-parent Adoption* (London, HMSO, 1983) 46.

and were routinely completed in the minimum allowable period; the court effectively rubber-stamped the application.[78] Being a step-father effectively qualified a
man to adopt his spouse's children, at least if there was no natural father with
parental responsibility who objected.[79] Following a change in policy in the 1970s,
step-parent adoption became regarded as inappropriate because of its potential to
cut a child off from the natural father and his family, replace the father with a
step-father, and confuse birth and adoptive relationships. As an alternative, provision was made for forms of joint custody which allowed the step-father to obtain
parental responsibility whilst preserving the child's existing legal and social relationships.[80] Step-parent adoption was not abolished but assimilated with other
non-agency placements and subjected to closer scrutiny. Where step-families were
willing and able to establish the quality of their parenting and could justify
excluding the father, adoption was still available but it was considered neither necessary nor desirable for step-parents to go to these lengths.[81]

Joint custody was not attractive; few step-parents acquired parental responsibility but the numbers of step-parent adoptions continued to fall. Step-parent adoption was re-assessed; it could be appropriate if 'the other parent had never acted
in a parental capacity and the child has never really known any member of that
side of the birth family.'[82] Failing to *do anything* as a parent justified substitution
by someone who demonstrated that they were *doing* parenting. However, there
was still concern about this use of adoption; the 1992 Adoption Review did not
want to prevent it but was concerned to discourage 'inappropriate applications'.[83]

The Adoption and Children Act 2002 includes a series of measures to enable
step-parents to obtain parental responsibility for their step-children or even the
status of parent. Acquiring status still depends on adoption, but this no longer
requires adoption by, or marriage to, the parent.[84] Thus the parent's same-sex
partner can, at least in theory, become a legal parent to his or her step-child by
adoption. Parents can make an agreement that grants parental responsibility to a
step-parent who is married to one of them,[85] but an unmarried partner who
wants parental responsibility must apply to the court for a residence order or
adoption. Thus *being a parent's spouse* can now lead to rights as well as liabilities,

---

[78] *Ibid.*

[79] *Ibid.*

[80] Children Act 1975, ss 10(3) and 33(3).

[81] See S Cretney, J Masson and R Bailey-Harris, *Principles of Family Law*, 7th edn (London, Sweet &
Maxwell, 2003) para 23.054. Approximately a quarter of adoptions are step-parent adoptions compared with more than 60% in the early 1970s.

[82] *Review of Adoption Law* (Department of Health and Welsh Office, 1992) para 19.2.

[83] *Ibid.*

[84] Adoption and Children Act 2002, s 52(2).

[85] Children Act 1989, s 4A. This provision extends to civil partners, Civil Partnership Act 2004, s
75(2).

and informal partners can obtain rights without liabilities by obtaining a residence order rather than adoption. The approach of the court to parental responsibility orders for step-parents will only become clear after the provisions have been implemented. However, the positioning of the provision in the Children Act and the parallels with parental responsibility for unmarried fathers suggest that the court may be relatively unconcerned about what the step-parent *does*, at least where his or her partner wants him or her to share parental responsibility.

Other people who want parental responsibility for a child must also apply to the court, and must show that they are entitled to do so. Entitlement depends on status, *being* the child's guardian, on *doing*, living with the child for a substantial period, or on having the leave of the court. Leave is granted to those who can justify their application. This depends on their relationship (legal or social) to the child and what they are proposing—the court thus considers aspects of *being and doing* in these applications.

E. Parenting by Doing, Parenting by Being and the Right to Family Life

The European Court of Human Rights has repeatedly stated that Article 8 protects real relationships. However, for parents, the right to family life seems to depend largely on their status, *on being*. The Court has imposed a very low hurdle for fathers seeking to challenge the complete non-recognition of any relationship with their child. In *Keegan v Ireland*[86] a father whose relationship with the mother had ended before the birth of their child and who had seen the child only twice, was held to have a right to respect for his family life with his child. Although family life arises only once a child is born, clearly events that occur before birth such as the planned pregnancy in *Keegan* can be highly relevant. In contrast, a man who donated sperm to a lesbian friend was held by the European Commission of Human Rights not to have Article 8 rights, despite contact with the child.[87] The English courts have recognised that mothers necessarily have family life with their children, even when they have rejected them at birth.[88] In relation to unmarried fathers, they have sought to protect their decisions from challenge on human rights grounds. They have assumed that most such fathers have rights to family life with their children but then determined that it may, nevertheless, be necessary

---

[86] Series A no 290 (1994) 18 EHRR 342.
[87] *G v the Netherlands* 16 EHRR CD 38.
[88] *Re B (Adoption by Natural Parent)* [2001] 1 FLR 589 (CA) paras 34–40; [2002] 1 FLR 196 (HL) para 30.

for the protection of the child's and the mother's rights to exclude a father completely from decisions about his child.[89]

The European Court of Human Rights has recognised that non-parents can have Article 8 rights, and even accepted that sometimes these may be accorded greater respect than those of parents.[90] For non-parents, family life depends on 'real relationships', on *doing* rather than *being*, because Article 8 ultimately protects ties of emotion.

F. The Right To Be (Recognised As) A Parent in the Context of Medically Assisted Reproduction

The above analysis serves to highlight the exceptional nature of the provision in the Human Fertilisation and Embryology Act 1990 which gives the status of parent to the unmarried (male) partner of a woman who is provided with fertility services using another man's sperm. He has no genetic relationship with the child *and* no legal relationship with the woman; his suitability for parenthood is not assessed, nor is he required to demonstrate care or commitment; yet he is recognised as the child's father and acquires rights and obligations to the child.

The parliamentary debates shed considerable light on how this curious arrangement came about. At report stage in the Lords, an amendment was proposed to secure the status of parent for the mother's unmarried partner. The aim of the amendment was to 'bolster and build up the family'[91] alongside a proposal to restrict access to fertility services to couples.[92] Giving status to the woman's partner was integral to making a man responsible for the child, and thus to creating 'proper' families. It was illogical for the government to be seeking to secure financial support for children through the creation of the Child Support Agency whilst at the same time allowing fatherless children to be born. Not all who spoke at report took such a narrow approach. A more liberal view was also put forward that treatment should be available to all who could benefit from it subject only to counselling and advice. If only couples could obtain treatment, clinics would be required to make intrusive inquiries about the relationships of those seeking services[93] and these were

---

[89] *Re M (Adoption: Rights of Natural Father)* [2001] 1 FLR 745.

[90] *Söderbäck v Sweden* Reports of Judgments and Decisions 1998–VII [1999] 1 FLR 250.

[91] Lord Ashbourne, *Hansard* Lords vol 516, col. 1146, 6 March 1990.

[92] Amendment 16: *Hansard* Lords vol 516, col. 1101, 6 March 1990. Lord Ashbourne, who also put this amendment forward, sought to have the use of donated gametes outlawed but did not press this because of the 'weight of opposition'.

[93] Baroness Warnock, *Hansard* Lords vol 516, col. 1103, 6 March 1990. The idea that the child's welfare is separate from the relationships of the person caring for the child is not one which would be accepted by family lawyers.

unnecessary because the clinic was already being required to consider the welfare of any child who might be born as a result of treatment.[94] Even a requirement that the man attends or consents could be too intrusive. The Lord Chancellor undertook to consider the question of providing a status for the unmarried father. He did not wish to promote relationships outside marriage, 'thus perhaps undermining marriage',[95] but recognised that there was a case for imposing responsibility where fertility services were provided to an unmarried couple.[96]

The government brought forward its own amendment on non-genetic paternity for unmarried fathers at third reading in the Lords. The Lord Chancellor explicitly stated that liability for the man would 'discourage irresponsible use of treatments' by unmarried couples. Recognising the man as a father also provided three further benefits to any child born as a result of treatment. He or she would gain inheritance rights; have a father; and: '[F]ormal recognition of the man's fatherhood may help to cement and strengthen the relationship within the informal family and reduce the risks of breakdown and its consequences for the child and ... the taxpayer.'[97]

Thus conservatives who sought to prevent treatment of single women combined with liberals who wanted to provide equality for married and unmarried couples, to secure parental status for male partners and rights for children. In this way, treating single women would be less likely to be seen as satisfying the welfare requirement[98] and less likely to take place.

Deeming informal partners to be fathers (and thus making them liable for their children's maintenance) appeared to be a win-win solution for the government. Either such men would refuse to participate and clinics would not treat women alone, or they would do so and take responsibility for any children born. Indeed, giving them a status (even though parental responsibility did not automatically attach to it) was seen as encouraging men to take on a fathering role. The distinction between married and unmarried fathers was maintained so that marriage itself was not 'undermined'. Married couples could be allowed to undertake donor insemination anywhere, and without medical intervention, but unmarried couples (and single women)[99] would be dependent on licensed clinics.

However, the compromise achieved by s 28(3) of the HFE Act 1990 was substantially flawed. It was not based on a clear test that could ensure certainty of paternity from the moment of the child's birth; it did not ensure that the child was born into a legally recognised family unit including both parents and it maintained

---

[94] Baroness Faithful, *Hansard* Lords vol 516, col. 1103, 6 March 1990.

[95] *Hansard* Lords vol 517, col. 210.

[96] *Hansard* Lords vol 516, col. 1106, 6 March 1990.

[97] *Hansard* Lords vol 517, col. 210.

[98] HFE Act 1990, s 13(5) specifically refers to 'the child's need for a father'.

[99] Only through the use sperm obtained through a licensed clinic could a single woman secure that the donor would not claim paternity and seek to be involved in the child's life.

differential treatment of children born outside marriage and their 'fathers' which was arguably not compliant with the European Convention on Human Rights.

The desire to provide a father has resulted in a provision without a clear basis for identifying the man who is deemed to be the father. Much reliance is placed on clinics to inform and advise the potential father. However, a close examination of the HFEA *Code of Practice* indicates that the clinic actually has to do relatively little. It must 'try to obtain written acknowledgement that a man is being treated together with a woman and that donated sperm is to be used.'[100] It follows that a man may be being 'treated together' even if he fails to sign such a document, or not be being 'treated together' despite having signed on an earlier occasion.[101] The document does not have to be witnessed, nor does the identity of the man have to be established. Far less care is taken in securing the man's status as father than with granting parental responsibility by agreement, despite the acquisition of status having far wider consequences.[102]

If one considers the position of a child seeking to establish paternity for inheritance purposes the difficulties the test creates are even more obvious. How is a child to know that the man he regards as his father satisfies this test? Children are unlikely to know that their conception was achieved using donor insemination.[103] Even if they do, the HFEA's power to disclose information is limited in the case of a minor to disclosing whether an intended marriage partner is related. An adult child could find out whether they might have been born as a result of treatment services to their mother, but without evidence that the child could not have been naturally conceived, or is genetically related to the sperm donor, it may not be possible to establish that a man whose partner received fertility treatment is the child's legal father. This issue does not arise with married couples because the presumption of paternity can only be rebutted by proof that the husband did not consent. However, if a couple use fertility services outside the scope of s 28(3) the man will not be the father even if they marry before the child's birth. There is no retrospection in these provisions.[104] The problem of uncertainty about the man's status could be solved either by basing fatherhood for unmarried partners on the intended father's consent to the treatment in a formal document registered with the HFEA or the Registrar General on the child's birth, or, alternatively, by creating a formal status for unmarried couples and requiring those

---

[100] HFEA *Code of Practice*, 6th edn (2004) para 6.36 but note the greater emphasis on obtaining consent in para 6.34 relating to husbands.

[101] *Re R (IVF: Paternity of Child)* [2003] 1 FLR 1183 (CA), *sub nom Re D (a child)* [2005] UKHL 33.

[102] Status gives inheritance rights to both father and child whereas parental responsibility merely gives a right to take decisions unless objection is made.

[103] S Golombok *et al*, 'The European Study of Assisted Reproduction Families: The Transition to Adolescence' (2002) 17 *Human Reproduction* 830.

[104] But if the man's sperm was used and the couple later married, the man would obtain parental responsibility on marriage.

seeking treatment as a couple to obtain it as a condition of the man acquiring the status of father.

Consent is accepted as the basis for non-genetic fatherhood in a number of countries which allow donor insemination. The UK is alone amongst European countries in recognising a man as father without either a genetic link or explicit consent to become one.[105] Consent provides a clear basis for linking the man to the child, and imposing obligations on him, but does not secure family ties between the adults which will protect the child in the event of relationship break-down.

English law is looking increasingly isolated in its failure to provide formal recognition to unmarried couples either by allowing them to register their status or imposing one following the birth of a child.[106] In the UK, full recognition of a relationship between people depends on marriage. A marriage-like relationship will also be available to same-sex couples under the Civil Partnership Act 2004. Without marriage or civil partnership, there is no recognition of the relationship, but behaviour commonly associated with marriage such 'living together as husband and wife' or being maintained, leads a partner or former partner to qualify for some protection in the event of his or her partner's death.[107] However, informal couples have no obligations to support each other, and no access to the adjustive jurisdiction of the family courts if their relationship fails. The loss lies where it falls, although the court has limited powers to order capital payments and property transfer in favour of children of the relationship.[108] This can be used to make unmarried fathers provide a home for their children, but the courts have not interpreted these powers to secure a home for the mother when the children have grown up.[109] Whilst securing a father for a woman's children, parliament did not impose on the man the obligations which could provide security for the children's mother.

This is not just an issue in assisted reproduction but applies equally to adoptions by unmarried couples. Parliament required that these should only be granted to unmarried couples with an 'enduring family relationship' but secured no

---

[105] Council of Europe, *Medically Assisted Procreation and the Protection of the Human Embryo: Comparative Study of the Situation in 39 Countries* (1998) CBDI/INF (98) 8. As was pointed out in the text, the question whether a woman receiving donor insemination was being 'treated together' with her partner in a UK licensed clinic—the HFE Act's criterion for becoming the non-genetic legal father of a child born from donated gametes to an unmarried couple—is very different from the question whether the man consented to becoming the legal father of the child.

[106] See Law Society, *Cohabitation: The Case for Clear Law* (2002) appendix 1 and 2.

[107] For example, the right to make an application under the Fatal Accidents Act 1976, the right to succeed to various types of tenancy, and the right to seek family provision in the event of death (see Law Society *ibid.*).

[108] Children Act 1989, Sch 1.

[109] *H v P (Illegitimate Child: Capital Provision)* [1993] Fam Law 515; *J v C (Child: Financial Provision)* [1999] 1 FLR 152.

protection for the child if the family should fail. The parents have a relationship with each other only through the child, their obligations are to the child even though it is well established that a child's well-being is largely dependent on that of his or her carers. The need for a formal relationship was recognised—the government initially suggested that adoption by unmarried couples should only be permitted once a formal legal relationship was available to them, but it withdrew its opposition after an amendment had been accepted in the Commons.

Restricting s 28(3) to men in a formal relationship with the child's mother would provide certainty, but at the expense of providing a father for some children where the mother's partner was either unable or unwilling to enter such an arrangement. This too could benefit the children. The context of the child's conception would be known—it clearly was not to the woman in *U v W*[110] nor to the man in *Re R*.[111] Clinics could determine their treatment policies on this basis. Should the woman subsequently establish a formal partnership (or marry), her partner or husband would become the child's step-father with a duty to maintain and the possibility of parental responsibility.

Another question is whether status also ought to be accorded to the same-sex partner of the woman who obtains treatment with donor gametes. The Adoption and Children Act 2002 allows a same-sex couple (whether in a civil partnership or not) to adopt a child and be registered as first and second parents. Each parent has an equal status and legal relationship *vis-a-vis* the child. No similar provision exists outside adoption.[112] The policy of securing a father for children born through donor insemination has not extended to securing a second parent when a lesbian woman with a partner seeks treatment. A justification for this difference in treatment could arise from the very different process for assessing parents-to-be in adoption and in medically assisted reproduction. Adopters have to show that they can parent. The partner who is treated together with a woman who wants to achieve pregnancy through donor insemination does not. However, looked at in another way this arrangement seems discriminatory in terms of Articles 8 and 14. The difference between a lesbian or heterosexual partner of a woman undergoing DI is purely one of gender. The lesbian woman can have a stronger legal relationship than the man through a civil partnership, yet she can only be recognised as a step-parent, whereas he will be a parent, with the additional rights (and liabilities) that brings. It may be too soon for the European Court of Human Rights to accept

---

[110] [1997] 2 FLR 282. In this case, the unmarried partner of the woman was not recognised as the child's legal father. The child had been conceived with donated sperm and s 28(3) HFE Act was held to be inapplicable because the treatment had not taken place in a UK licensed clinic.

[111] [2001] 1 FLR 247 (FD); [2003] 1 FLR 1183 (CA); *sub nom Re D (a child)* [2005] UKHL 33.

[112] Following the extension of adoption to unmarried and same-sex couples there is a clear need for amendment to HFE Act 1990, s 30 to enable them to apply for parental orders following surrogacy arrangements where one of the couple is genetically related to the child.

that such distinctions amount to unlawful discrimination and to a failure to respect family life. However, a law of parentage which is such a patchwork and generally applies such limited tests makes justification of exclusions difficult.

G. Non-genetic Fatherhood Within and Outside the 'DI Context': The Way Forward

Concern for clarity in determining parenthood has focused on refining the definition of father in cases of non-genetic parenting.[113] But the 'treatment together' test endorsed by the HFE Act fails to indicate what the unmarried man has to do.[114] Relying on licensed clinics means that protection is denied to children who are born and brought up in the UK simply because they were conceived overseas.

Shifting to a test based on written consent, as has been suggested elsewhere,[115] would be clearer although no doubt disputes would shift to issues of whether consent was informed and freely given. Consent would also go some way to base parenting on *doing* for such men, albeit an action before conception only. Consent-based parenthood is possibly justifiable where there is no genetic link, but would be most inappropriate in other cases—leading to arguments that men should have no responsibility where they believed that the woman was using contraception, or that they themselves were infertile.[116] The negative consequences for children, and for the state, could be very serious.

An alternative would be to strengthen the parallel with married fathers, and to make becoming a legal father in cases of non-genetic parenthood dependent on a formal relationship between the mother and the man. Such a formal status does not currently exist outside marriage for heterosexual couples, civil partnership being confined to same-sex couples so as not to undermine marriage. However, until a formal status is provided, all children born to, or adopted by, unmarried heterosexual couples will remain disadvantaged if their parents' relationship ends. The fact that it is not possible to prevent children being born outside marriage

---

[113] S Bridge, 'Assisted Reproduction and Parentage in Law' in A Bainham, S Day Sclater and MPM Richards (eds), *What is a Parent? A Socio-legal Analysis* (Oxford, Hart Publishing, 1999) 73, 86; C Lind, '*Re R (Paternity of IVF Baby)*—Unmarried Paternity under the Human Fertilisation and Embryology Act 1990' (2003) 15 *Child and Family Law Quarterly* 327.

[114] *Re Q (Parental Order)* [1996] 1 FLR 369.

[115] C Barton and G Douglas, *Law and Parenthood* (Cambridge, CUP, 1995); M Shulz, 'Reproductive Technology and Intent-based Parenthood: An Opportunity for Gender Neutrality' [1990] *Wisconsin L Rev* 297; J Hill, 'What Does it Mean to be a "Parent"? The Claims of Biology as the Basis of Parental Rights' (1991) 66 *NYU L Rev* 353; Bridge, 'Assisted Reproduction and Parentage in Law', above n 113, 86.

[116] S Sheldon, '"Sperm Bandits", Birth Control and the Battle of the Sexes' (2001) 21 *Legal Studies* 460.

does not justify failing to protect children who are placed with unmarried couples in adoption or born to them through DI. Merely requiring clinics 'to consider the child's need for a father'[117] or adoption agencies to ensure that the applicants are 'living in an enduring family relationship' provides inadequate financial security for the parent left to bring up the children should the relationship fail. Indeed, as the law now stands, a child who grows up as 'a child of the family' is better protected (even without adoption) than a child conceived by donor insemination whose mother was not treated together with her partner in a licensed clinic.

A requirement to enter a formal relationship could not protect all children. Whereas it is possible to control most legal adoptions by UK couples whether they are carried out at home or overseas, this could never be the case with conceptions through the use of fertility services. But why should the creation of a legal bond between mother and father be additional to the creation of the link between parent and child? The impact on the parent with care of caring for a child is well established, as is the link between parental adversity and less good outcomes for children. Therefore, the fact that a couple have produced a child together should make them responsible for each other as well as for the child. Many jurisdictions already have provision for recognising *de facto* relationships.[118] These usually distinguish between couples with and without children. Mutual obligations arise because of a period of cohabitation, or if the couple have a child. And where relationships break down, there is provision for financial adjustment which may be very similar to that available to divorcing couples.[119]

Such a system would not do away with the need to be clear that two people are a couple when reproductive services are provided so that the man becomes the (non-genetic) father of the child. There would be no requirement for such couples to obtain treatment from a UK licensed clinic, so the partner would be the father wherever treatment took place. Clinics would be expected to obtain written consent from both parties; if the man does not consent he does not become the father. Women seeking treatment (and clinics) would then need to decide if it was appropriate to go ahead on the basis that the child would only have one parent.

H. Conclusion

The desire to maintain the special status of marriage, and to impose a father in every possible arrangement has produced an incoherent system for establishing

---

[117] HFE Act 1990, s 13(5).

[118] Council of Europe, *Medically Assisted Procreation and the Protection of the Human Embryo: Comparative Study of the Situation in 39 Countries* (1998) CBDI/INF (98).

[119] De Facto Relationships Act 1984 (New South Wales); Property (Relationships) Act 1976 (New Zealand). This approach is also taken in the Civil Partnership Act 2004.

parenthood, and one which leaves unprotected a large minority of children whose parents cohabit rather then marry. Clarity about both who will be the child's parents and the legal status of the relationship the child is born into are highly relevant for the child's welfare. However, the system for determining parentage of children born as a result of medically assisted reproduction involving the use of donated gametes has ignored these issues and instead reified the child's need for a father. A more rational system would focus on making clear, before the procedure takes place, whether the mother intends to parent alone and, if she does not, her partner ought to have the status of second parent. The least that should be expected of the second parent is a relationship with the mother, which is recognised in law and supported with legal remedies in case of breakdown.

9

Birthrights? The Rights and Obligations Associated with the Birth of a Child

ANDREW BAINHAM*

Five years ago a remarkable case came before the English courts.[1] A married couple failed to conceive a child together owing to the husband's low sperm count. Not for them the anonymous sperm donor, they sought the help of an old friend. He had been an usher at their wedding but was now to contribute to the marriage in an altogether more intimate manner. For several months the wife had regular sexual intercourse with the friend and with her husband but no pregnancy resulted. Then a decade down the line, and with the biological clock relentlessly ticking, the wife decided to launch another attempt. The old friend reappeared but, unbeknown to him, so did three other men. The wife had decided to maximise her chances of pregnancy during what she calculated would be her 'conception window'. These other men made their respective contributions on 28 April, 29 April and 30 April. And it worked. A child was conceived and in due course the wife gave birth to a child who was then raised as the child of the marriage.

Rumours then circulated around the family and wider community that there were doubts about the child's paternity. The old friend, by this time no longer a friend, publicly declared that he was the father on his citizens-band radio and produced a placard to that effect. For his part the husband asserted his own paternity. Perhaps inevitably the dispute ended in the courts.

* I would like to thank Alastair Bissett-Johnson for his helpful insights on an earlier version of this paper. I am solely responsible for the views presented and for any errors which remain.
[1] *Re T (Paternity: Ordering Blood Tests)* [2001] 2 FLR 1190.

How should the legal system respond to such a case? What rights and obligations should be generated by the birth of this child? Should the mother remain in control? Is she entitled to preserve confidentiality regarding her sexual relationships? Should she alone determine which of these five men should be recognised as the father? What of the men themselves? Should the husband, undoubtedly performing the social role of father, be protected from intrusion by outsiders? Or should the man claiming to be the father have the right, or indeed the duty, to establish his connection with the child? What of the child? Was it the child's right to have the stability of the family preserved, or was it his right to know his true identity by getting at the biological truth? And what about the state? Should this be a purely private matter or does the state have some right or obligation to intervene?

I want to attempt to address some of these questions by considering the rights and obligations which do, or which should, arise on the birth of a child. The focus of my chapter is therefore not on the right to reproduce, or the right not to reproduce, but on the *consequences of having reproduced.* My concern is with reproductive *responsibility* rather than with reproductive choice.

As we all know, the birth of a child may be a matter of choice but may equally not be. However, leaving aside the exceptional cases of assisted reproduction and adoption, in general legal rights and obligations arise as a matter of status once the biological connection between the child and the mother or father is established. And this is irrespective of the particular circumstances of conception. The philosophical basis for the obligations which parents have to care for their children is elusive and was the subject of a seminal article by John Eekelaar in 1991.[2] But, whatever their true basis, this has not stopped the international community from asserting parental obligations or from casting them increasingly in terms of children's rights. I therefore want to begin by briefly sketching what the two main conventions, the United Nations Convention on the Rights of the Child (CRC)[3] and the European Convention on Human Rights (ECHR)[4] have to say about the birth of a child.

A. The International Conventions

Article 7 of the CRC requires that the child be registered immediately after birth and that the child should have *from birth* the right to acquire a nationality and, as

---

[2] J Eekelaar, 'Are Parents Morally Obliged to Care for Their Children?' (1991) 11 *Oxford Journal of Legal Studies* 340.
[3] United Nations Convention on the Rights of the Child, adopted by General Assembly Resolution 44/25 of 20 November 1989 and entered into force on 2 September 1990.
[4] Convention for the Protection of Human Rights and Fundamental Freedoms, ETS No 5, adopted on 4 November 1950 and entered into force on 3 September 1953.

far as possible, the right to know and be cared for by his parents.[5] Article 8 then goes on to require that states:

> respect the right of the child to *preserve* his or her identity, including nationality, name and [importantly for the purposes of this paper] *family relations* as recognized by law without unlawful interference (emphasis added).[6]

Commentators have tended to concentrate on the 'right to know' aspect of Article 7 and the issue of the identity rights of the child. But Article 7 is about much more than the child's right to know his or her parents. I want to focus in this chapter on some aspects of Article 7 which, in my view, have been rather neglected. First, the Article is concerned with the child's relationship with the parents *from birth*; not tomorrow, not the next day, not some weeks, months or years down the line and certainly not on the child's 18th birthday, but *from birth*. This raises a fundamental question about exactly *when* children should be told the truth of their biological origins—what I will call the temporal question. Secondly, the article is not merely concerned with knowing the identity of parents but also with, as far as possible, the child's right to *be cared for* by his or her parents. This underlines the child's right not merely to knowledge of parents but also to an ongoing relationship with them. Thirdly, Article 7 does not refer to the *mother* or the *father* but to the child's *parents*. It takes a gender-neutral view of parentage. The child's rights apply equally to the relationship with the mother and the father.[7] In general this is also true of English domestic legislation which increasingly refers to 'parents' and only occasionally distinguishes between mothers and fathers.[8] The new adoption legislation, which for the first time allows adoption of a child by a same-sex couple, was more or less bound to refer to the gender-neutral parent, rather than provide expressly that the child should have two mothers or two fathers.[9]

---

[5] Art 7 CRC provides as follows:

(1) The child shall be registered immediately after birth and shall have the right from birth to a name, the right to acquire a nationality and, as far as possible, the right to know and be cared for by his or her parents. (2) States Parties shall ensure the implementation of these rights in accordance with their national law and their obligations under the relevant international instruments in this field in particular where the child would otherwise be stateless.

[6] Art 8 para 1 CRC.

[7] This gender-neutral approach to parents is reinforced by other articles of the CRC. Art 18(1), for example, requires States Parties to 'use their best efforts to ensure recognition of the principle that *both parents have common responsibilities* for the upbringing and development of the child' (emphasis added).

[8] An uncommon exception is s 2 of the Children Act 1989 which gives sole parental responsibility to *the mother* of a child where the parents were unmarried at the time of the child's birth.

[9] Section 68(3) of the Adoption and Children Act 2002 provides: 'A reference (however expressed) to the adoptive mother and father of a child adopted by—(a) a couple of the same sex, or (b) a partner of the child's parent, where the couple are of the same sex, is to be read as a reference to the child's adoptive *parents*' (emphasis added). The provisions governing adoption by a married couple have now also been extended to civil partners, by s 79 Civil Partnership Act 2004.

This right of the child to establish and maintain a relationship with both biological parents is reflected also in the European Convention on Human Rights.
But, here it arises in conjunction with *parents' own rights*. Whereas the CRC is
concerned only with children's rights, the ECHR is concerned with the rights of
all parties, the mother, the father and the child. This concern is expressed princi-
pally through the concept of 'family life' in Article 8.[10] All three have the right to
respect for their family life. Any interference by the state with this right must be in
accordance with the law, justified by a legitimate state aim and must be proportion-
ate and necessary to that aim. And states not only have this *negative* obligation—
not to interfere with family life—but also *positive* obligations to foster family life.[11]
The broad effect of Article 8 at the time of the child's birth has been summarised in
this way by Marie-Thérèse Meulders: 'Article 8 lays upon States the *positive* obligation to provide in their legislation a legal protection ensuring the child's integration into its legitimate or natural family, grandparents included, as from its
birth ... . In other words, a right to the establishment of its maternal and paternal
affiliation in or out of wedlock'.[12]

I shall argue that English law is deficient and fails to give effect to these obligations. I will try to demonstrate this by focusing separately on the respective positions of the mother, the father and the child.

B. The Mother

The fact of birth will usually establish the identity of the mother. In certain cases
of assisted reproduction there may be a philosophical argument about whether
the claim to motherhood should be based more on carrying the child and giving
birth or on the genetic connection.[13] But, leaving aside that exceptional situation,
we still need to make a number of qualifications to an apparently straightforward
proposition.

First, where the mother relinquishes the child within a short time of birth, the
legal relationship between her and the child depends crucially on an effective system of birth registration. We are concerned primarily here with English law and

---

[10] Art 8(1) provides: 'Everyone has the right to respect for his private and family life, his home and
his correspondence'.

[11] A principle reiterated many times by the European Court of Human Rights. See particularly
Marckx v Belgium Series A no 31 (1979) 2 EHRR 330; *X and Y v the Netherlands* Series A no 91 (1986)
8 EHRR 235; and *Kroon v the Netherlands* Series A no 297 (1994) 19 EHRR 263.

[12] M-T Meulders-Klein, 'Family Law, Human Rights and Judicial Review in Europe' in P Lødrup and
E Modvar (eds), *Family Life and Human Rights* (Oslo, Gyldendal Academisk, 2004) 477, 486.

[13] The law is, however, quite clear. It is the carrying or gestational mother who is the legal mother.
See s 27 Human Fertilisation and Embryology Act 1990.

with developed societies. But we should note that UNICEF has estimated that approximately 40 million children world wide do not have birth registration—and this despite birth registration being described as the child's first right; the right on which so many other rights are dependent.[14] In some countries, registration of birth has been deliberately frustrated or falsified where unscrupulous individuals have seen the opportunity to make some easy money out of children. There is clear evidence, for example, that Romanian mothers have been coerced, sometimes while still pregnant, to hand over their children in maternity hospitals for the trade in international adoption. For those concerned in such practices it was extremely convenient to pretend that the identity of the mother was unknown and that she had abandoned the child.[15] The new Romanian laws (passed by the Romanian parliament in June 2004) impose duties on the health authorities, the police and the child protection authorities to establish the identity of the mother, by investigation where necessary, and to ensure proper registration of the birth; duties backed up by criminal sanctions.[16]

French law, as is well known, makes provision for a mother to give birth anonymously.[17] The European Court of Human Rights has held by majority (in the *Odièvre*[18] case) that this does not violate the Convention. The ruling is, in my view, plainly inconsistent with what is required under the CRC and is in conflict with the court's own earlier decision in *Marckx v Belgium*.[19] There the court had

[14] For further discussion see L Hauwen, 'The Child's Right to Birth Registration: International and Chinese Perspectives' in P Lødrup and E Modvar (eds), *Family Life*, above n 12, 441.

[15] For the author's views on the scandals surrounding international adoption from Romania see A Bainham, 'International Adoption from Romania: Why the Moratorium should Not be Ended' (2003) 15 *Child and Family Law Quarterly* 223; and A Bainham, 'Child Protection, Adoption and the Moratorium: An Important Crossroads for Romania' (2003) 3 *Romanian Journal of Society and Politics* 54.

[16] Law no 272/2004 on the Protection and Promotion of the Rights of the Child, Romanian Official Gazette, Part I, no 557. Art 9 of the new law, *inter alia*, requires maternity and paediatric units to employ a social worker and police authorities to appoint individuals responsible for taking the necessary steps to establish the identity of abandoned babies. Under Art 10 the child's birth must be certified within 24 hours and that article also places the medical authorities who assisted in the birth under a legal obligation to ensure this. Under Art 11, where the child is abandoned in a maternity hospital, that institution is required to report the matter by telephone and in writing to the General Department for Social Security and Child Protection and the police within 24 hours of the mother's disappearance. These authorities will then be under a statutory obligation to arrange for the emergency placement of the child and to take steps to trace the mother.

[17] For discussion of the French position and the debates on the issue in Germany see K Scheiwe, 'Legal Provisions that Allow Women to Give Birth Anonymously—Apt to be Exported from France to Germany?' in P Lødrup and E Modvar (eds), *Family Life*, above n 12, 681.

[18] *Odièvre v France* (GC) ECHR 2003–IV. For commentary on the case see E Steiner, 'Desperately Seeking Mother—Anonymous Births in the European Court of Human Rights' [2003] 15 *Child and Family Law Quarterly* 425; and A Pedain, 'Condemned to Lifelong Ignorance' (2003) 62 *Cambridge Law Journal* 269.

[19] Series A no 31 (1979) 2 EHRR 330.

held that family life between mother and child arose *from the moment of birth*. English law in contrast does require that maternity is established and there are clear statutory obligations on the mother to register the birth.[20]

Where a new controversy, in my view, may be looming in England is in relation the mother's traditional right to give her child up for adoption within a short time of birth. When adoption was first introduced in England in the 1920s it had a good deal to do with providing an opportunity for unmarried mothers to give up their children and thereby escape the stigma of illegitimate birth.[21] In one (admittedly exceptional) recent case[22] the mother wished to relinquish her parental status by consenting to the father adopting the child on his own. Ultimately the adoption order made by the judge was upheld by the House of Lords. But in the Court of Appeal Hale LJ (as she then was), deciding against allowing the adoption, made robust comments to the effect that it was generally in the best interests of children to have two legal parents and two legal families. She emphasised that the relationship of mother and child was *in itself* sufficient to establish family life between them from birth. Such comments surely call into question more broadly the right of the mother to give up her child for adoption in an era of human rights. The uncomfortable question which we need to pose here was put starkly by John Eekelaar in 1991: 'Does a mother who gives a child over for adoption fail in a moral duty towards her child?'[23]

This question has become more complicated in recent years by an awareness of human rights and also by the emergence in the last decade or so of an apparently new kind of man; no longer the man whose only involvement with the courts is about dodging child support obligations, but the man who is seeking to assert his relationship with a child.

C. The Father

The CRC does not distinguish between mothers and fathers, but one inevitable practical distinction must be made. Whereas the identity of the mother is usually

---

[20] Section 10 Births and Deaths Registration Act 1953. Where the parents are *married* the statutory obligation is placed on both mother and father. Where they are *unmarried* it is on the mother alone.

[21] By the Adoption of Children Act 1926 following the recommendations of the *Report of the Child Adoption Committee* (Cmd 2401, 1925), (Cmd 2469, 1926) (the 'Tomlin Report'). An earlier Report, *The Report of the Committee on Child Adoption* (Cmd 1254, 1921) (the 'Hopkinson Report') had been followed by a number of unsuccessful legislative attempts to introduce adoption.

[22] *Re B (Adoption: Natural Parent)* [2002] 1 FLR 196 (HL); *Re B (Adoption by One Natural Parent to Exclusion of Other)* [2001] 1 FLR 589 (CA). For the author's views on the case see A Bainham, 'Unintentional Parenthood: The Case of the Reluctant Mother' (2002) 61 *Cambridge Law Journal* 288.

[23] J Eekelaar, 'Are Parents Morally Obliged to Care for Their Children?' (1991) 11 *Oxford Journal of Legal Studies* 340, 350.

clear from the fact of birth, this same fact of birth does not reveal the identity of the father. Although therefore the CRC upholds the right of the child to a relationship with the father *from the moment of birth*, this right cannot crystallise for the child, or for the father, until the identity of the father is known. Yet it is surely arguable that the *only* thing preventing the mutual rights of father and child from coming into being at the moment of birth is this practical limitation. In many cases there will be more than a clue about the identity of this man, perhaps encapsulated in the traditional characterisation of such a man as the *putative* father. Looked at in this way, we might reasonably label these rights as 'inchoate' and capable of perfection as and when paternity is established. After all, this is precisely what happens in relation to the *obligation* of child support. There too, the only thing preventing the obligation from arising at the moment of birth is the practical concern that the identity of the father may be unknown. Could it not therefore be argued that what holds good for obligations also holds good for rights?

The concept of inchoate rights in family law, especially in relation to fathers, is not a new one. It has been utilised by the English courts in the (admittedly quite different) context of international child abduction.[24] In that context the view has been taken that *certain* unmarried fathers, though lacking the formal legal status which goes with the acquisition of parental responsibility, nonetheless may have 'rights of custody' for the purposes of the Hague Convention governing child abduction. Such rights can arise by virtue of having primary *de facto* care of a child or from having a reasonable prospect of successfully obtaining a court order in their favour; in short, inchoate rights capable of being perfected. By analogy, my argument here is that the factual existence of the genetic connection between the father and child is sufficient to create inchoate rights which should then be perfected and converted into recognisable rights at the moment when paternity is established through legal process. They exist from the moment of birth but remain in 'legal limbo' until paternity is proved.

The legal procedures for establishing paternity are therefore critical; and they differ markedly between different jurisdictions. How well do our procedures stand up to examination alongside the situation elsewhere? It is my position that both English law and the judgments of the European Court of Human Rights (which are by now an integral part of English law) fail to uphold the rights of the child and the rights of the father.

I will concentrate on the issues surrounding births outside marriage, now standing at around 40% of the total of live births in England.[25] However, I will begin with a brief comment on births within marriage. Here the common law

---

[24] *Re B (A Minor) (Abduction)* [1994] 2 FLR 249; *Re F (Abduction: Unmarried Father: Sole Carer)* [2003] 1 FLR 839.
[25] *Population Trends* 108 (2002) Table 3.2.

presumption reigns that the husband is the genetic and therefore the legal father of the child. The presumption may be rebutted on the balance of probabilities and increasingly the courts have been inclined to direct scientific tests to get at the truth. Although this remains a matter for the courts' discretion, the previous concern for the stability of marriage[26] seems to have been largely supplanted by an emphasis on the right to know the truth.[27] The courts have taken the position that it is by no means clear that biological revelations will be the catastrophe which they once were. Changes in society mean that it may now be possible to recognise the biological position without necessarily fatally undermining a marriage. The various adults concerned may be expected to come to terms with the child having both a biological and a social father.[28] In some cases of assisted reproduction, however, where the husband is co-operating in the treatment we can see legal and genetic parentage expressly divorced from one another.[29] At least at the present time, a fiction is maintained to the outside world that they are coincidental. That is to say, no-one apart from the couple concerned, may have reason to believe that the husband does not have legal, social and genetic parentage.

In births outside marriage there is no legal presumption of paternity, even where the mother is in a stable cohabitation with the man who presents as the father. Paternity is a matter of proof, most obviously through registration of a man as the father on the child's birth certificate.

English law upholds the right of the mother to withhold the name of the man she knows or believes to be the father of her child, though this right is qualified where she is in receipt of state benefits.[30] There is no statutory obligation on her to include the name of the father on the child's birth certificate and neither may a man be included if he does not consent. Essentially, the mother and the man concerned must co-operate in birth registration. Yet English law has withheld from the father a full parental status in relation to the child. Although the fact of paternity gives rise to the legal relationship of parent and child, it does not automatically give to the father parental responsibility—the legal device for conveying the powers and duties necessary for raising the child.[31] A major change in English law brought about by the Adoption and Children Act 2002, and implemented in December 2003, will result in many more unmarried fathers acquiring parental

---

[26] See, for example, *Re F (A Minor: Paternity Test)* [1993] 1 FLR 598.

[27] See particularly *Re T (Paternity: Ordering Blood Tests)* [2001] 2 FLR 1190; and *Re H and A (Paternity: Blood Tests)* [2002] 1 FLR 1145.

[28] A view strongly expressed by Ward LJ in *Re H (Paternity: Blood Test)* [1996] 2 FLR 65.

[29] Under s 28 Human Fertilisation and Embryology Act 1990.

[30] In benefit cases there is a qualified legal obligation to provide information designed to enable the Secretary of State to identify or trace the non-resident parent. See s 6 Child Support Act 1991 as amended.

[31] Section 2 Children Act 1989.

responsibility on being registered.[32] The process of birth registration in this sense assumes a new significance, for the father, the mother and the child. But there is no change to the rule that the mother effectively controls the process of registration. Indeed there has been some speculation about whether some mothers may be *less* inclined to register a man as the father, given the wider legal consequences of doing so.

The decisions of the European Court of Human Rights do not uphold, any more than English law does, the notion that the child has a right to a relationship with the father from birth. The answer which the Court has given to the question 'Is there family life between the father and the child?' is 'maybe'. The test which the Court has employed is whether there are 'certain ties' between father and child which make the relationship one of sufficient constancy for family life to have arisen.[33] Whether family life has been established is therefore a factual test. Is the connection between father and child considered strong enough to justify the conclusion that they had a family life together? We should note, however, that no such question of fact arises where the father is married.[34] There is a certain irony perhaps in the result that some husbands, who are not genetic fathers and may in some cases even be estranged from their wives, will have 'family life' with the children concerned, whereas some unmarried men who are undeniably the genetic fathers will not. The European Court of Human Rights has nonetheless taken the view that the genetic connection does not by itself give rise to family life between the father and the child. Thus a sperm donor does not have family life with the resulting child.[35] More controversially, the English courts have held, applying Article 8, that family life may not arise where the relationship between the mother and father broke down, perhaps while the mother was pregnant, and especially in circumstances where the father remained unaware of the pregnancy and birth until some time later.[36]

The most striking feature of English law's attitude to the father's legal status is the extent to which it is content to leave this under the control of the mother. It is for *the mother* to decide whether or not she wishes to disclose the name of the father at the time of registration and now also, by virtue of this same decision, to determine whether or not he should acquire parental responsibility. While it is

---

[32] Section 4(1)(a) Children Act 1989 as inserted by the Adoption and Children Act 2002.

[33] Among the leading cases are *Söderbäck v Sweden* Reports of Judgments and Decisions 1998–VII [1999] 1 FLR 250; *Kroon v the Netherlands* Series A no 297 [1994] 19 EHRR 263 and, more recently, *Lebbink v the Netherlands* ECHR 2004- [2004] 2 FLR 463.

[34] Here it is just assumed that the existence of the *legal* tie arising from marriage will of itself suffice.

[35] *G v the Netherlands* 16 EHRR CD 38 (Application no 16944/90). See also *Mikulic v Croatia* [2002] 1 FCR 20 which held that a purely casual sexual relationship did not give rise to family life.

[36] Contrast, for example, the results in the two conjoined appeals in *Re H; Re G (Adoption: Consultation of Unmarried Fathers)* [2001] 1 FLR 646. For a general review of the case law, see A Bainham, 'Can We Protect Children and Protect their Rights?' (2002) *Family Law* 279.

true that a man claiming to be the father does have the option of bringing the matter before the courts,[37] this is a serious step and it represents a significant hurdle which may or may not be crossed depending on the court's view of the child's best interests. The central question which perhaps needs to be addressed is whether this level of control by the mother is consistent with the notion that the child and the father have independent rights in relation to paternal affiliation. And we should remember in this respect that failure to establish affiliation with the father also amounts to failure to generate the kinship links between the child and the wider paternal family which derive from the relationship of parent and child.[38] Hale LJ (as she then was) was mindful of these wider kinship links, though in the context of the mother's family, when she offered the view that a child needs two families. Unless we can therefore find a rational basis for distinguishing between the potential significance of the maternal and paternal families, it is questionable why the maternal family should be thought indispensable, while the paternal family should be viewed as an optional extra.

Other countries have laws which view the determination of paternity as a more urgent matter. The tradition in civil law jurisdictions is to provide mechanisms whereby a man claiming to be the father may formally 'recognise' or 'acknowledge' a child as his own.[39] It is true that the mother may dispute such recognition, but the onus will be on her to bring the matter before the court and not, as in England, on the father. In some countries considerable significance is attached to paternal affiliation. In Argentina an action for damages will lie against a man who fails to recognise his child based on the psychological harm thereby caused to the child.[40] An action has also succeeded against a married woman and her lover who culpably 'passed off' the three children of their extra-marital relations as the genetic children of the woman's husband. In this case the husband was awarded 60,000 dollars on appeal for the mental and psychological harm suffered in believing throughout the marriage that the children were his.[41] In the Nordic countries

---

[37] Under s 4 Children Act 1989 he may apply to the court for a 'parental responsibility order'. The courts have on the whole granted such orders quite liberally except where the father is thought to pose some sort of threat to the child's welfare. The leading case is the Court of Appeal's decision in *Re S (Parental Responsibility)* [1995] 2 FLR 648.

[38] It should be emphasised that these legal kinship relations are derived from the relationship of parent and child, do not depend on possessing parental responsibility and are not created merely by the acquisition of parental responsibility.

[39] For a review of paternity procedures in the countries of continental Europe see M-T Meulders, 'The Position of the Father in European Legislation' (1990) 4 *International Journal of Law and the Family* 131.

[40] See CP Grosman and AM Chechile 'Argentina: Recent Judicial Decisions Giving Effect to the Convention on the Rights of the Child' in A Bainham (ed), *The International Survey of Family Law*, 2004 edn (Bristol, Jordans, 2004) 21, 22–29.

[41] The case is discussed in detail by CP Grosman and M Herrera, 'Argentina: The Right to One's Identity in Recent Judicial Decisions on Filiation and Adoption' in A Bainham (ed), *The International Survey of Family Law*, 2005 edn (Bristol, Jordans, 2005) 23, 24–27.

there is concern for determining paternity in as many cases as possible. Thus, in Sweden a government agency is charged with the responsibility for ensuring that, wherever possible, the name of the child's genetic father is recorded as a matter of public record.[42] In Norway, too, legislation enacted in 2002 is grounded in the basic philosophy that it is in the best interests of the child that the biological father should also be the legal father, even if that means that an existing father's parent-hood is challenged.[43] In 2001 Denmark enacted a new Children Act (in force since 1 July 2002) which is based, *inter alia*, on the fundamental principle that each child shall to the farthest possible extent have both a father and a mother. The leg-islation provides that, *prima facie*, it is the obligation of the mother always to dis-close the name of the father.[44] Australia has given the equivalent of parental responsibility to all unmarried fathers on proof of paternity since 1975 and most of the countries of Eastern Europe have done so since World War II, at the same time taking the opportunity to abolish illegitimacy.[45]

The common denominator is that all these countries take the question of the legal relationship between the genetic father and the child more seriously than we do in England. Of course it might be argued that we have got it right and they have all got it wrong. We have a law which in essence attaches first importance to the mother's right of confidentiality or, expressed in terms of the ECHR, her right to respect for her 'private life'. Yet we surely ought to question why the mother's interests should be elevated over competing interests in this way.

D. The Child

There are essentially two aspects to the rights of the child; first, to have a relation-ship established with his or her father and mother and to have knowledge of their identity and, second, the right to have those relationships fostered and preserved.

As to the first right—the right to know, and to establish a relationship with, one's parents—I want to return briefly to what I have called the temporal ques-tion. Exactly when should the child be entitled to have this information? Where the child has been adopted, access to the original birth certificate is allowed only

---

[42] See A Eriksson and Å Saldeen, 'Parenthood and Science' in J Eekelaar and P Šarcevic (eds), *Parenthood in Modern Society: Legal and Social Issues for the Twenty-First Century* (Dordrecht, Martinus Nijhoff, 1993) 75.

[43] See P Lødrup, 'Challenges to an Established Paternity—Radical Changes in Norwegian Law' in A Bainham (ed), *The International Survey of Family Law*, 2003 edn (Bristol, Jordans, 2003) 353.

[44] For a full discussion of the new rules see I Lund-Andersen, 'Denmark: Focus on Legal Status Between Children and Parents' in A Bainham (ed), *The International Survey of Family Law*, 2005 edn (Bristol, Jordans, 2005) 203, 205–8.

[45] Discussed further by the author in A Bainham, 'Family Rights in the Next Millenium' (2000) 53 *Current Legal Problems* 471.

on the child attaining majority.[46] At the present time, where the child was conceived by gametes donated before April 2005, only non-identifying information
about donors is available, again on attaining majority.[47] Donors who donate
gametes after 1 April 2005 lose their anonymity.[48] But the child has no legal right
to be told that he or she was adopted[49] or the product of donated gametes. The
question I want to pose is: why 18? The child's right to knowledge of parents,
according to the CRC, arises *at birth*. The New Zealand Law Commission[50] has
recently questioned whether the attainment of adulthood is an appropriate
threshold for the receipt of this information. In particular, the Commission points
out that, elsewhere in the law, certain capacities of adolescents arise when the
child has attained a sufficient age and understanding to be able to assess the implications of what is involved.[51] It could also be argued that to deny access to information to those under 18 is a form of age discrimination.[52] It could be said that a
child who is old enough to ask for the information is old enough to know the
truth.

I want to go further than this. I doubt that a test of maturity would provide all
the answers to this temporal question. What about babies and young children
caught up in paternity disputes? In that context it has been largely accepted judicially that the sooner the truth is established the better.[53] The thinking appears to
be that it is better for all concerned to know where they stand and for an opportunity to be provided for a relationship between the child and the biological parent to develop. It is worth considering how much more difficult it is likely to be
for the child where he or she has the first opportunity to seek out this relationship
only in adulthood. So, there is a question here about why the child's right or interest in establishing the identity of the biological parent is greater or different in the
case of a paternity dispute than it is in the context of assisted reproduction or
adoption. If it is important to establish the truth in one context as soon as possible why wait in the other context?

[46] A right introduced by the Children Act 1975.
[47] Section 31 Human Fertilisation and Embryology Act 1990. At 16 information may be given which
would prevent a potential marriage within the prohibited degrees.
[48] *Human Fertilisation and Embryology Authority (Disclosure of Donor Information) Regulations
2004*. The effect of the regulations is that children born of gametes donated after April 2005 will have
the right to identifying information about the donor on attaining the age of 18.
[49] It was proposed by the Adoption Review of the 1990s that the child should have a statutory right to
be told that he or she was adopted but such a right has not been enshrined in the Adoption and Children
Act 2002. See *Review of Adoption Law* (Department of Health and Welsh Office, 1992) para 4.9.
[50] Law Commission Preliminary Paper 54 *New Issues in Legal Parenthood: A Discussion Paper*
(Wellington, New Zealand, 2004).
[51] Increasingly so following the landmark decision of the House of Lords in *Gillick v West Norfolk
and Wisbech Area Health Authority* [1986] 1 AC 112.
[52] Law Commission Preliminary Paper 54 *New Issues in Legal Parenthood: A Discussion Paper*
(Wellington, New Zealand, 2004) para 5.65.
[53] A principle forcefully propounded by Ward LJ in *Re H (Paternity: Blood Test)* [1996] 2 FLR 65.

There are many aspects to what we may view as the second right of the child—to preserve family relations. I want to focus briefly on just two which have proved controversial in England and which are still the subject of considerable debate. The first is the issue of contact and the second is adoption.

E. Contact

Fostering and maintaining contact between the child and a parent from whom that child has been separated is an important principle in international conventions.[54] The ECHR requires the state to provide a serious justification for curtailing it or terminating it. Where the child is in care, this is conceived as a temporary arrangement and there is a strong duty on the state to make strenuous efforts to bring about reunification of the family.[55] It has often been denied by commentators that parents have a right of contact with their children, yet it is crystal clear that such a right exists under international conventions. Most recently, the Council of Europe has produced a Convention on Contact concerning Children.[56] Article 4 of this Convention sets it out in plain English that 'a child and *his or her parents* shall have the right to obtain and maintain regular contact with each other' (emphasis added). It goes on to provide that 'such contact may be restricted or excluded only where necessary in the best interests of the child'. The explanatory notes to the Convention set out in uncompromising tones the very limited circumstances under which the state is permitted to restrict or exclude contact between children and parents: '[I]t must be beyond any doubt that such restriction or exclusion of what essentially is a human right is necessary in the best interests of the child concerned'. And it is further stated: 'The more the right of contact is to be restricted, the more serious the reasons for justifying such restriction must be'.[57]

These principles apply both to the situation where the child is in state care and to private disputes between parents.[58] There has also been a great deal of debate

---

[54] It is regarded as a right arising from the right to respect for family life which both parent and child have under Art 8 of the ECHR.

[55] See especially the judgments of the European Court of Human Rights in *Johansen v Norway* Reports of Judgments and Decisions 1996–I (1996) 23 EHRR 33; *K and T v Finland* (GC) ECHR 2001–VII [2000] 2 FLR 79 and *S and G v Italy* [2000] 2 FLR 771.

[56] Convention on Contact concerning Children, ETS No 192, adopted on 15 May 2003 (not yet entered into force). The United Kingdom has not yet signed and ratified the Convention. In 2004, the Department for Constitutional Affairs conducted a consultation on whether the UK ought to become a member to the Convention. The outcome of the consultation process has not yet been made public. See http://www.dca.gov.uk/consult/contconveur/contactconv.htm.

[57] *Ibid*, Art 4.

[58] On the right of contact in the private law context see *Hokkanen v Finland* Series A no 299–A [1996] 1 FLR 289; and, more recently, *Kosmopoulou v Greece* [2004] 1 FLR 800; and *Hansen v Turkey* [2004] 1 FLR 142. And see now the Draft Children (Contact and Adoption) Bill 2005.

in this country about whether contact orders should be enforced by the courts.[59] Yet the position under the ECHR is quite clear. The state *must* take all reasonable steps to enforce such orders as an aspect of the *positive* obligations imposed by Article 8. It is at least questionable whether our current contact regime complies with these requirements. It is important too, in my view, that any increase in the use of mediation for resolving contact disputes—as is currently proposed[60]— should be conducted with an appreciation by those involved in mediation of the fundamental rights which are the backdrop to the mediation.

F. Adoption

Recent changes to adoption law in England[61] can be criticised for failing to take seriously enough the child's interests in maintaining links with the birth family. Where an adoption is sought in the face of parental objection, the new law replaces the primary test of whether that parent is withholding consent unreasonably with a straightforward welfare test.[62] Is adoption in the best interests of the child? The change goes against the official recommendations of a Review of Adoption Law in the 1990s.[63] It had always been thought, before this change, that termination of the fundamental relationship of parent and child was too serious a matter to be governed solely by a welfare test. The former grounds had reflected the significance of what was at stake for the *parent* as well as for the child.[64]

---

[59] See particularly the argument of Carol Smart and Bren Neale that the courts have been over-zealous in their enforcement of contact (C Smart and B Neale, 'Arguments against Virtue—Must Contact be Enforced?' [1997] *Family Law* 332).

[60] By the government in its Green Paper, *Parental Separation: Children's Needs and Parents' Responsibilities* (Cmd 6273, 2004).

[61] Brought about by the Adoption and Children Act 2002. The Act was preceded by the White Paper from the Department of Health, *Adoption: A New Approach* (Cmd 5017, 2000) and by a paper produced by the Performance and Innovation Unit, *Prime Minister's Review: Adoption: Issued for Consultation* (Cabinet Office, July 2000).

[62] Adoption and Children Act 2002, s 51(2)(b). The only other ground for granting an adoption order without parental consent is in s 51(2)(a) and covers the rather exceptional situation where 'the parent or guardian cannot be found or is incapable of giving consent'.

[63] The review had instead favoured a test which would have required the court to be satisfied that the advantages to the child of becoming part of a new family and having a new legal status were so significantly greater than the advantages to the child of any alternative option as to justify overriding the wishes of a parent or guardian. See *Review of Adoption Law* (Department of Health and Welsh Office, 1992), para 12.6.

[64] Significantly, there were still cases being reported right up to the enactment of the 2002 legislation in which the higher courts had held that a parent was not unreasonably withholding consent to adoption. See, for example, *Re M (Adoption or Residence Order)* [1998] 1 FLR 570; and *Re B (Adoption Order)* [2001] 2 FLR 26.

A related issue is post-adoption contact with the birth family. Post-adoption contact is certainly possible under the new law, but what is absent from the new legislation and from the government's White Paper which preceded it, is any real sense that this is being officially encouraged.[65] More fundamentally the policy of the legislation, of seeking to drive up adoption figures in relation to children in public care, is questionable.[66] The evidence that adoption is better than other long-term alternatives which preserve the child's legal relationship with the birth family is inconclusive at best.[67] In my view, in terms of complying with international obligations, the conventions are much more about avoiding adoption where possible than they are about encouraging it.

G. Conclusion

None of the arguments in this chapter should be taken as detracting from the proposition that those looking after a child should be given the legal powers and duties associated with that role. I am all in favour of the law giving appropriate recognition and support to social parents. But I part company with those who argue that social parents should become legal parents. In general, it is my view that it is unnecessary and undesirable to go this far. The distinction between being a legal parent and having parental responsibility is an important one. What social carers need are the legal powers to enable them to get on with the job of raising the child. In England we have a perfectly good legal device for this purpose, namely parental responsibility. This will enable the social carer to take all major decisions in relation to the child's upbringing, for example those relating to education or a medical operation. It is a positive feature of the new adoption legislation that it enables certain categories of long-term carers of children, notably step-parents, to acquire parental responsibility more easily than has been

---

[65] A rather half-hearted little subsection (s 46(6)) merely provides that before making an adoption order the court must consider whether there should be arrangements for allowing any person contact with the child.

[66] The government's target as expressed in its White Paper is by 2004/2005 to increase by 40% the number of children looked after by local authorities who are adopted.

[67] For a critique of the government's policy see J Eekelaar, 'Contact and the Adoption Reform' in A Bainham *et al* (eds), *Children and Their Families: Contact, Rights and Welfare* (Oxford, Hart Publishing, 2003) 253. On the very different policies followed in France, the Netherlands and Sweden, all of which eschew domestic adoption, see A Warman and C Roberts, *Adoption and Looked after Children: An International Comparison*, Working Paper 2003/1, Oxford Centre for Family Law and Policy, Department of Social Policy, University of Oxford (2003). A 'pro-adoption' policy in relation to children in long-term substitute care was also recently rejected in South Australia, as to which see P Parkinson, 'Child Protection, Permanency Planning and Children's Right to Family Life' (2003) 17 *International Journal of Law, Policy and the Family* 147.

the case in the past.[68] And the new status of special guardianship should better protect long-term carers against the threat of removal of the child from their care by the birth parents.[69] But this does not mean that the law should take the ultimate step of making the carer the legal parent, for that is to confuse the function of legal parentage with that of parental responsibility. The purpose of legal parentage is to recognise the fundamental kinship connection between the child and the parent and the child and that parent's wider family. The effect of making social parents legal parents, as the New Zealand Law Commission has recently pointed out, is to create 'a legal fiction by hiding the fact that the child's genetic parents are not the social parents'.[70]

I find myself in agreement with some of the central aims and issues identified by the New Zealand Law Commission in its discussion paper on Legal Parenthood. In particular the following seem to me to be important guiding principles identified by the Commission:

1. *Children have a right to know the circumstances of their conception and birth.*
2. *Persons raising children should have the legal responsibilities and rights necessary to nurture and rear the child.*
3. *A child can have a number of committed and co-operative adults involved in his or her upbringing, provided that these people always have clear lines of responsibility and mechanisms for dealing with conflict.*[71]

The third of these guiding principles reflects an important social phenomenon which also needs to be reflected in the legal regime governing parenthood. The law needs to be *inclusive* and to give appropriate recognition to *all* those adults who are making a contribution, in their various ways, to the life of the child. Increasingly, the law is not going to be faced with a stark choice between genetic or social parents. It is not so much a matter of choosing between the two as finding the right legal formula for acknowledging that the child may have an interest or right in securing the relationship with *both*. It is no longer necessarily the case that to discover the truth of genetic parentage will undermine or cause the collapse of the child's relationships with the social parents. It is not necessarily the case either that to allow some contact between the child and the birth family will

---

[68] The 2002 Act gives a boost to a number of 'alternatives for permanence'. Section 114 inserts a new s 12(5) into the Children Act 1989 allowing applications to extend residence orders to the age of 18; s 113 amends s 9(3) Children Act 1989 to relax the residential requirement for local authority foster parents wishing to apply for orders in relation to a foster child and s 112 inserts a new s 4 A into the Children Act to enable step-parents to acquire parental responsibility by agreement with the parent(s) or by a parental responsibility order.

[69] Section 115 Adoption and Children Act 2002, creating a new status of special guardianship to be regulated by new ss 14 A-G Children Act 1989.

[70] Law Commission Preliminary Paper 54 *New Issues in Legal Parenthood: A Discussion Paper* (Wellington, New Zealand, 2004).

[71] *Ibid.*

destabilise the position of long-term carers. These perceived conflicts may be more attitudinal than real. In my view they are much more likely to be about the psychological insecurities of adults than they are about children's ability to adapt. As it becomes more accepted that children are able to relate to a range of adults, some genetically related to them and some not, it becomes more necessary to find *inclusive* legal concepts and to move away from the all or nothing approaches which appear previously to have characterised legal solutions.

The growing internationalisation of family law dictates that there should be a much sharper appreciation of the obligations of the state. These are manifestly not private matters to be kept within the family. The international conventions confer rights and it is the obligation of the state to respect and give effect to those rights. Determining who are the child's birth parents is not a matter of choice for the state. It is an obligation imposed by the CRC. Taking steps to preserve contact between the child and those parents is not a matter of choice for the state either. It is required, *inter alia*, by Article 8 of the ECHR.

The legal regime should be clearly seen to be giving effect to what I believe would be accepted by the vast majority of people both here and elsewhere—that the relationships between mother, father and child are fundamental. They arise at birth and are truly terminated only by death. As Margaret Thatcher once famously, or infamously, put it: 'Parenthood is for life'.

10

Reproductive Choice: Men's Freedom and Women's Responsibility?

SALLY SHELDON

In this chapter, I hope to offer some insights into the influence of gender on how we think about reproductive responsibilities. By 'reproductive responsibilities', I intend a bundle of (perceived) obligations relating to what one can and should do before conception and birth to safeguard the health of one's future child; decisions regarding whether to conceive and if so when; the choice of whether to go ahead with a pregnancy; and decisions about how to act during birth, pregnancy and prior to conception in order to ensure fetal/child health. All of these decisions may be more or less carefully planned, made more or less 'responsibly' with varying levels of regard for fetal/child welfare, and given more or less priority *vis-a-vis* other aspects of life. Such responsibilities can be enforced in a range of ways, from criminal sanctions to warnings in increasingly large fonts on cigarette packets to the social disapproval which may be felt when a heavily pregnant woman is seen drinking alcohol. Considering the influence of gender on reproductive responsibilities raises a host of interesting ethical questions, but here my interest is sociological rather than normative. I am concerned to flesh out some aspects of the ways in which we think about these responsibilities, and how that thinking has reflected gendered assumptions. And I am particularly interested to track the footprints of these assumptions in law.

In a first section, I lay some theoretical groundwork regarding sex, gender, and reproductive biology. With this in place, I go on to suggest that a number of gendered assumptions are commonly made regarding reproductive responsibilities: first, that reproduction is 'women's business', a far more important matter for women than for men; secondly, that the female reproductive system is more fragile than that of men and this renders it potentially more dangerous to the fetus/future child; and thirdly that coition is almost entirely a recreational practice for men, while its importance for women is more closely linked to a desire for procreation. Finally, I will suggest that the carer/breadwinner divide also enjoys an important influence on our ideas about reproductive responsibilities. In a second section, I make use of two legal case studies to illustrate some of these assumptions. Thirdly and inevitably more speculatively, however, I go on to sketch some changes to the social and medical context, which may serve to challenge current understandings of male and female reproductive responsibilities.

A. Sex, Gender and Reproductive Biology

Before I go on to sketch the four assumptions noted above, I need to clarify one basic point. My focus on a 'gendered' underpinning to our thinking on reproductive biology should not be taken as a denial of the existence of basic biological differences between men and women in the context of reproduction. Biological asymmetry does exist and, moreover, it provides a clear basis for suggesting that men's and women's responsibilities in the context of reproductive decision-making must therefore also be asymmetrical. Nonetheless, biological asymmetry itself cannot adequately explain the differences in how we think about men's and women's reproductive responsibilities: gender is an important prism through which these are read. As such, our understandings of sexed differences are 'situational ... explicable only within the context of battles over gender and power'.[1] To claim that our understandings of sex are so influenced, is not to claim that material bodies and material differences between them do not exist, rather, it is to assert that there is no reference to a pure, objectively knowable, body.[2]

My starting point, then, is in the recognition that beliefs about gender are fundamental to how we read sex. One often cited illustration of this point is Emily Martin's telling description of the way in which research into human reproductive biology reproduces stereotypes of appropriate gender behaviour.[3] Martin presents

[1] J Butler, *Bodies that Matter: On the Discursive Limits of 'Sex'* (London, Routledge, 1993) 11.

[2] *Ibid*, 10. Butler makes this statement in the context of asking herself how one should respond to the idea that there are at least certain minimal sexually differentiated parts, activities, capacities, hormonal and chromosomal differences which could be conceded without reference to construction: 'although at this moment I want to offer an absolute reassurance [that such biological differences exist] some anxiety prevails. To concede the undeniability of "sex" or its "materiality" is always to concede some version of "sex", some formation of "materiality"', *ibid*. In other words, Butler does not deny that we are/have material bodies which differ from each other in a variety of ways. However in seeking to map and catalogue these differences, to order them along certain axes, to describe the objective 'reality' of bodies, the descriptor will inevitably impose particular understandings and values to construct a particular version of what is described. The elaboration of objective truth is a laudable scientific aspiration, but sociologically speaking it remains an impossibility: there is no unmediated access to a pre-social unconstructed 'reality' of the body.

[3] E Martin, 'The Egg and the Sperm: How Science has Constructed a Romance Based on Stereotypical Male-Female Roles' (1991) 16 *Signs: Journal of Women in Culture and Society* 485.

two different biological accounts of human conception, both equally clearly displaying evidence of gendered imagery. On the one hand, scientists describe conquering, active 'macho' sperm which would race and fight with each other in their attempts to be the first to penetrate a waiting egg. This clearly gendered imagery parallels a particular understanding of appropriate male and female roles during sexual relationships: whilst men chase, conquer and penetrate, women are passive, waiting for the male advance and submitting to penetration. A second and more recent strand of scientific writing has challenged this model, putting forward the theory of the 'seductive egg' which selects an appropriate sperm. Again this draws on a particular, though different, understanding of a sexual encounter where it is the woman who initiates the sex, enticing a man into her bed:

> A human egg cell does not idle languidly in the female reproductive tract, like some Sleeping Beauty waiting for a sperm Prince Charming to come along and waken it for fertilization. Instead, new research indicates that most eggs actively beckon to would-be partners, releasing an as-yet-unidentified chemical to lure sperm cells.[4]

Of interest here is not the vivid language used to present these findings, but the extent to which gendered understandings influence what the scientists actually see. The 'seductive egg' model would seem to have at least as much to do with the presentation of a different understanding of gender relationships (where women enjoy a less passive role), as it has to do with a different account of the biological 'facts' of human reproduction. As such, Martin's work should not be read as an attack on individual scientists who have, in some way, failed to do their work properly. Rather it demonstrates the constraints on scientific understanding: in seeking to see, describe or understand the world scientists, like all of us, will inevitably rely on ideas and conceptual frameworks which are already available to them. Any scientific study cannot help but be informed by existing beliefs.

In this chapter, I follow Martin in attempting to uncover a number of assumptions which have influenced the way we think about human reproduction. I am happy to acknowledge at the outset that none of these assumptions are universally accepted, that all are subject to challenge and, very possibly, that their cultural resonance (and impact in law) is diminishing. I do suggest, however, that they retain some continued cultural power and legal relevance.

First, then, we are often told that reproduction is women's business: women are far more interested in reproduction than are men and far more closely

---

[4] *Science News*, cited in C Daniels 'Between Fathers and Fetuses: The Social Construction of Male Reproduction and the Politics of Fetal Harm' (1997) 22 *Signs: Journal of Women in Culture and Society* 579.

involved in every aspect of it.[5] At worst, men are seen as absent, uninterested and uninvolved. At best, their relationship to reproduction is secondary and vicarious, mediated through their partner's experiences.[6] Even to talk of men and reproductive capacity in the same sentence seems to risk straying into the realms of the oxymoronic. Reproduction seems to be a peculiarly, palpably *female* activity. It is the woman's body that carries and nourishes a fetus and visibly swells to accommodate its growth. And it is this bodily connection to the growing fetus which has generally grounded claims that women need to control contraception and have the right to make decisions about continuing or terminating pregnancies:

> [The pregnant woman] is sick, pulled out of shape, moves clumsily and worries about falling. She is tested and then makes conscious choices in response to those tests. She ponders over the effects of the simplest drug that might relieve a headache, often enough struggles against possibly damaging addictive habits, and frequently worries and then feels guilty about what she eats, drinks, or smokes. She is apprehensive of the pain she will almost surely suffer, yet (if she has the time and the money) selects anaesthetics and labor practices conducive to her infant's health. Typically, she expects to take on the greater share of the child tending on which parental visions ultimately depend; anxiously she devises strategies for getting the services she and her child will require and imagines ways in which she might maintain her job or pursue her career and still enjoy the friendships, projects and pleasures of her pre-maternal adult life.[7]

The responsibilities of motherhood are seen to extend far back into pregnancy and even precede conception, involving a complex range of prescriptions (*do* pay attention to your diet, take folic acid, listen to soothing music; but *don't* drink alcohol, smoke, take drugs, eat soft cheese, do vigorous exercise, expose yourself to stress or sustained high temperatures). By comparison, the man's involvement before birth appears insignificant, amounting to nothing more than the ejaculation of a small amount of seminal fluid.

---

[5] For the popular currency of such ideas, see C Lewis, *Becoming a Father* (Milton Keynes, Open University Press, 1986) 35–36. Lewis' interviews with one hundred married fathers in the 1980s, found that many couples had drifted into pregnancy, but that wives were three times more likely to have raised the subject, and men were likely to feel that they should defer to them on it. Lewis also cites an earlier study of infertile couples, which suggested that however much men wanted children, their main concern in attending an infertility clinic was to provide a child for their wife, whose social status very much depended on her role as mother.

[6] For men's experience of pregnancy as mediated through partners, see J Draper, 'Blurring, Moving and Broken Boundaries: Men's Encounters with the Pregnant Body' (2003) 25 *Sociology and Health and Illness* 743. For fathers' relationships with their children as mediated through mothers, see C Smart and B Neale, *Family Fragments?* (Cambridge, Polity, 1999).

[7] S Ruddick, 'Thinking about Fathers' in M Hirsch and E Fox Keller (eds), *Conflicts in Feminism* (London, Routledge, 1990) 222, 228.

Secondly, closely related to this understanding of reproduction, is the belief that it is only the woman's body which is liable to pose any risk to the fetus. Women's reproductive bodies are seen as porous and volatile, dangerous places for the developing embryo and fetus which will require every protection which can be offered by medical science.[8] As one prominent legal commentator puts it: '[i]n most circumstances, the unborn child is much more likely to be harmed, not by a third party but by his [sic] own mother.'[9] It is thus the woman who must moderate her actions in the interests of the well being of her future child.

> It is now well known, for example, that the excessive consumption of drugs or alcohol and the excessive smoking of cigarettes by the pregnant mother is hazardous to the health of her unborn child. There are many other sources of potential harm: safeguards are commonly taken against unsuitable or inadequate maternal diet and workplace hazards such as exposure to radiation or harmful chemicals of various kinds.[10]

Thirdly, men's involvement in the business of sex is often codified in conventional wisdom as primarily a sexual act, rather than a reproductive one: the idea being that whilst women are interested in coition at least in part as a means to a reproductive end, men invariably desire it exclusively in terms of sexual gratification. An illustration of this point is provided by Adrienne Burgess' discussion of what doctors consider important when making decisions about how to treat intersex children: to create a girl, they remove penile tissue, even though the resulting 'girl' will be unable to experience orgasm; to create a boy, they remove the ovaries but keep the penis, even if the ejaculate will be infertile.[11] Here sexual ability is protected for those patients selected to be male and reproductive capacity for those designated female. This same prioritisation is evident in Graycar's discussion of Australian loss of consortium cases.[12] When damage to women's sexual ability or enjoyment is at issue, Graycar notes, talk often turns to her (residual) reproductive capacity. For a man, however, comments are more typically about loss of sexual ability or enjoyment.

---

[8] See S Sheldon, '*Re*Conceiving Masculinity: Imagining Men's Reproductive Bodies in Law' (1999) 26 *Journal of Law and Society* 129 for a more detailed exposition of these understandings of the woman's body as porous, volatile and hence dangerous. See further E Grosz, *Volatile Bodies: Toward a Corporeal Feminism* (Indianapolis, IN, Indiana University Press, 1994); M Shildrick, *Leaky Bodies and Boundaries: Feminism, Postmodernism and Bioethics* (London, Routledge, 1997).

[9] J Fortin, 'Legal Protection for the Unborn Child' (1988) 51 *Modern L Rev* 54, 75.

[10] *Ibid.*

[11] A Burgess, *Fatherhood Reclaimed: The Making of the Modern Father* (London, Vermillion, 1997) 102–3. See also Michael Thomson's discussion of the advertising discourses surrounding erectile dysfunction and Viagra, noting a focus on the importance of recreational sexual activity for men, with discussion of any procreative function very much absent (M Thomson, 'Viagra Nation: Sex and the Prescribing of Familial Masculinity' (forthcoming 2005) *Law, Culture and Humanities*).

[12] The action in loss of consortium traditionally protected a husband who had been deprived of his wife's society, for example through her hospitalisation or changes in her personality consequent on an accident caused by the negligence of another, see *eg Oakley v Walker* (1977) 121 SJ 619.

It seems that when it comes to women, 'sex' and 'reproduction' are interchangeable. That is, the natural consequence of women having sex seems to be having children. So, if sex is painful, but she can still have it (even if it is painful and/or unpleasant) and get pregnant and give birth, it is sometimes difficult for a court to see that there has been any injury at all. For men, however ... sex is sex and is integral to men's sense of self.[13]

This point is also illustrated by the first Californian case where a wife (rather than husband) successfully sued for loss of consortium. The plaintiff, Mary Anne Rodriguez describes various ways in which she has suffered as a result of the paralysis of her husband, Richard, including the pain of '[being] deeply in love with each other and [having] no way of physically expressing this love'. However, the loss which she emphasises most strongly is that of the possibility to bear children. She explains: 'I have lost what I consider is the fulfilment of my existence because my husband can't make me pregnant so to bear children and have a family'.[14] Can we imagine a male plaintiff also describing the ability to have a family as 'the fulfilment of his existence'? Without seeking to deny that some men want to have children, it seems unlikely.

The potential impact of these assumptions is well illustrated by a recent study of (heterosexual) HIV+ men, which found that while HIV+ women are routinely given reproductive advice, HIV+ men were given very little such information.[15] This was not because the men were not interested: over half of those interviewed stated that they would value consultations regarding fertility and fathering. That sexual intercourse would continue to play a role in HIV+ men's lives is assumed: information is regularly provided regarding safer sexual practices. Thus, these men are seen as sexual but not as reproductive agents. Reproduction is presented as a less central matter of concern for men and, while women are expected to be responsible reproductive decision-makers, far less is expected of men and far less assistance (and surveillance) is provided of their reproductive decision-making.[16]

Finally, it seems to me that understandings of reproductive responsibilities have also been influenced by beliefs regarding an appropriate gendered division of labour after birth. We know that parenting practice remains a highly gendered activity. Single parent households are overwhelmingly likely to be headed by a

---

[13] See R Graycar 'Sex, Golf and Stereotypes: Measuring, Valuing and Imagining the Body in Court' (2002) 10 *Torts Law Journal* 205, 211.

[14] *Rodriquez v Bethlehem Steep Corp* 525 P 2d 669 (Cal 1974) 671. For further discussion of this case and the action for loss of consortium, see A Hyde, *Bodies of Law* (Princeton, NJ, Princeton University Press, 1997) 100–5.

[15] L Sherr and N Barry, 'Fatherhood and HIV-positive Men' (2004) 5 *HIV Medicine* 258.

[16] It is also often assumed that contraception is a woman's responsibility, with the needs of men overlooked. See JM Swanson, 'Men and Family Planning' in S Hanson and F Bozett (eds), *Dimensions of Fatherhood* (London, Sage, 1985) 21.

woman.[17] Where a pregnancy results from a casual encounter, a man may not even know that he is a father. Where he has a child in the context of a relationship but then separates from his partner, he may lose contact with both, while remaining liable for the financial support of his genetic child. And where the couple live in the same household, the man is highly unlikely to be forced to sacrifice his career in order to take on more childcare responsibilities. Far from spending more time at home, men tend to increase their working hours after the birth of a child to meet the increase in household expenses.[18] The breadwinner/carer divide thus still retains a powerful grip on the reality of parenting in modern Britain. What is less recognised is that this division of labour has an important impact on our understandings of responsibilities towards a child who has not yet been born, possibly not even yet been conceived. This final gendered assumption is demonstrated by the two case studies in the following section. The case studies also provide further illustration of the other assumptions discussed above.

B. Enforcing Reproductive Responsibilities: Two Case Studies

Once the possibility of causing injury to a child by one's actions during pregnancy or before conception is acknowledged, the existence of duties to avoid such harm (and if and how they should be enforced) becomes at issue. In the US, a number of criminal prosecutions have been brought against women (but not men) for their antenatal behaviour.[19] In the UK, no such prosecutions have been reported and, were they to be attempted, it has been suggested that they would be unlikely to succeed.[20] However, this is not to say that there has been no interest in the issue of antenatal responsibilities. Two examples can provide an illustration of how law has approached male and female reproductive responsibility: fetal protection legislation and policies, and parental liability for congenital disability in tort. These will serve as illustration of the assumptions set out above, particularly the relevance of the breadwinner/carer divide.

---

[17] See the 2001 census data, available at www.statistics.gov.uk.

[18] N Charles, *Gender in Modern Britain* (Oxford, OUP, 2002) 69. Moreover, the hours of work for fathers are increasing: J Brannen and P Moss, *Managing Mothers: Dual Earner Households after Maternity Leave* (London, Unwin Hyman, 1991).

[19] For a discussion of some of these cases, see C Daniels, *At Women's Expense: State Power and the Politics of Fetal Rights* (Cambridge, MA, Harvard University Press, 1993); and LE Gomez, *Misconceiving Mothers: Legislators, Prosecutors, and the Politics of Prenatal Drug Exposure* (Philadelphia, PA, Temple University Press, 1997).

[20] See M Brazier, 'Parental Responsibilities, Foetal Welfare and Children's Health' in C Bridge (ed), *Family Law: Towards the Millennium: Essays in Honour of PM Bromley* (London, Butterworths, 1997) 263.

1. Fetal Protection Legislation and Policies

A range of statutes and regulations prohibit employers from allowing pregnant women or women of reproductive capacity to work in contact with certain toxic substances.[21] Further, some employers have implemented what are known as 'fetal protection policies' to exclude fertile women from work which involves exposure to any toxic substances potentially dangerous to fetal health. Such substances may affect the fetus by producing defects in the conceptus (teratogens), or may cause mutation in the genetic structure of either sperm cells or the ova leading to hereditable genetic defects which may result in spontaneous abortion or birth defects (mutagens).

Today, it is broadly accepted that the fetus can also be at danger from male exposure and, as such, those policies which operate to exclude women alone from these workplaces have become increasingly difficult to justify.[22] As is discussed in more detail below, scientific research into male transmission of toxic substances has shown that male transmission can occur through the passing on of fetal toxins which are carried home to pregnant partners on the clothes or in the hair of male workers. Equally, male exposure to mutagens can affect sperm and hence the development of the fetus. Male reproductive exposures are now proven or strongly suspected of causing not only fertility problems but also miscarriage, low birth weight, congenital abnormalities, cancer, neurological problems, and other childhood health problems.[23]

There has been only one reported, unsuccessful, attempt to challenge a fetal protection policy in the UK. In *Page*, the Employment Appeals Tribunal upheld the legality of an employer's decision to dismiss a 23 year old female tanker

---

[21] The Factories Act 1961, the Control of Lead at Work Regulations 1980 and the Ionizing Radiation Regulations 1985 specify a maximum level of exposure for all workers, yet fertile women are treated differentially in that they are subject to a lower maximum level, see M Thomson, 'Employing the Body: the Reproductive Body and Employment Exclusion' (1996) 5 *Social & Legal Studies* 243. Likewise, the Management of Health and Safety at Work Regulations 1994 (which implemented the European Directive on Pregnant Workers) requires employers of all women of child-bearing age to take account of risks to new and expectant mothers and their babies. If the employer's risk assessment shows any substance, work process or working conditions that could damage the health and safety of the mother or child, action must be taken to remove the hazard or, failing that, the risk must be controlled through adjusting the working conditions or offering suitable alternative work. If this is not possible, paid leave must be given for as long as necessary. The approach here is more defensible in terms of the available scientific evidence (as it is not assumed that all women intend to be pregnant); however it is still flawed in that it focuses exclusively on pregnant and new mothers (of six months or less). The possibility of mutagenic harm to female or male workers is ignored, as is the possibility of indirect teratogenic harm (where male workers transport home toxins to their female partners).

[22] For example, see the scientific studies cited in E Draper, 'Fetal Exclusion Policies and Gendered Constructions of Suitable Work' (1993) 40 *Social Problems* 90.

[23] *Ibid*; RH Blank, *Fetal Protection in the Workplace* (New York, NY, Columbia University Press, 1993); M Thomson, 'Employing the Body', n 21 above; M Thomson, *Reproducing Narrative: Gender, Reproduction and the Law* (Aldershot, Ashgate, 1998); C Daniels, *At Women's Expense,* n 19 above, R Roth, *Making Women Pay: the Hidden Costs of Fetal Rights* (Ithaca, NY, Cornell University Press, 2000).

driver who would be brought into contact with a particular chemical believed dangerous to pregnant women. The woman's claim that she did not wish to become pregnant and was willing to provide her employer with an indemnity to that effect did not help her given the judge's view that she was 'clearly of a child-bearing age'.[24]

While *Page* makes clear the implications of fetal protection policies for women, neither are they without consequences for men. This is best demonstrated by a case from across the Atlantic. The Johnson Controls Company, a manufacturer of batteries, was sued in the United States courts following its introduction of a fetal protection policy excluding women who are pregnant or capable of bearing children from jobs involving exposure to lead on the basis that such exposure could harm their reproductive capacity and result in children being born with congenital defects. Thus excluded were '[a]ll women except those whose inability to bear children is medically documented.'[25] Some women chose to become sterilised in order to avoid losing their jobs, others accepted transfers to other positions with lower pay. A group of the company's employees responded by taking their employers to court and, eventually, the United States Supreme Court held that the company's policy constituted sex discrimination and was therefore unlawful.[26]

Not surprisingly, the company's actions provoked a storm of critical comment, tending to focus on the dreadful dilemma facing those women forced to choose between their jobs and their reproductive capacity.[27] It was also noted that fetal protection policies have most often been used to exclude women from traditionally male industries, such as chemical and heavy manufacturing works, whilst retaining men in them.[28] Less widely discussed was the fact that one of the plaintiffs in this case was a man. Donald Penney had complained that he was denied a request for leave of absence for the purpose of lowering his lead level because he intended to become a father. Whilst the dangers to male reproductivity resulting from lead exposure were already well known at this time, Penney found himself subject to discrimination of a different kind. He was refused the possibility of taking advantage of the very health measures which were being indiscriminately imposed on his female colleagues.

Fetal protection policies assume that where a woman chooses to act 'irresponsibly', that is in contradiction to what the legislature or her employers see as the best interests of her fetus, such 'responsible' behaviour can be forced on her (as in

---

[24] *Page v Freight Hire (Tank Haulage Co) Ltd* [1981] IRLR 13. For more discussion of this case, see S Sheldon, 'ReConceiving Masculinity', n 8 above.

[25] *International Union, United Automobile Workers v Johnson Controls Inc* 499 US 187 (1991).

[26] Under Title VII of the Civil Rights Act 1964.

[27] See the authors cited above, n 23.

[28] See M Thomson, 'Employing the Body', n 21 above; and S Sheldon, 'ReConceiving Masculinity', n 8 above.

the case of *Page*). In other words, a woman's reproductive destiny 'trumps' any other choices which she may wish to make.[29] As Karen Messing notes:

> The reproductive system of working women 'belongs' to society in a way that men's does not. If they wish, men may have many children without their colleagues and superiors being aware of it, but pregnancy is visible. In addition, while sperm are generally considered to belong to the male worker alone, pregnancy concerns not only the woman but the fetus, which may sometimes be considered to be a member of the general population (for example, in regulations regarding radiation exposure).[30]

Fetal protection policies on both sides of the Atlantic have thus sometimes assumed the paramount importance of reproduction to women. Equally, they have denied its importance to men. Donald Penney's agency is also ignored. He is refused the possibility of prioritising his body's reproductive capacity over and above its ability to labour, as surely as this prioritisation is forced on his female colleagues.[31] As a man, he is expected to continue in employment in order to act as breadwinner for his family, with other considerations marginalised. Both men and women may thus find their reproductive choices severely constrained, albeit in different ways, reflecting the heavily gendered assumptions of the policy maker. The policies can also serve to exaggerate the risk of female mediated harm to the fetus/child whilst often ignoring the possibility of male mediated harm.[32]

2. Liability for Congenital Disability

A second case study reflecting similar assumptions can be found in the law regarding civil liability for congenital disability. As was noted above, women have not

---

[29] Michael Thomson has expressed this well:

[t]he indiscriminate nature of the policies constructs all women as potentially pregnant, as primarily bearers and rearers of children, first and foremost 'biological actors'. A woman's reproductive role is seen as considerably more important than her economic role, regardless of the impact of unemployment on herself, her pregnancy or her existing children. In defining women by their generative organs, as primarily breeders, women become homogenized. Foetal protection policies ignore individuality and the existence of autonomous interests beyond the traditional family group. The possibility that women may choose not to have children, or may plan when to have them, is not recognized. Women may only participate in the public/economic sphere within the terms of heterosexuality and traditional views of womanhood. (*Ibid*, 259).

[30] K Messing, *One-eyed Science: Occupational Health and Women Workers* (Philadelphia, PA, Temple University Press, 1998) 138. Or as Elaine Draper puts it: 'Fetal exclusion policies place women's interests as mothers in opposition to their interests as workers' ('Fetal Exclusion Policies', n 22 above, 97).

[31] Draper's overview of US fetal exclusion policies produces the following interesting insights: first that discussions of excluding groups of men to protect them from reproductive hazards are rare; secondly in those unusual cases where such discussion does occur, employers generally see other men—not women—as the replacement workers; thirdly, the idea of excluding fertile men is not implemented, *ibid*, 96.

[32] Some of the scientific evidence that underpins this claim is discussed below (nn 53–57 and accompanying text).

been prosecuted for their antenatal drug and alcohol use in the UK.[33] The issue of whether mothers and fathers should be liable to pay damages to their future off-spring for harm suffered as a result of their pre-conceptual and antenatal actions has, however, been fully considered and is subject to the provisions of the Congenital Disabilities (Civil Liability) Act 1976. This statute provides that a child who survives for at least 48 hours will be able to sue in negligence for an occur-rence before its birth which results in some physical or mental disability. The 'occurrence' envisaged by the legislation includes anything which 'affected either parent in his or her ability to have a normal, healthy child' or which 'affected the mother during her pregnancy, or affected her or the child in the course of its birth'.[34]

The 1976 Act derives largely from the recommendations made by the Law Commission in 1974. Specifically, it incorporates the Law Commission's sugges-tion that, except in the case of negligent driving (where insurance payments would be available), a woman will not be liable to her eventual child for antenatal injury. The same exclusion, however, does not apply to the father. Four reasons cited in support of the exclusion of maternal liability were thus clearly believed not to be equally applicable to fathers. First, the Law Commission noted that the relationship between a mother and disabled child is one of the most stressful that can exist and to add legal liability to pay compensation would be bound to increase tension. Secondly, some possible allegations such as smoking and gin-drinking were thought to be 'unseemly' and potentially difficult to prove. Thirdly, it was noted that there would often be no fund from which the mother's liability could be paid without hardship to the rest of the family. Creation of a right of action that could seldom be satisfied would 'exacerbate the bitterness which a dis-abled child so often feels when it grows conscious of its condition'. Finally, it was felt that the existence of such an action might become a weapon between parents in a matrimonial conflict, to the further detriment of a disabled child.[35]

Although the Law Commission clearly saw the greatest threat of injury as occurring through the body of the pregnant woman, it did recognise that muta-genic harm to either genitor could be the cause of abnormalities in a child subse-quently conceived; noting, in particular, the threat posed by radiation. However, it saw no need to extend the same special exemption from liability to fathers. There was neither the same 'physical identification' between father and fetus, nor

---

[33] Although such behaviour may be taken into account when making decisions about whether a child need be taken into care. In *D v Berkshire CC* [1987] 1 All ER 20, the House of Lords held that a baby girl born with drug withdrawal symptoms to a drug dependent mother could be taken into care at birth, because of the mother's prior neglect coupled with the threat of future neglect.

[34] Section 1(2)(a) and (b).

[35] Law Commission, *Report on Injuries to Unborn Children* (Cmd 60, 1974). These reasons were adopted from the Bar Council's response to the Law Commission's Working Paper, *Injuries to Unborn Children* (Working Paper No 47, 1973).

the same enormous variety of ways in which paternal conduct could cause a congenital disability. Neither was it felt that the dangers of legal action or threat of such being used in matrimonial disputes was as great in the context of paternal liability, as available allegations would be far more limited and, presumably, not so 'unseemly' in nature. It was clearly felt that the damage that would result from litigation within a close familial relationship should not automatically rule out the possibility of suing the father. Indeed, to fail to recognise the child's action against its biological father might mean that a 'family' (a child, acting with the support of its social parents) would be precluded from suing the woman's lover or even her rapist.

Implicit in this reasoning is an assumption that women are more closely involved in reproduction and that female reproductive biology is more dangerous and far more likely to injure a child. A bewildering range of female activities were felt to be potentially dangerous.[36] The assumption of a male breadwinner/female carer is also clear, with the exclusion of maternal liability grounded in beliefs regarding parenting arrangements following birth. The Law Commission focuses exclusively on preventing disruption to the woman's familial role, being persuaded that maternal liability should be limited because of the dangers to the family, and particularly the mother/child relationship, which would result from allowing it. The child's possibility of suing is denied on the basis of a construction of its future relationship with the mother who will be its primary carer (this is implicit in the Law Commission's positing of the mother/disabled child relationship as the *most* stressful one), a relationship that should be characterised by love rather than litigation. The mother's lack of paid employment is assumed: she is felt unlikely to have an independent income to meet a claim for damages. Further, although the Law Commission is aware of the available literature setting out appropriate behaviour for the pregnant woman, it sees legal enforcement of such behaviour as liable to provoke 'unseemly' accusations. Allegations that harm was caused by the father's occupational exposure or dangerous lifestyle choices are, by implication and in contrast, acceptable. The refusal to allow an action which can bring bitterness, or contribute to tension in the child's relationship with its mother (primary carer), can thus be contrasted with a willingness to accept the legitimacy of an

---

[36] As illustrated by the two following interventions in the parliamentary debates: 'though a mother, knowing that she is pregnant goes, for example on the big dipper at Battersea Fun Fair, though she goes galloping on her horse, though she takes drugs which she knows may be dangerous to the child' Weitzman, 910 HC Debs Col 720(30 April 1976); '[t]here are the extraordinary things that women do to themselves. Further, we do not yet know whether there will be any effect on the next generation from such things as air fresheners, hair sprays and spray wood polishes', Gow, 910 HC Debs Col 755 (30 April 1976). These interventions also present an interesting image of the figure of the mother as housewife. Risks to the fetus come from household labour, beauty products and frivolous recreational activities.

action where the child's father (financial provider) has acted irresponsibly. Tort's role is to impose financial responsibility for one's harmful actions and, in some circumstances, omissions. This fits easily with the man's responsibilities to his child which are envisaged as primarily economic.

The 1976 Act reflects the same highly gendered assumptions regarding men's and women's responsibilities towards their children as were evident in the fetal protection laws and policies discussed above. Within this vision, a man's responsibilities for his biological children are those of financial provision, and a woman's are those of love and bodily care. Thus, a woman can be excluded from employment (via fetal protection policies) because of the paramount duty to provide a safe environment for her fetus. However, she cannot be sued by her child for her antenatal behaviour as that would introduce financial considerations into what is prized as an exclusively and uniquely affective relationship. The man will not be excluded from employment (nor allowed to remove himself from potentially hazardous work) given that his primary duty is to provide financially for his family. However, in principle, where he has negligently injured his unborn child, he should make financial reparation for that damage. Reproduction is seen as altogether a more important part of women's existence (and therefore women, but not men, should prioritise it above paid labour). Further, female reproductive biology is more fragile and, therefore, more susceptible both to be harmed and to harm than that of men.

While there is always scope for creative judicial interpretation, law inevitably fossilises the understandings and values of the era in which it is created. While still in force today, the Congenital Disabilities (Civil Liability) Act 1976 was drafted more than thirty years ago and reflects the common-sense assumptions of that era. It is far from clear that a contemporary parliament would vote to draw a distinction between mothers' and fathers' liabilities along these same lines and, if it did so choose, that distinction might be justified in rather different terms.[37] Likewise, the one reported challenge to a UK fetal protection policy discussed above, was brought almost 25 years ago. At the beginning of the 21st century, it is possible (though by no means inevitable) that a judge might feel less confident in opining

---

[37] Current concerns would no doubt lead to discussions less focused on the problems of gin drinking, furniture polish and 'those extraordinary things which women do to themselves', and more on the dangerous possibilities of cocaine, ecstasy and alcohol abuse. And debates focused in such a way might produce rather different conclusions. The US debates have centred on alcohol and crack cocaine use and, as was noted above, have played out very differently, with women often held responsible (and sometimes criminally liable) for causing harm to their fetus/future child, and men exonerated. The focus on crack cocaine means these debates are inevitably heavily racially coded. See C Daniels 'Between Fathers and Fetuses', n 4 above; C Daniels, *At Women's Expense*, n 19 above; D Roberts, *Killing the Black Body: Race, Reproduction and the Meaning of Liberty* (New York, NY, Vintage Books, 1997). Those prosecutions which are successful at state level are invariably overturned on appeal.

that a woman who is 'clearly of child-bearing age' cannot be taken seriously when she declares that she will have no further children.[38] However, while the assumptions which underpin these legal provisions may still hold some considerable sway, I would suggest that there are some signs that they are coming under challenge. This will be explored in the following section.

C. Men, Women and Reproductive Decision-making

I have suggested above that the legal regulation of reproductive responsibilities is clearly influenced by certain gendered assumptions regarding the relative importance of reproduction to men and women, the relative fragility and liability to harm of male and female reproductive bodies and an appropriate post-natal division of labour. Here, however, I want to suggest that while this view of male and female reproductive responsibilities retains a grip on the legal and popular imagination, it may be under attack.[39] In this final section, I seek to demonstrate the existence of growing medical and lay recognition both of the importance of reproduction to men and of the vulnerability of male reproductive bodies. The result is that men, like women, are likely to find themselves increasingly asserting their need for information and, where available, treatment to enable them to act as responsible reproductive agents. Further men, like women, may find these responsibilities imposed upon them.

In their extensive review of men's influence on female reproductive health, Dudgeon and Inhorn note a 'slowly changing perception that men are only tangentially involved in the mother-fetus health package'.[40] Here, they join the authors of the HIV study discussed above and a number of other commentators in arguing

---

[38] Though it should be noted that the author of this judgment, Gordon Slynn, has only very recently stopped sitting in the House of Lords.

[39] Elsewhere, I have discussed the phenomenon of birth control fraud or 'sperm banditry' where women lie about contraceptive use or fertility in order to trick men into unprotected sexual intercourse which results in the birth a child and male financial liability, see S Sheldon, '"Sperm Bandits", Birth Control Fraud and the Battle of the Sexes' (2001) 21 *Legal Studies* 460. While there is no way of knowing if these kinds of practices are widespread, substantial media attention may have contributed to a specific sense of male reproductive vulnerability, of a different kind than that discussed below. As Sara Ruddick has put it:

A man's increasingly traceable sperm is used to bind him to economic relations he would not have chosen and often cannot sustain. Now, like a woman, a man can be made materially accountable for, yet socially alienated from, his sexual activities; he may therefore feel that, like a woman (though surely less painfully) he is a victim of his procreative body. ('Thinking About Fathers', n 7 above, 232).

[40] MR Dudgeon and MC Inhorn, 'Men's Influences on Women's Reproductive Health: Medical Anthropological Perspectives' (2004) 59 *Social Science & Medicine* 1379, 1387.

that men's reproductive health needs are underemphasised in current reproductive health policy discussions.[41] A fast expanding body of literature is now exploring men's influence in pregnancy and childbirth and has revealed men's involvement in reproduction to be highly relevant to their partners' well-being and decision-making. In US-based health studies, male partners have been shown to affect timing of first pregnancy, women's prospective desire for becoming pregnant, feelings on learning of pregnancy, and subsequent changes in women's evaluation of how much a pregnancy is wanted.[42] This latter finding is born out in UK research showing that the decisions which women make regarding whether to continue with a pregnancy are highly influenced by a partner's wishes, whether he is supportive and the extent to which he is perceived as a suitable father.[43] However, men's involvement in reproduction is increasingly recognised as important not just in terms of female well-being, with attention also focused on the needs of fathers themselves.

That there has been a sea-change in attitudes to men's involvement in reproduction is most dramatically illustrated by statistics regarding fathers' presence at birth. The number of fathers attending labour and delivery has risen from 5% in the 1950s to 97% in the early 1990s, with the most rapid period of increase in the 1970s and 1980s. In the space of just these two decades, fathers' birth presence rose from 35% to 90%.[44] Before the 1970s, some hospitals had formally excluded fathers with the medical profession expressing a number of objections to their presence, including the risk of infection and fathers' propensity to faint. While the presence of fathers in the birth room may now seem entirely normal, that their admittance was anything but uncontroversial is well illustrated by an exchange in the *British Medical Journal*. A letter published in 1961 suggesting 'a more enlightened attitude to normal obstetrics ... where the father is welcomed and encouraged to be present at the delivery' provoked a response characterised by a rather different idea of the father's proper place:

> Let us not pander to morbid curiosity and sensationalism, nor to those featherbrains who wish to be in the van of a new fashion, by encouraging a highly unnatural trend with the mumbo-jumbo of pseudo-psychology. The proper place for the father, if not

---

[41] The authors of the HIV study note: 'Provision regarding reproduction is usually concentrated on women. This is short-sighted ... and the needs of men should be incorporated into provision.' They end on a plea for men to be given better information so that they, like women, can exercise responsible reproductive agency (L Sherr and N Barry, 'Fatherhood and HIV-positive Men', n 15 above).

[42] MR Dudgeon *et al*, 'Men's Influences on Women's Reproductive Health', n 40 above, 1386.

[43] M Lattimer, *Abortion Discourses: An Exploration of the Social, Cultural and Organisational Context of Abortion Decision-making in Contemporary Britain* (Unpublished PhD Thesis, University of Sussex, 2001).

[44] J Smith, 'The First Intruder: Fatherhood, a Historical Perspective' in P Moss (ed), *Father Figures: Fathers in the Families of the 1990s* (Edinburgh, HMSO, 1995) 17, 21.

at work, is the 'local' whither instinct will usually guide him. Family men may be baby-sitting, unless ejected by mother-in-law.[45]

The motives of those men who did wish to attend the delivery were frequently questioned. Burgess cites the 1994 case of a man who missed a court appearance to attend the birth of his first child and found himself arrested and castigated by the magistrate that 'women have been giving birth for millennia without men there.'[46] In clear contrast, reports of the recent UK election campaign saw little adverse comment on the delay of the launch of the Liberal Democrats' manifesto in order to allow the party leader to attend the birth of his child.[47] This is not to suggest that men now feel like equal partners in their encounters with the providers of what are, after all, still called 'maternity' services.[48] But the change is nonetheless marked.

Medicine's increasing concern for men's reproductive health can also be seen in other areas. Infertility has often been viewed as a female problem and this under-standing still pervades popular beliefs. All of the infertile men in one recent study reported having assumed that their wives' failure to conceive would have been due to female infertility and experienced shock and disbelief on finding out that the prob-lem lay with them: 'Obviously it wasn't my problem, it had to be hers .... Infertility is not a male problem, it's a female problem. The woman can't have the baby. Not the man, it's the woman .... The woman is the one who needs to be tested, not the man.'[49]

---

[45] This exchange is reported in J Draper, 'Whose Welfare in the Labour Room? A Discussion of the Increasing Trend of Fathers' Birth Attendance' (1997) 13 *Midwifery* 132, 133; and in C Lewis, *Becoming a Father*, n 5 above, 57. Note the letter writer's assumption that if a man is looking after his own chil-dren (a task surely only occasioned by his wife's need to be away in hospital), then this is 'baby-sitting' which, by definition, involves looking after someone else's children. A 1958 British Medical Association conference on the rights of the father found opinion divided into two main groups: those who felt that that fathers should be excluded altogether and those who felt they should be excluded after the first stages of labour, see Lewis *ibid*, 59.

[46] A Burgess, *Fatherhood Reclaimed*, n 11 above, 121. Burgess provides a second example which also occurred in 1994: a football star who skipped a training session to be at his child's birth was dropped from his team.

[47] With one notable exception: Lord Beaumont of Whitley commented that 'you wouldn't have had a wimp taking days off to go and have babies in my day', see S Graudt, 'The Reckoning' *The Observer* (24 April 2005). Charles Kennedy's incoherent presentation of one of his party's key election pledges following a largely sleepless night with his new son was generally greeted rather less sympathetically.

[48] A burgeoning literature emerging primarily in the pages of nursing and midwifery journals relates that, despite the fact that fathers are now encouraged to attend their children's births, medical practice generally operates to limit their participation, with maternity services focused heavily on the well-being of mother and child: see Draper, 'Fetal Exclusion Policies', n 22 above; R Early, 'Men as Consumers of Maternity Services: A Contradiction in Terms' (2001) 25 *International Journal of Consumer Studies* 160; K Vehvilainen-Julkunen and A Liukkonen, 'Fathers' Experiences of Childbirth' (1998) 14 *Midwifery* 10; C Lewis, *Becoming a Father*, n 5 above, ch 4. For a lively account of one man's own experiences, see N Johnstone, 'Push Comes to Shove' *The Observer*, 11 April 2005.

[49] RE Webb and JC Daniluk, 'The End of the Line: Infertile Men's Experience of Being Unable to Produce a Child' (1999) 2 *Men and Masculinities* 6, 13. This was a small, qualitative study involving only six men.

While the men in this study undoubtedly give voice to popular beliefs, the most comprehensive epidemiological study of infertility to date suggests that men are the sole cause or a contributing factor to infertility in more than half of all couples around the globe.[50] And it has now become accepted medical practice to refer not to infertile women or men but to 'infertile couples', conceptualising the problem as a shared one.[51] Occupational health specialist, Karen Messing, notes a marked shift in scientific understandings. In 1989, a presentation given on environmental causes of male infertility to a local fertility clinic was greeted with astonishment, with the doctors who attended saying that they only treated women. Less than 20 years later, while most infertility clinics still concentrate on the female partner, the idea of protecting sperm from workplace hazards has been taken more and more seriously.[52]

Perhaps, most relevantly to the case studies given above, there is also a growing body of medical research which suggests that it is not just women's bodies which can pose risks to child/fetal health, but also those of men. The American political scientist Cynthia Daniels provides a particularly rich and insightful survey of the development of scientific research in this area.[53] She notes that, for a long time, scientists assumed that only female transmission of mutagens (toxins which affect the fetus or the sperm/ova which create it) was possible. Men were believed either to be invulnerable to harm from the toxicity of drugs, alcohol, environmental or occupational hazards, or to be rendered completely infertile by any vulnerability to risk. In particular, sperm which crossed the line from virile to vulnerable by being damaged by reproductive toxins were assumed to be incapable of fertilisation.[54] The converse was also true: men not rendered infertile by their toxic exposures were assumed to be immune from any other forms of reproductive risk.[55] Daniels provides the example of Gladys Friedler, a scientist working at Boston University in the 1970s who was the first to document a link in mice between paternal exposure to morphine and birth defects in their offspring. At that time, cultural constructions of male reproduction made Friedler's work simply unbelievable and, as such, its scientific validity was challenged.[56] More recently,

---

[50] See MR Dudgeon and MC Inhorn, 'Men's Influences on Women's Reproductive Health', n 40 above, 1388, discussing a WHO sponsored study of 5800 couples in 33 centres in 22 countries.

[51] See *eg* R Winston, *Infertility: A Sympathetic Approach* (London, Martin Dunitz, 1986).

[52] *One-eyed Science*, n 30 above, 146.

[53] C Daniels, 'Between Fathers and Fetuses', n 4 above. See also the works cited in n 23 above.

[54] *Ibid.* Catherine Waldby reached similar conclusions regarding the heterosexual male body in her study of AIDS. Biomedical understanding of HIV transmission is focused around bodily boundaries and bodily permeability, whereas the idealised phallic body is effectively a prophylactic device—immunologically perfect. See C Waldby, *AIDS and the Body Politic: Biomedicine and Sexual Difference* (London, Routledge, 1996) 13.

[55] C Daniels, *ibid*.

[56] *Ibid*, 591.

Messing reports, it has become well known that various substances affect sperm and male fertility including pesticides, radiation, metals, and heat exposure. She further notes that the scientific community's growing interest in male genetic damage has made it an increasingly 'hot' topic, a good area for getting research funding.[57]

An enhanced sense of male reproductive fragility has also entered the public consciousness by way of the extensive media attention paid to the claims of Gulf War veterans in the UK and US, who have alleged that toxic exposure suffered during military service has resulted in injury not just to their own health but also that of their children. While the scientific basis for these claims remains fiercely contested, the publicity attendant on veterans' efforts to secure redress has contributed to an enhanced popular acceptance that men, like women, are reproductively vulnerable.[58] Concerns about Gulf War Syndrome fit within a growing stream of other health scares about male reproductivity, such as concern at declining sperm counts attributed to overly tight underpants, 'gender-bending' chemicals in the environment, certain industrial toxins or an increase in dietary fat.[59] The media attention paid to these reports of male reproductive harm may contribute to pressure on men, as well as women, to worry about disability in their future children, and to seek to make informed reproductive choices on this basis. Significantly, men as well as women are now called upon to moderate their behaviour in order to improve their chances of a successful conception, as a cursory review of the advice available on the internet will confirm. To take just one example, the UK Baby Centre suggests a number of steps which can be taken to improve the chances of conception, including:

> *Look at your diet and lifestyle*: Both of you need to follow a good, healthy diet and also to lose any excess weight if you are significantly overweight. If you are underweight, you may need to put some weight on—ideally your Body Mass Index (BMI) should be between about 20 and 25 ... . Also take a look at our guidelines for a healthy diet for mum-to-be and healthy diet for dad-to-be. Smoking is known to reduce fertility in both men and women, so try to cut down or stop altogether if you smoke. Keep an eye on your alcohol intake, especially prospective dads-to-be, and take a look at our lifestyle advice for parents trying for a baby for the first time—it still applies to you.[60]

[57] *One-eyed Science*, n 30 above, 146–47.

[58] There has been substantial discussion of whether 'Gulf War Syndrome' exists but an independent British inquiry conducted by Lord Lloyd found substantial evidence for it, see *The Guardian*, 19 November 2004. One large scale survey has found a small increased risk of infertility among Gulf War veterans. If the men's partners did become pregnant, conception had taken longer to achieve, and the pregnancy was less likely to run full term. See N Maconochie, P Doyle and C Carson, 'Infertility among Male UK Veterans of the 1990–91 Gulf War: Reproductive Cohort Study' (2004) 329 *BMJ* 196.

[59] See, for example, S Connor 'The Facts of (Modern) Life' *The Independent*, 4 February 2004; and S Boseley, 'Pollutants "Damage Men's Fertility"' *The Guardian*, 28 April 2005.

[60] http://www.babycentre.co.uk/refcap/563485.html#1 (visited 14 April 2005).

Finally, developments in genetic medicine are also playing an important role in highlighting reproductive responsibilities. Increasing knowledge in the area of genetics calls on all of us to be responsible citizens who will make appropriate reproductive choices with a view to the health of our future offspring. Crucially, as Novas and Rose argue, genetic risk does not imply resignation in the face of an implacable biological destiny but rather introduces new and active relations to oneself and one's future, generating a new form of 'genetic responsibility'.[61] Novas and Rose's research focused on a web chat room for Huntingdon's Disease (HD) sufferers, where one of the most frequently posed ethical questions concerns the decision to have children in the light of knowledge of being genetically at risk or pre-symptomatic.

> One example of the ways in which quite complex molecular genetic knowledge has begun to permeate the field of reproductive decision making concerns paternal transmission of HD. In the case of HD, fathers at risk for HD have the potential to transmit more severe and earlier onset forms of HD to their offspring. This clearly serves to complicate the decision to have children for such men, and also for their actual or potential partners ... Once the field of reproductive decision-making becomes structured by knowledge of molecular risk, each individual becomes obliged to inform themselves of the potential genetic risks that may be transmitted in the course of reproducing their genetic selves.[62]

What is interesting for current purposes is that the new genetic diagnostic technologies clearly implicate both men and women in responsible reproductive decision-making. Indeed, fathers at risk of HD have the potential to transmit more severe and earlier onset forms of HD to their offspring. Men, like women, are thus called upon to manage their own genetic health and to act responsibly with regard to the health of their future offspring. This impetus to act as a responsible reproductive agent may be implicitly enforced via various social and medical mechanisms and mediated through other people's expectations of the *right* thing to do. For example, even a gay man with no desire for children may feel obliged to accept a reproductive advice session with a genetic counsellor in order to be seen to act responsibly.[63] In *Page*, we saw reproductive responsibility imposed on a woman who had no reproductive intentions. Here, we see something similar happening with regard to men. In a clear contrast to the study of HIV+ men discussed above, men like women are here obliged to consider themselves as reproductive agents. They may expect to be judged on how well they exercise the responsibility which goes with that agency, possibly facing medical, familial and other forms of disapproval if they make irresponsible choices. The subject that is constructed in the

---

[61] C Novas and N Rose, 'Genetic Risk and the Birth of the Somatic Individual' (2000) 29 *Economy and Society* 485.

[62] *Ibid*, 504.

[63] See S Sheldon, '*Re*Conceiving Masculinity', n 8 above, 148 for an account of such an incident.

contemporary genetic consultation is not then merely a subject at genetic risk, but also a responsible subject who exercises choices wisely for himself and for others.[64] Individuals can no longer focus just on their own health, but are forced to think of themselves in a complex genealogical web of connections. For both men and women, the norms of reproductive health suggested by genetics are shaped in terms of a concern for others.[65]

D. Conclusion

The opposition of 'men's freedom' to 'women's responsibility' in the title of this chapter is overly blunt and deliberatively provocative. Nonetheless, it does capture a particular world-view in which, to coin a military metaphor used by one US author, men are often *volunteers* in reproduction whereas women are *draftees*.[66] As Gillian Douglas has argued, men enjoy significantly more freedom with regard to reproduction, experiencing it as a series of choices that women simply do not enjoy.[67] While these writers are concerned primarily with parenting practices, it seems to me that their analysis also speaks to some assumptions which have commonly been made about reproductive responsibilities. It is suggested above that a number of dominant and highly gendered assumptions have had a clear impact on the way in which we think about such responsibilities. Men have been understood as having less fragile reproductive systems, as being less concerned with reproduction than are women, as better able to disassociate sex and reproduction, and as expected to prioritise their duties as breadwinners over other forms of familial responsibility. While constrained by the expectation of paid labour, men are nonetheless thus seen to have enjoyed a significant level of reproductive freedom that has historically been denied to women. Women have found themselves significantly more burdened and constrained by the demands of reproduction, with widely accepted responsibilities for fetal/child well-being which extend long back into pregnancy and even precede conception. While biological asymmetry may explain some of this disparity in our thinking, I have argued that it can by no means explain all of it.

---

[64] C Novas and N Rose, 'Genetic Risk', n 61 above, 495 (references omitted).

[65] *Ibid*, 504.

[66] K Czapanskiy, 'Volunteers and Draftees: The Struggle for Parental Equality' (1991) 38 *University of California L Rev* 415.

[67] In the UK, noting the increased relevance of 'intention to parent' in determining who should be considered the legal parents of a child, Gillian Douglas observes that it is in many ways a very male way of thinking about parenthood: the possibility of making a conscious decision of whether or not to recognise children as one's own or to participate in their upbringing, is not normally experienced by women. G Douglas 'The Intention to be a Parent and the Making of Mothers' (1994) 57 *Modern L Rev* 636.

However, I have also suggested above that this disparity has not gone unchallenged. Strict child support legislation, now buttressed by highly accurate paternity testing may see men feeling less able to disassociate sex and reproduction and made painfully aware of the procreative consequences of their sexual acts.[68] Further, men like women are also increasingly called upon to be aware of their reproductive fragility with concern about decline in sperm quality commanding widespread media attention. And men, like women, can find themselves called upon to make 'responsible' reproductive choices, not just in avoiding unwanted pregnancy, but also in taking appropriate measures to safeguard their own reproductive health and to avoid conception of a child likely to suffer from illness or disability.

Above, I suggested the impossibility of 'pure' scientific endeavour that produces results unmediated by pre-existing assumptions. It is worth noting by way of conclusion that there is a striking fit between the challenges to the reproductive assumptions outlined above and the current rethinking of men's and women's responsibilities with regard to parenting.[69] What can be seen in the shift sketched above is a movement towards conceptualising reproduction as a matter of more central concern for men, with male bodies more closely implicated in fetal health. This presents a clear parallel to the evolution in contemporary understandings of the family as requiring a father who is more than just a breadwinner and remote disciplinarian, and whose daily involvement and hands-on parenting is integral to child welfare. While there is no space here to explore the existence of a causal relationship between these two trends, it is possible that as a rhetoric of more involved fathering gains dominance in discussions of parenting practices, a similar trend may also be seen in understandings of reproductive responsibilities.

---

[68] See S Sheldon, '"Sperm Bandits"', n 39 above.
[69] See C Lewis, *Becoming a Father*, n 5 above, on evolution in understandings of the fathers' role.

INDEX